THE ESSENTIAL DALE CARNEGIE

Often hailed as the father of 'self-help', Dale Carnegie was an American author, speaker and developer of courses in self-improvement. His notable works include *How to Win Friends and Influence People*, *The Quick and Easy Way to Effective Speaking*, *How to Stop Worrying and Start Living* and *Little Known Facts about Well-Known People*. His works form the basis of Dale Carnegie Training, a programme founded in 1912 to help people develop and hone their interpersonal and business skills.

THE ESSENTIAL DALE CARNEGIE

Curated Wisdom from
3 Bestselling Books

hachette
INDIA

This specially curated edition first published in 2016 by Hachette India
(Registered name: Hachette Book Publishing India Pvt. Ltd)
An Hachette UK company
www.hachetteindia.com

SRD

How to Win Friends and Influence People first published in 1936
by Simon and Schuster, New York
How to Stop Worrying and Start Living first published in 1948
by Simon and Schuster, New York
The Quick and Easy Way to Effective Speaking (fourth revised edition of
Public Speaking and Influencing Men in Business) first published in 1962
by Association Press, New York

ISBN 978-93-5195-156-8

Hachette Book Publishing India Pvt. Ltd
4th & 5th Floors, Corporate Centre,
Plot No. 94, Sector 44,Gurgaon – 122003, India

Typeset in 10.5/13.5 Minion Pro by
SŪRYA, New Delhi

Printed and bound in India by
Manipal Technologies Limited, Manipal

MIX
Paper | Supporting responsible forestry
FSC™ C043100
FSC www.fsc.org

Contents

Publisher's Note

Author and motivational speaker Dale Carnegie's name has become synonymous with self-made success. Born into poverty in a rural village in Missouri, USA, Carnegie worked his way up the social ladder, armed with nothing but salesmanship, charisma and his legendary interpersonal skills. After his enormous success as a lecturer, he published the now iconic *How to Win Friends and Influence People*, which has sold over 30 million copies worldwide, and has been translated into over 31 languages. He went on to write several other bestsellers, and his works have been devised into the Dale Carnegie Course, a popular training programme that is represented in more than 90 countries.

What is remarkable about Carnegie's books is how well they've stood the test of time. Even after years of being in print, his advice is universal, and relatable. In this book, we have brought together curated learnings from three of his most popular books in a form that is contemporary and easy-to-use. *The Quick and Easy Way to Effective Speaking* will help you build your public speaking skills – from developing the confidence to speak in front of an audience to writing and practising the perfect speech and, finally, delivering your pitch in a way that guarantees maximum impact. *How to Win Friends and Influence People* will teach you how to make a great first impression: a skill that is as priceless in the workplace as in your personal life. It will also guide you through the art of winning people over to your way of thinking; becoming a better leader; and critiquing others without giving offence. The selections from *How to Stop Worrying and Start Living* are perhaps the most relevant in today's times, because they will teach you how to develop work habits to get rid of resentment and frustration; how to stop letting stress and anxiety control your decisions; and how to make the change towards a positive, more mindful, outlook in life and work.

THE QUICK AND EASY WAY TO EFFECTIVE SPEAKING

1

Acquiring the Basic Skills

I started teaching classes in public speaking in 1912, the year the Titanic went down in the icy waters of the North Atlantic. Since then, more than 7,50,000 people have been graduated from these classes.

In the demonstration meetings preceding the first session of the Dale Carnegie Course, people are given the opportunity of telling why they intend to enrol and what they hope to gain from this training. Naturally, the phraseology varies; but the central desire, the basic want in the vast majority of cases, remains surprisingly the same: 'When I am called upon to stand up and speak, I become so self-conscious, so frightened, that I can't think clearly, can't concentrate, and can't remember what I intended to say. I want to gain self-confidence, poise, and the ability to think on my feet. I want to get my thoughts together in logical order, and I want to be able to talk clearly and convincingly before a business or social group.'

Doesn't this sound familiar? Haven't you experienced these same feelings of inadequacy? Wouldn't you give a small fortune to have the ability to speak convincingly and persuasively in public? I am sure you would. The very fact that you have begun reading the pages of this book is proof of your interest in acquiring the ability to speak effectively.

I know what you are going to say, what you would say if you could talk to me: 'But Mr Carnegie, do you really think I could develop the confidence to get up and face a group of people and address them in a coherent, fluent manner?'

I have spent nearly all my life helping people get rid of their fears and develop courage and confidence. I could find many books with stories of the miracles that have taken place in my classes. It is not, therefore, a question of my thinking. I know you can, if you practise the directions and suggestions that you will find in this book.

Is there the faintest shadow of a reason why you should not be able to think as well in a perpendicular position before an audience as you can sitting down? Is there any reason why you should play host to butterflies in your stomach and become a victim of the 'trembles' when you get up to address an audience? Surely, you realize that this condition can be remedied, that training and practice will wear away your audience-fright and give you self-confidence.

This book will help you to achieve that goal. It is not an ordinary textbook. It is not filled with rules concerning the mechanics of speaking. It does not dwell on the physiological aspects of vocal production and articulation. It is the distillation of a lifetime spent in training adults in effective speaking. It starts with you as you are, and from that premise works naturally to the conclusion of what you want to be. All you have to do is cooperate – follow the suggestions in this book, apply them in every speaking situation, and persevere.

In order to get the most out of this book, and to get it with rapidity and dispatch, you will find these four guideposts useful:

- Take heart from the experience of others
- Keep your goal before you
- Predetermine your mind to success
- Seize every opportunity to practise

TAKE HEART FROM THE EXPERIENCE OF OTHERS

There is no such animal, in or out of captivity, as a born public speaker. In those periods of history when public speaking was a refined art that demanded close attention to the laws of rhetoric and the niceties of delivery, it was even more difficult to be born a public speaker. Now we think of public speaking as a kind of enlarged conversation. Gone forever is the old grandiloquent style and the stentorian voice. What we like to hear at our dinner meetings, in our church services, on our TV sets and radios, is straightforward speech, conceived in common sense and dedicated to the proposition that we like speakers to talk with, and not at, us.

Despite what many school texts would lead us to believe, public speaking is not a closed art, to be mastered only after years of perfecting the voice and struggling with the mysteries of rhetoric. I have spent almost all of my teaching career proving to people that it is easy to speak in public, provided they follow a few simple, but important, rules. When I started to teach at the 125th Street YMCA in New York City back in 1912, I didn't know this any more than my first students knew it. I taught those first classes pretty much the way I had been taught in my college years in Warrensburg, Missouri. But I soon discovered that I was on the wrong track; I was trying to teach adults in the business world as though they were college freshmen. I saw the futility of using Webster, Burke, Pitt, and O'Connell as examples to imitate. What the members of my classes wanted was enough courage to stand on their hind legs and make a clear, coherent report at their next business meeting. It wasn't long before I threw the textbooks out of the window, got right up there on the podium and, with a few simple ideas, worked with those fellows until they could give their reports in a convincing manner. It worked, because they kept coming back for more.

I wish I could give you a chance to browse through the files of testimonial letters in my home or in the offices of my representatives in various parts of the world. They come from industrial leaders whose names are frequently mentioned in the business section of the *New York Times* and the *Wall Street Journal*, from governors of states and members of parliaments, from college presidents, and from celebrities in the world of entertainment. There are thousands more from housewives, ministers, teachers, young men and women whose names are not well known yet – even in their own communities, executives and executive trainees, labourers – skilled and unskilled, union men, college students, and business women. All of these people felt a need for self-confidence and the ability to express themselves acceptably in public. They were so grateful for having achieved both that they took the time to write me letters of appreciation.

Of the thousands of people I have taught, one example comes to mind as I write because of the dramatic impact it had on me at the time. Some years ago, shortly after he joined my course, D.W. Ghent, a successful businessman in Philadelphia, invited me to lunch. He leaned across the table and said: 'I have sidestepped every opportunity to speak to various gatherings, Mr Carnegie, and there have been many. But now I am chairman of a board of college trustees. I must preside at their meetings. Do you think it will be possible for me to learn to speak at this late date in life?'

I assured him, on the basis of my experience with men in similar positions who had been members of my classes, that there was no doubt in my mind that he would succeed.

About three years later we lunched together again at the Manufacturers' Club. We ate in the same dining room and at the very same table we had occupied at our first meeting. Reminding him of our former conversation, I asked him whether my prediction had come true. He smiled, took a little red-backed notebook out of his pocket, and showed me a list of speaking engagements for the next several months. 'The ability to make these talks,' he confessed, 'the pleasure I get in giving them, the additional service I can render in the community – these are among the most gratifying things in my life.'

But that was not all. With a feeling of justifiable pride, Mr Ghent then played his ace card. His church group had invited the prime minister of England to address a convocation in Philadelphia. And the Philadelphian selected to make the introduction of the distinguished statesman, on one of his rare trips to America, was none other than Mr D.W. Ghent.

This was the man who had leaned across that same table less than three years before and asked me whether I thought he would ever be able to talk in public!

Here is another example. The late David M.L. Goodrich, chairman of the board of the B.F. Goodrich Company, came to my office one day. 'All my life,' he began, 'I have never been able to make a talk without being frozen with fear. As board chairman I have to preside at our meetings. I have known all the board members intimately for years, and I have no trouble talking to them when we are sitting around the table. But the moment I stand up to talk, I am terrified. I can hardly say a word. I have been that way for years. I don't believe you can do anything for me. My trouble is too serious. It has existed too long.'

'Well,' I said, 'if you don't think I can do anything for you, why did you come to see me?'

'For one reason only,' he replied. 'I have an accountant who takes care of my personal accounting problems. He is a shy chap, and to get into his little office, he has to walk through my office. He has been sneaking through my office for years, looking at the floor and hardly ever saying a word. But lately, he has been transformed. He walks into my office now with his chin up, a light in his eye, and he says, "Good morning, Mr Goodrich," with confidence and spirit. I was astonished at the change. So, I said to him: "Who has been feeding you meat?" He told me about taking your training course, and it is only because of the transformation I have witnessed in that frightened little man that I have come to see you.'

I told Mr Goodrich that if he attended the classes regularly and did what we asked him to do, within a few weeks he would enjoy speaking before audiences.

'If you can do that,' he replied, 'I'll be one of the happiest men in the country.'

He joined the course, made phenomenal progress, and three months later, I invited him to attend a meeting of 3,000 people in the ballroom of the Hotel Astor, and talk to them on what he had got out of our training. He was sorry – couldn't come due to a previous engagement. The next day he phoned me. 'I want to apologize,' he said. 'I have broken that engagement and I'll come and speak for you. I owe it to you – to tell the audience what this training did for me. I'll do it with the hope that my story will inspire some of the listeners to get rid of the fears that are devastating their lives.'

I asked him to speak for two minutes only. He spoke to 3,000 people for 11 minutes.

I have seen thousands of similar miracles worked in my courses. I have seen men and women whose lives were transformed by this training – many of them receiving promotions far beyond their dreams, or achieving positions of prominence in their business, profession, and community. Sometimes, this has been done by means of a single talk delivered at the right moment. Let me tell you the story of Mario Lazo.

Years ago, I received a cable from Cuba that astonished me. It read:

> Unless you cable me to the contrary, I am coming to New York to take training to make a speech.
>
> Mario Lazo

When Mr Lazo arrived in New York, he said: 'The Havana Country Club is going to celebrate the fiftieth birthday of the founder of the club; and I have been invited to present him with a silver cup, and to make the principal talk of the evening. Although I am an attorney, I have never made a public talk in my life. I am terrified at the thought of speaking. If I fail, it will be deeply embarrassing to my wife and myself socially; and, in addition, it might lower my prestige with my clients. That is why I have come all the way from Cuba for your help. However, I can stay only three weeks.'

During those three weeks, I had Mario Lazo going from one class to another speaking three or four times a night. Three weeks later, he addressed the distinguished gathering at the Havana Country Club. His address was so outstanding that *Time* magazine reported it under the head of foreign news and described Mario Lazo as a 'silver-tongued orator'.

Sounds like a miracle, doesn't it? It is a miracle – a twentieth-century miracle of conquering fear.

KEEP YOUR GOAL BEFORE YOU

When Mr Ghent spoke of the pleasure his newly acquired skill in public speaking gave him, he touched upon what I believe (more than any other factor) contributed to his success. It's true he followed the directions and faithfully did the assignments. But I'm sure he did these things because he wanted to do them, and he wanted to do them because he saw himself as a successful speaker. He projected himself into the future and then worked toward bringing that projection into reality. That is exactly what you must do.

Concentrate your attention on what self-confidence and the ability to talk more effectively will mean to you. Think of what it may mean to you socially, of the friends it will bring, of your increased capacity to be of service in your civic, social, or church group, of the influence you will be able to exert in your business. In short, it will prepare you for leadership.

In an article entitled, 'Speech and Leadership in Business,' S.C. Allyn, chairman of the board of the National Cash Register Company and chairman of UNESCO, wrote in the *Quarterly*

Journal of Speech: 'In the history of our business, many a man has drawn attention to himself by a good job done on the platform. A good many years ago a young man, who was then in charge of a small branch in Kansas, gave a rather unusual talk, and is today our vice-president, in charge of sales.' I happen to know that this vice-president is now the president of the National Cash Register Company.

There is no predicting how far the ability to speak on your feet will take you. One of our graduates, Henry Blackstone, president of the Servo Corporation of America, says, 'The ability to communicate effectively with others and win their cooperation is an asset we look for in men moving to the top.'

Think of the satisfaction and pleasure that will be yours when you stand up and confidently share your thoughts and feelings with your audience. I have travelled around the world several times, but I know of few things that give greater delight than holding an audience by the power of the spoken word. You get a sense of strength, a feeling of power. 'Two minutes before I begin,' said one of my graduates, 'I would rather be whipped than start; but two minutes before I finish, I would rather be shot than stop.'

Begin now to picture yourself before an audience you might be called upon to address. See yourself stepping forward with confidence, listen to the hush fall upon the room as you begin, feel the attentive absorption of the audience as you drive home point after point; feel the warmth of the applause as you leave the platform, and hear the words of appreciation with which individual members of the audience greet you when the meeting is over. Believe me, there is a magic in it and a never-to-be-forgotten thrill.

William James, Harvard's most distinguished professor of psychology, wrote six sentences that could have a profound effect on your life – six sentences that are the open sesame to Ali Baba's treasure cave of courage:

- In almost any subject, your passion for the subject will save you.
- If you care enough for a result, you will most certainly attain it.
- If you wish to be good, you will be good.
- If you wish to be rich, you will be rich.
- If you wish to be learned, you will be learned.
- Only then you must really wish these things and wish them with exclusiveness, and not wish one hundred other incompatible things just as strongly.

Learning to speak effectively to groups brings other benefits than merely the ability to make formal public speeches. As a matter of fact, if you never give a formal public speech in your life, the benefits to be derived from this training are manifold. For one thing, public speaking training is the royal road to self-confidence. Once you realize that you can stand up and talk intelligently to a group of people, it is logical to assume that you can talk to individuals with greater confidence and assurance. Many men and women have taken my course in effective speaking primarily because they were shy and self-conscious in social groups. When they found they were capable of speaking on their feet to their fellow class members without having the roof foil in, they became aware of the ridiculousness of self-consciousness. They began to impress others, their families, friends, business associates, customers, and clients, with their newly found poise. Many of our graduates, like Mr Goodrich, were impelled to take the course by the remarkable change in the personalities of those around them.

This type of training also affects the personality in ways that are not immediately apparent. Not long ago I asked Dr David Allman, the Atlantic City surgeon and former president of the American Medical Association, what, in his opinion, were the benefits of public speaking training in terms of mental and physical health. He smiled and said he could best answer that question by writing a prescription that 'no drugstore can fill. It must be filled by the individual; if he thinks he can't, he is wrong.'

I have the prescription on my desk. Every time I read it, I am impressed. Here it is, just as Dr Allman jotted it down:

> Try your best to develop an ability to let others look into your head and heart. Learn to make your thoughts, your ideas, clear to others, individually, in groups, in public. You will find, as you improve in your effort to do this, that you – your real self – are making an impression, an impact on people, such as you never made before.
>
> You can reap a double benefit from this prescription. Your self-confidence strengthens as you learn to speak to others, and your whole personality grows warmer and better. This means that you are better off emotionally, and if you are better off emotionally, you are better off physically. Public speaking in our modern world is for everybody – men and women, young and elderly. I do not know personally about its advantages to one in business or industry. I only hear that they are great. But, I do know its advantages in health. Speak when you can, to a few or to many; you will do it better and better, as I have found out, myself; and you will feel a buoyancy of spirit, a sense of being a whole, rounded person, such as you never felt before.
>
> It is a wonderful sense to have, and no pill ever made can give it to you.

The second guidepost, then, is to picture yourself as successfully doing what you fear to do now, and to concentrate on the benefits you will receive through your ability to talk acceptably before groups. Remember the words of William James: 'If you care enough for a result, you will most certainly attain it.'

PREDETERMINE YOUR MIND TO SUCCESS

I was asked once, on a radio programme, to tell in three sentences the most important lesson I have ever learned. This is what I said: 'The biggest lesson I have ever learned is the stupendous importance of what we think. If I knew what you think, I would know what you are, for your thoughts make you what you are. By changing our thoughts, we can change our lives.'

You have set your sights on the goal of increased confidence and more effective communication. From now on, you must think positively, not negatively, about your chances to succeed in this endeavour. You must develop a buoyant optimism about the outcome of your efforts to speak before groups. You must set the seal of determination upon every word and action that you devote toward the development of this ability.

Here is a story that is dramatic proof of the need for resolute determination on the part of anyone who wants to meet the challenge of more expressive speaking. The man I am writing about has come up the management ladder so far that he has become a big business legend. But the first time he stood up to speak in college, words failed him. He couldn't get beyond the middle of the five-minute talk his teacher had assigned. His face went white, and he hurried off the platform in tears.

The man who had that experience as a young student didn't let that failure frustrate him. He was determined to become a good speaker and didn't stop in that determination until he became a world-respected economic consultant to the government. His name is Clarence B. Randall. In one of his thoughtful books, *Freedom's Faith*, he has this to say about public speaking: 'I have service stripes all the way up one sleeve and all the way down the other from appearances before luncheons and dinners of manufacturers' associations, chambers of commerce, rotary clubs, fundraising campaigns, alumni organizations, and all the rest; I talked myself into the First World War by a patriotic address in Escanaba, Michigan; I have brainstormed for charity with Mickey Rooney, and for education with President James Bryant Conant of Harvard, and Chancellor Robert M. Hutchins of the University of Chicago; and I have even made an after-dinner speech in very bad French.

I think I know something about what an audience will listen to, and how they want it said. And there is nothing whatever about it that a man worthy to bear important responsibility cannot learn if he will.

I agree with Mr Randall. The will to succeed must be a vital part of the process of becoming an effective speaker. If I could look into your mind and ascertain the strength of your desire and the light and shadow of your thought, I could foretell, almost with certainty, the swiftness of your progress toward your goal of improved communicative skills.

In one of my classes in the Middle West, a man stood up the first night and unabashedly said that as a builder of homes he wouldn't be content until he became a spokesman for the American Home Builders' Association. He wanted nothing more than to go up and down this country and tell everybody he met the problems and achievements of his industry. Joe Haverstick meant what he said. He was the kind of class member that delights an instructor. He was in dead earnest, he wanted to be able to talk, not on local issues only, but on national ones, and there was no half-heartedness about his desires. He prepared his talks thoroughly, practised them carefully, and never missed a single session, though it was the busy season of the year for men in his business. He did precisely what such a class member always does – he progressed at a rate that surprised him. In two months he had become one of the outstanding members of the class. He was voted its president.

The instructor handling that class was in Norfolk, Virginia, about a year later, and this is what he wrote: 'I had forgotten all about Joe Haverstick back in Ohio when, one morning while I was having breakfast, I opened the *Virginia Pilot*. There was a picture of Joe and a write-up about him. The night before, he had addressed a large meeting of area builders, and I saw that Joe was not just a spokesman for the National Home Builders Association; he was its president.'

To succeed in this world, you need qualities that are essential in any worthwhile endeavour:

- Desire amounting to enthusiasm
- Persistence to wear away mountains
- The self-assurance to believe that you will succeed

When Julius Caesar sailed over the channel from Gaul and landed with his legions in what is now England, what did he do to ensure the success of his army? A very clever thing – he halted his soldiers on the chalk cliffs of Dover; and, looking down over the waves 200 feet below, they saw red tongues of fire consume every ship in which they had crossed. In the enemy's country, with the last link with the Continent gone, the last means of retreat burned, there was but one thing left for them to do – to advance and to conquer. That is precisely what they did.

Such was the spirit of the immortal Caesar. Why not make it yours, too, as you set out to conquer your fear of audiences? Throw every shred of negative thought into the consuming fires and slam doors of steel upon every escape into the irresolute past.

SEIZE EVERY OPPORTUNITY TO PRACTISE

The course I gave in the 125th Street YMCA before the First World War has been changed almost beyond recognition. Every year new ideas have been woven into the sessions and old ones cast away. But, one feature of the course remains unchanged. Every member of every class must get up once, and in the majority of cases, twice, and give a talk before his fellow members. Why? Because no one can learn to speak in public without actually speaking in front of people any more than a person can learn to swim without getting in the water. You could read every volume ever written about public speaking – including this one – and still not be able to speak. This book is a thorough guide. But you must put its suggestions into practice.

When George Bernard Shaw was asked how he learned to speak so compellingly in public, he replied: 'I did it the same way I learned to skate – by doggedly making a fool of myself until I got used to it.' As a youth, Shaw was one of the most timid persons in London. He often walked up and down the Embankment for 20 minutes or more before venturing to knock at a door. 'Few men,' he confessed, 'have suffered more from simple cowardice or have been more horribly ashamed of it.'

Finally, he hit upon the best and quickest and surest method ever yet devised to conquer timidity, cowardice, and fear. He determined to make his weak point his strongest asset. He joined a debating society. He attended every meeting in London where there was to be a public discussion, and he always arose and took part in the debate. By throwing his heart into the cause of socialism, and by going out and speaking for that cause, George Bernard Shaw transformed himself into one of the most confident and brilliant speakers of the first half of the twentieth century.

Opportunities to speak are on all sides. Join organizations and volunteer for offices that will require you to speak. Stand up and assert yourself at public meetings, if only to second a motion. Don't take a back seat at departmental meetings. Speak up! Teach a Sunday school class. Become a Scout leader. Join any group where you will have an opportunity to participate actively in the meetings. You have but to look around you to see that there is scarcely a single business, community, political, professional, or even neighbourhood activity that does not challenge you to step forward and speak up. You will never know what progress you can make unless you speak, and speak, and speak again.

'I know all about that,' a young business executive once said to me, 'but I hesitate to face the ordeal of learning.'

'Ordeal!' I replied. 'Put that thought out of your mind. You've never thought of learning in the right – the conquering – spirit.'

'What spirit is that?' he asked.

'The spirit of adventure,' I told him, and I talked to him a little about the path to success through public speaking, and the warming up, the unfolding, of one's personality.

'I'll give it a try,' he finally said. 'I'll head into this adventure.'

As you read on in this book, and as you put its principles into practice, you, too, will be heading into adventure. You will find it is an adventure in which your power of self-direction and your vision will sustain you. You will find it is an adventure that can change you, inside and out.

> You will never know what progress you can make unless you speak, and speak again.

2

Developing Confidence

'Five years ago, Mr Carnegie, I came to the hotel where you were conducting one of your demonstrations. I walked up to the door of the meeting room and then stopped. I knew if I entered that room and joined a class, sooner or later I'd have to make a speech. My hand froze on the doorknob. I couldn't go in. I turned my back and walked out of the hotel. If I had only known then how you make it easy to conquer fear, the paralysing fear of an audience, I wouldn't have lost these past five years.'

The man who spoke these revealing words wasn't talking across a table or a desk. He was directing his remarks to an audience of some 200 people. It was the graduation session of one of my courses in New York City. As he gave his talk, I was particularly impressed by his poise and self-assurance. Here was a man, I thought, whose executive skills will be tremendously increased by his newly acquired expressiveness and confidence. As his instructor, I was delighted to see that he had dealt a death blow to fear, and I couldn't help thinking how much more successful, and what is more, how much happier this man would have been if his victory over fear had come five or ten years before.

Ralph Waldo Emerson said, 'Fear defeats more people than any other one thing in the world.' Oh, how I have been made aware of the bitter truth of that statement! And how grateful I am that during my life I have been able to rescue people from fear. When I started to teach my course in 1912, little did I realize that this training would prove to be one of the best methods ever yet devised to help people eliminate their fears and feelings of inferiority. I found that learning to speak in public is nature's own method of overcoming self-consciousness, and building up courage and self-confidence. Why? Because speaking in public makes us come to grips with our fears.

In years of training men and women to speak in public, I have picked up some ideas to help you quickly overcome stage fright and develop confidence in a few short weeks of practice.

GET THE FACTS ABOUT FEAR OF SPEAKING IN PUBLIC

Fact Number One: You are not unique in your fear of speaking in public.

Surveys in colleges indicate that 80 to 90 per cent of all students enrolled in speech classes suffer from stage fright at the beginning of the course. I am inclined to believe that the figure is higher among adults at the start of my course – almost 100 per cent.

Fact Number Two: A certain amount of stage fright is useful.

It is nature's way of preparing us to meet unusual challenges in our environment. So, when you notice your pulse beating faster and your respiration speeding up, don't become alarmed. Your body, ever alert to external stimuli, is getting ready to go into action. If these physiological preparations are held within limits, you will be capable of thinking faster, talking more fluently, and generally speaking with greater intensity, than under normal circumstances.

Fact Number Three: Many professional speakers never completely lose all stage fright.

It is almost always present just before they speak, and it may persist through the first few sentences of their talk. This is the price these men and women pay for being like race horses and not like draft horses. Speakers who say they are 'cool as a cucumber' at all times are usually as thick-skinned as a cucumber and about as inspiring as a cucumber.

Fact Number Four: The chief cause of your fear of public speaking is simply that you are unaccustomed to speak in public.

'Fear is misbegotten of ignorance and uncertainty,' says Professor Robinson, in *The Mind in the Making*. For most people, public speaking is an unknown quantity, and consequently one fraught with anxiety and fear factors. For the beginner, it is a complex series of strange situations, more involved than, say, learning to play tennis or drive a car. To make this fearful situation simple and easy – practise, practise, and practise. You will find, as thousands upon thousands have, that public speaking can be made a joy instead of an agony merely by getting a record of successful speaking experiences behind you.

The story of how Albert Edward Wiggam, the prominent lecturer and popular psychologist, overcame his fear, has been an inspiration to me ever since I first read it. He tells how terror-struck he was at the thought of standing up in high school and delivering a five-minute declamation.

'As the day approached,' he writes, 'I became positively ill. Whenever the dreadful thought occurred to me, my whole head would flush with blood and my cheeks would burn so painfully that I would go out behind the school building and press them against the cold brick wall to try to reduce their surging blushes. It was the same way with me in college.

On one occasion, I carefully memorized a declamation

beginning, "Adams and Jefferson are no more." When I faced the audience, my head was swimming so I scarcely knew where I was. I managed to gasp out the opening sentence, stating that Adams and Jefferson have passed away. I couldn't say another word, so I bowed and walked solemnly back to my seat amid great applause. The president got up and said, "Well, Edward, we are shocked to hear the sad news, but we will do our best to bear up under the circumstances." During the uproarious laughter that followed, death would surely have been a welcome relief. I was ill for days afterward.

Certainly, the last thing on earth I ever expected to become was a public speaker.'

A year after he left college, Albert Wiggam was in Denver. The political campaign of 1896 was raging over the issue of Free Silver. One day he read a pamphlet explaining the proposals of the Free Silverites; he became so incensed over what he considered the errors and hollow promises of William Jennings Bryan and his followers, that he pawned his watch for enough money to get back to his native Indiana. Once there, he offered his services to speak on the subject of sound money. Many of his old school friends were in the audience. 'As I began,' he writes, 'the picture of my Adams and Jefferson speech in college swept over me. I choked and stammered and all seemed to be lost. But, as Chauncey Depew often said, both the audience and I managed, somehow, to live through the introduction; and encouraged by even this tiny success, I went on talking for what I thought was about fifteen minutes. To my amazement, I discovered I had been talking an hour and a half!

As a result, within the next few years, I was the most surprised person in the world to find myself making my living as a professional public speaker. I knew at first-hand what William James meant by the habit of success.'

Yes, Albert Edward Wiggam learned that one of the surest ways of overcoming the devastating fear of speaking before groups is to get a record of successful experiences behind you.

You should expect a certain amount of fear as a natural adjunct of your desire to speak in public, and you should learn to depend on a limited amount of stage fright to help make you give a better talk.

If stage fright gets out of hand and seriously curtails your effectiveness by causing mental blocks, lack of fluency, uncontrollable tics, and excessive muscular spasm, you should not despair. These symptoms are not unusual in beginners. If you make the effort, you will find the degree of stage fright soon reduced to the point where it will prove a help and not a hindrance.

PREPARE IN THE PROPER WAY

The principal speaker at a New York Rotary Club luncheon several years ago was a prominent government official. We were looking forward to hearing him describe the activities of his department.

It was obvious almost at once that he had not planned his speech. At first he tried to talk impromptu. Failing in that attempt, he pulled out of his pocket a sheaf of notes which evidently had no more order than a flatcar full of scrap iron. He fumbled a while with these, all the time becoming more embarrassed and inept in his delivery; minute by minute he became more helpless, and more bewildered. But he kept on floundering, apologizing, trying to make some semblance of sense out of his notes and raising a glass of water with a trembling hand to his parched lips. He was a sad picture of a man completely overcome by fright, due to almost total lack of preparation. He finally sat down, one of the most humiliated speakers I have ever seen. He made his talk as Rousseau says a love letter should be written: he began without knowing what he was going to say, and finished without knowing what he had said.

Since 1912, it has been my professional duty to evaluate over five thousand talks a year. From that experience, one great lesson stands out like Mt Everest, towering above all the others: only the prepared speaker deserves to be confident. How can anyone ever hope to storm the fortress of fear if he goes into battle with defective weapons, or with no ammunition at all? 'I believe,' said Lincoln, 'that I shall never be old enough to speak without embarrassment when I have nothing to say.'

If you want to develop confidence, why not do the one thing that will give you security as a speaker? 'Perfect love,' wrote the Apostle John, 'casteth out fear.' So does perfect preparation. Daniel Webster said he would as soon think of appearing before an audience half-clothed as half-prepared.

Never Memorize a Talk Word for Word

By 'perfect preparation' do I mean that you should memorize your talk? To this question I give back a thunderous NO. In their attempts to protect their egos from the dangers of drawing a mental blank before an audience, many speakers fall headlong into the trap of memorization. Once a victim of this type of mental dope addiction, the speaker is hopelessly bound to a time-consuming method of preparation that destroys effectiveness on the platform.

When H.V. Kaltenborn, the dean of American news commentators, was a student at Harvard University, he took part in a speech contest. He selected a short story entitled, 'Gentlemen, the King'. He memorized it word for word and rehearsed it hundreds of times. The day of the contest he announced the title, 'Gentlemen, the King.' Then his mind went blank. It not only went blank; it went black. He was terrified. In desperation he started telling the story in his own words. He was the most surprised boy in the hall when the judges gave him first prize. From that day to this, H. V. Kaltenborn has never read nor memorized a speech. That has been the secret of success in his broadcasting career. He makes a few notes and talks naturally to his listeners without a script.

> The man who writes out and memorizes his talks is wasting his time and energy, and courting disaster.

All our lives we have been speaking spontaneously. We haven't been thinking of words. We have been thinking of ideas. If our ideas are clear, the words come as naturally and unconsciously as the air we breathe.

Even Winston Churchill had to learn that lesson the hard way. As a young man, Churchill wrote out and memorized his speeches. Then one day, while delivering a memorized talk before the British Parliament, he stopped dead in his mental tracks. His mind went blank. He was embarrassed, humiliated! He began his last sentence all over again. Again his mind went blank and his face scarlet. He sat down. From that day on, Winston Churchill never attempted to deliver a memorized talk.

If we memorize our talk word for word, we will probably forget it when we face our listeners. Even if we do not forget our memorized talk, we will probably deliver it in a mechanical way. Why? Because it will not come from our hearts, but from our memories. When talking with people privately, we always think of something we want to say, and then we go ahead and say it without thinking of words. We have been doing that all our lives. Why attempt to change it now? If we do write out and memorize our talk, we may have the same experience that Vance Bushnell had.

Vance was a graduate of the Beaux Arts School in Paris, and later became vice-president of one of the largest insurance companies in the world – the Equitable Life Assurance Society. Years ago, he was asked to address a conference of two thousand Equitable Life representatives from all over America at a meeting in White Sulphur Springs, West Virginia. At that time, he had been in the life insurance business for only two years, but he had been highly successful, so he was scheduled to make a twenty-minute talk.

Vance was delighted to do so. He felt it would give him prestige. But, unfortunately, he wrote out and memorized his talk. He rehearsed forty times in front of a mirror. He had everything down pat – every phrase, every gesture, every facial expression. It was flawless, he thought.

However, when he stood up to deliver his address, he was terrified. He said: 'My part in this programme is...' His mind went blank. In his confusion, he took two steps backward and tried to start all over again. Again, his mind went blank. Again he took two steps back and tried to start. He repeated this performance three times. The platform was four feet high; there was no railing at the back; and there was a space five feet wide between the back of the platform and the wall. So, the fourth time he stepped back, he toppled backwards off the platform and disappeared into space. The audience howled with laughter. One man fell off his chair and rolled in the aisle. Never before nor since, in the history of the Equitable Life Assurance Society, has anyone ever given such a comic performance. The astonishing part of the story is that the audience thought it was really an act. The old-timers of the Equitable Life are still talking about his performance.

But what about the speaker, Vance Bushnell? Vance Bushnell himself told me it was the most embarrassing occasion of his life. He felt so disgraced that he wrote out his resignation.

Vance Bushnell's superiors persuaded him to tear up his resignation. They restored his self-confidence, and Vance Bushnell, in later years, became one of the most effective speakers in his organization. But he never memorized a talk again. Let us profit by his experience.

I have heard countless scores of men and women try to deliver memorized talks, but I don't remember even one speaker who wouldn't have been more alive, more effective, more human, if he had tossed his memorized talk into the waste basket. If he had done that, he might have forgotten some of his points. He might have rambled, but at least he would have been human.

Abe Lincoln once said: 'I don't like to hear a cut-and-dried sermon. When I hear a man preach, I like to see him act as if he were fighting bees.' Lincoln said he wanted to hear a speaker cut loose and get excited. No speaker ever acts as if he were fighting bees when he is trying to recall memorized words.

Assemble and Arrange Your Ideas Beforehand

What, then, is the proper method of preparing a talk? Simply this – search your background for significant experiences that have taught you something about life; and assemble your thoughts, your ideas, and your convictions, that have welled up from these experiences. True preparation means brooding over your topics. As Dr Charles Reynold Brown said some years ago in a memorable series of lectures at Yale University: 'Brood over your topic until it becomes mellow and expansive…then put all these ideas down in writing, just a few words, enough to fix the idea… put them down on scraps of paper. You will find it easier to arrange and organize these loose bits when you come to set your material in order.' This doesn't sound like such a difficult programme, does it? It isn't. It just requires a little concentration and thinking to a purpose.

Rehearse Your Talk with Your Friends

Should you rehearse your talk after you have it in some kind of order? By all means. Here is a sure-fire method that is easy and effective. Use the ideas you have selected for your talk in everyday conversation with your friends and business associates. Instead of going over the ball scores, just lean across the luncheon table and say something like this: 'You know, Joe, I had an unusual experience one day. I'd like to tell you about it.' Joe will probably be happy to listen to your story. Watch him for his reactions. Listen to his response. He may have an interesting idea that may be valuable. He won't know that you are rehearsing your talk, and it really doesn't matter. But he probably will say that he enjoyed the conversation.

Allan Nevins, the distinguished historian, gives similar advice to writers: 'Catch a friend who is interested in the subject and talk out what you have learned at length. In this way you discover facts of interpretation that you might have missed, points of arguments that had been unrealized, and the form most suitable for the story you have to tell.'

PREDETERMINE YOUR MIND TO SUCCESS

In the first chapter, you remember, this sentence was used in reference to building the right attitude toward public speaking training in general. The same rule applies to the specific task now facing you, that of making each opportunity to speak a successful experience. There are three ways to accomplish this:

Lose Yourself in Your Subject

After you have selected your subject, arranged it according to plan, and rehearsed it by 'talking it out' with your friends, your preparation is not ended. You must sell yourself on the importance of your subject. You must have the attitude that has inspired all the truly great personages of history – a belief in your cause. How do you fan the fires of faith in your message? By exploring all phases of your subject, grasping its deeper meanings, and asking yourself how your talk will help the audience to be better people for having listened to you.

Keep Your Attention Off Negative Stimuli that May Upset You

For instance, thinking of yourself making errors of grammar or suddenly coming to an end of your talk somewhere in the middle of it is certainly a negative projection that could cancel confidence before you started. It is especially important to keep your attention off yourself just before your turn to speak. Concentrate on what the other speakers are saying, give them your wholehearted attention and you will not be able to work up excessive stage fright.

Give Yourself a Pep Talk

Unless he is consumed by some great cause to which he has dedicated his life, every speaker will experience moments of doubt about his subject matter. He will ask himself whether the topic is the right one for him, whether the audience will be interested in it. He will be sorely tempted to change his subject. At times like these, when negativism is most likely to tear down self-confidence completely, you should give yourself a pep talk. In clear, straightforward terms tell yourself that your talk is the right one for you, because it comes out of your experience, out of your thinking about life. Say to yourself that you are more qualified than any member of the audience to give this particular talk and, by George, you are going to do your best to put it across. Is this old-fashioned couch teaching? It may be, but modern experimental psychologists now agree that motivation based on autosuggestion is one of the strongest incentives to rapid learning, even when simulated. How much more powerful, then, will be the effect of a sincere pep talk based on the truth?

ACT CONFIDENT

The most famous psychologist that America has produced, Professor William James, wrote: 'Action seems to follow feeling, but, really, action and feeling go together; and by regulating the action, which is under the more direct control of the will, we can indirectly regulate the feeling, which is not.

'Thus, the sovereign voluntary path to cheerfulness, if our spontaneous cheerfulness be lost, is to sit up cheerfully and to act and speak as if cheerfulness were already there. If such conduct does not make you feel cheerful, nothing else on that occasion can.

'So, to feel brave, act as if we were brave, use all of our will to that end, and a courage-fix will very likely replace the fit of fear.'

Apply Professor James' advice. To develop courage when you

are facing an audience, act as if you already had it. Of course, unless you are prepared, all the acting in the world will avail but little. But granted that you know what you are going to talk about, step out briskly and take a deep breath. In fact, breathe deeply for 30 seconds before you ever face your audience. The increased supply of oxygen will buoy you up and give you courage. The great tenor, Jean de Reszke, used to say that when you had your breath so you 'could sit on it' nervousness vanished.

> Draw yourself up to your full height and look your audience straight in the eyes, and begin to talk as confidently as if every one of them owed you money. Imagine that they do. Imagine that they have assembled there to beg you for an extension of credit. The psychological effect on you will be beneficial.

If you doubt that this philosophy makes sense, you would change your mind after a few minutes conversation with almost any of the class members who have preceded you in following the ideas on which this book is based. Since you can't talk to them, take the word of an American who will always be a symbol of courage. Once he was the most timorous of men; by practising self-assurance, he became one of the boldest; he was the trust-busting, audience-swaying, big-stick-wielding President of the United States, Theodore Roosevelt.

'Having been a rather sickly and awkward boy,' he confesses in his autobiography, 'I was, as a young man, at the first both nervous and distrustful of my powers. I had to train myself painfully and laboriously not merely as regards my body but as regards my soul and spirit.'

Fortunately, he has disclosed how he achieved the transformation. 'When a boy,' he wrote, 'I read a passage in one of Marryat's books which always impressed me. In this passage, the captain of some small British man-of-war is explaining to the hero how to acquire the quality of fearlessness. He says that at the outset almost every man is frightened when he goes into action, but that the course to follow is for the man to keep such a grip on himself that he can act just as if he were not frightened. After this is kept up long enough, it changes from pretence to reality, and the man does, in very fact, become fearless by sheer dint of practising fearlessness when he does not feel it.

'This was the theory upon which I went. There were all kinds of things of which I was afraid at first, ranging from grizzly bears to "mean" horses and gun-fighters; but, by acting as if I were not afraid I gradually ceased to be afraid. Most men can have the same experience if they choose.'

Overcoming fear of public speaking has a tremendous transfer value to everything that we do. Those who answer this challenge find that they are better persons because of it. They find that their victory over fear of talking before groups has taken them out of themselves into a richer and fuller life.

A salesman wrote: 'After a few times on my feet before the class, I felt that I could tackle anyone. One morning I walked up to the door of a particularly tough purchasing agent and before he could say no, I had my samples spread out on his desk, and he gave me one of the biggest orders I have ever received.'

A housewife told one of our representatives: 'I was afraid to invite the neighbours in for fear that I wouldn't be able to keep the conversation going. After taking a few sessions and getting up on my feet, I took the plunge and held my first party. It was a great success. I had no trouble stimulating the group along interesting lines of talk.'

At a graduating class, a clerk said: 'I was afraid of the customers. I gave them a feeling that I was apologetic. After speaking to the class a few times, I found that I was speaking up with more assurance and poise, I began to answer objections with authoritativeness. My sales went up 45 per cent the first month after I started to speak to this class.'

They discovered that it was easy to conquer other fears and anxieties and to be successful where they may have failed before. You, too, will find that speaking in public will enable you to face what each day presents with a sure touch that confidence brings. You will be able to meet the problems and conflicts of life with a new sense of mastery. What has been a series of insoluble situations can become a bright change to increase pleasure in living.

3

Speaking Effectively the Quick and Easy Way

I seldom watch television in the daytime. But a friend recently asked me to listen to an afternoon show that was directed primarily to housewives. It enjoyed a very high rating, and my friend wanted me to listen because he thought the audience participation part of the show would interest me. It certainly did. I watched it several times, fascinated by the way the master of ceremonies succeeded in getting people in the audience to make talks in a way that caught and held my attention. These people were obviously not professional speakers. They had never been trained in the art of communication. Some of them used poor grammar and mispronounced words. But all of them were interesting. When they started to talk they seemed to lose all fear of being on camera and they held the attention of the audience.

Why was this? I know the answer because I have been employing the techniques used in this programme for many years. These people, plain, ordinary men and women, were holding the attention of viewers all over the country; they were talking about themselves, about their most embarrassing moments, their most pleasant memory, or how they met their wives or husbands. They were not thinking of introduction, body, and conclusion. They were not concerned with their diction or their sentence structure. Yet, they were getting the final seal of approval from the audience – complete attention in what they had to say. This is dramatic proof of what to me is the first of three cardinal rules for a quick and easy way to learn to speak in public:

- Speak about something you have earned the right to talk about through experience or study
- Tell us what life has taught you
- Look for topics in your backyard

SPEAK ABOUT SOMETHING YOU HAVE EARNED THE RIGHT TO TALK ABOUT THROUGH EXPERIENCE OR STUDY

The men and women whose live flesh-and-blood stories made that television programme interesting were talking from their own personal experience. They were talking about something they knew. Consider what a dull programme would have resulted if they had been asked to define communism or to describe the organizational structure of the United Nations. Yet, that is precisely the mistake that countless speakers make at countless meetings and banquets. They decide they must talk about subjects of which they have little or no personal knowledge and to which they have devoted little or no attention. They pick a subject like patriotism, or democracy, or justice, and then, after a few hours of frantic searching through a book of quotations or a speaker's handbook for all occasions, they hurriedly throw together some generalizations vaguely remembered from a political science course they once took in college, and proceed to give a talk distinguished for nothing other than its length. It never occurs to these speakers that the audience might be interested in factual material bringing these high-flown concepts down to earth.

At an area meeting of Dale Carnegie instructors in the Conrad Hilton Hotel in Chicago some years ago, a student speaker started like this: 'Liberty, equality, fraternity. These are the mightiest ideas in the dictionary of mankind. Without liberty, life is not worth living. Imagine what existence would be like if your freedom of action would be restricted on all sides.'

That is as far as he got, because he was wisely stopped by the instructor, who then asked him why he believed what he was saying. He was asked whether he had any proof or personal experience to back up what he had just told us. Then, he gave us an amazing story.

He had been a French underground fighter. He told us of the indignities he and his family suffered under Nazi rule. He described in vivid language how he escaped from the secret police and how he finally made his way to America. He concluded by saying: 'When I walked down Michigan Avenue to this hotel today, I was free to come or go, as I wished. I passed a policeman and he took no notice of me. I walked into this hotel without having to present an identification card, and when this meeting is over I can go anywhere in Chicago I choose to go. Believe me, freedom is worth fighting for.' He received a standing ovation from that audience.

Tell Us What Life Has Taught You

Speakers who talk about what life has taught them never fail to keep the attention of their listeners. I know from experience that speakers are not easily persuaded to accept this point of view – they consider using personal experiences as too trivial and too restrictive. They would rather soar into the realms of general ideas and philosophical principles, where unfortunately, the air is too rarefied for ordinary mortals to breathe. They give us editorials when we are hungry for the news. None of us is averse to listening to editorials, when they are given by a man who has earned the right to editorialize – an editor or publisher of a newspaper. The point, though, is this – speak on what life has taught you and I will be your devoted listener.

It was said of Emerson that he was always willing to listen to any man, no matter how humble his station, because he felt he could learn something from every man he met. I have listened to more adult talks, perhaps, than any other man west of the Iron Curtain, and I can truthfully say that I have never heard a boring talk when the speaker related what life had taught him, no matter how slight or trivial the lesson may have been.

To illustrate, some years ago, one of our instructors conducted a course in public speaking for the senior officers of New York City banks. Naturally, the members of such a group, having many demands upon their time, frequently found it difficult to prepare adequately, or to do what they conceived of as preparing. All their lives they had been thinking their own individual thoughts, nurturing their own personal convictions, seeing things from their own distinctive angles, living their own original experiences. They had spent forty years storing up material for talks. But it was hard for some of them to realize that.

One Friday, a certain gentleman connected with an uptown bank – for our purposes we shall designate him as Mr Jackson – found 4.30 p.m. had arrived, and what was he to talk about? He walked out of his office, bought a copy of *Forbes* magazine at a newsstand, and in the subway coming down to the Federal Reserve Bank where the class met, he read an article entitled, 'You Have Only Ten Years to Succeed'. He read it, not because he was interested in the article especially, but because he had to speak on something to fill his quota of time.

An hour later, he stood up and attempted to talk convincingly and interestingly on the contents of this article.

What was the result, the inevitable result?

He had not digested, had not assimilated what he was trying to say. 'Trying to say' – that expresses it precisely. He was trying. There was no real message in him seeking for an outlet; and his whole manner and tone revealed it unmistakably. How could he expect the audience to be any more impressed than he himself was? He kept referring to the article, saying the author said so and so.

There was a surfeit of *Forbes* magazine in it, but regrettably little of Mr Jackson.

After he finished his talk, the instructor said, 'Mr Jackson, we are not interested in this shadowy personality who wrote that article. He is not here. We can't see him. But we are interested in you and your ideas. Tell us what you think, personally, not what somebody else said. Put more of Mr Jackson in this. Would you take this same subject next week? Read this article again, and ask yourself whether you agree with the author or not. If you do, illustrate the points of agreement with observations from your own experience. If you don't agree with him, tell us why. Let this article be the starting point from which to launch your own talk.'

Mr Jackson reread the article and concluded that he did not agree with the author at all. He searched his memory for examples to prove his points of disagreement. He developed and expanded his ideas with details from his own experience as a bank executive. He came back the next week and gave a talk that was full of his own convictions, based on his own background. Instead of a warmed-over magazine article, he gave us ore from his own mine, currency coined in his own mint. I leave it to you to decide which talk made a stronger impact on the class.

Look for Topics in Your Background

Once a group of our instructors were asked to write on a slip of paper what they considered was the biggest problem they had with beginning speakers. When the slips were tallied, it was found that getting beginners to talk on the right topic was the problem most frequently encountered in early sessions of my course.

What is the right topic? You can be sure you have the right topic for you if you have lived with it, made it your own through experience and reflection. How do you find topics? By dipping into your memory and searching your background for those significant aspects of your life that made a vivid impression on you. Several years ago, we made a survey of topics that held the attention of listeners in our classes. We found that the topics most approved by the audience were concerned with certain fairly defined areas of one's background:

Early Years and Upbringing

Topics that deal with family, childhood memories, schooldays, invariably get attention because most of us are interested in the way other people met and overcame obstacles in the environment in which they were reared.

Whenever possible, work into your talk's illustrations and examples from your early years. The popularity of plays, movies, and stories that deal with the subject of meeting the challenges of the world in one's early years attests to the value of this area for subject matter of talks. But how can you be sure anyone will be interested in what happened to you when you were young? There's one test. If something stands out vividly in your memory after many years have gone by, that almost guarantees that it will be of interest to an audience.

Early Struggles to Get Ahead

This is an area rich in human interest. Here again, the attention of a group can be held by recounting your first attempts to make your mark on the world. How did you get into a particular job or profession? What twist of circumstances accounted for your career? Tell us about your setbacks, your hopes, your triumphs when you were establishing yourself in the competitive world. A real-life picture of almost anyone's life, if told modestly, is almost sure-fire material.

Hobbies and Recreation

Topics in this area are based on personal choice and, as such, are subjects that command attention. You can't go wrong talking about something you do out of sheer enjoyment. Your natural enthusiasm for your particular hobby will help get this topic across to any audience.

Special Areas of Knowledge

Many years of working in the same field have made you an expert in your line of endeavour. You can be certain of respectful attention if you discuss aspects of your job or profession based on years of experience or study.

Unusual Experiences

Have you ever met a great man? Were you under fire during the war? Have you gone through a spiritual crisis in your life? These are experiences that make the best kind of speech material.

Beliefs and Convictions

Perhaps you have given a great deal of time and effort to thinking about your position on vital subjects confronting the world today. If you have devoted many hours to the study of issues of importance, you have earned the right to talk about them. But when you do, be certain that you give specific instances for your convictions. Audiences do not relish a talk filled with generalizations. Please don't consider the casual reading of a few newspaper articles sufficient preparation to talk on these topics. If you know little more about a subject than the people in your audience, it is best to avoid it. On the other hand, if you have devoted years of study to some subject, it is undoubtedly a topic that is made to order for you. By all means, use it.

* * *

The preparation of a talk does not consist merely in getting some mechanical words down on paper, or in memorizing a series of phrases. It does not consist in lifting ideas second-hand from some hastily read book or newspaper article. But it does consist in digging deep into your mind and heart and bringing forth some of the essential convictions that life has stored there. Never doubt that the material is there. It is! Rich stores of it, waiting for you to discover it. Do not spurn such material as too personal, too slight for an audience to hear. I have been highly entertained and deeply moved by such talks, more entertained and more moved than I have been by many professional speakers.

Only by talking about something you have earned the right to talk about will you be able to fulfil the next requirements for learning to speak in public quickly and easily.

- Be sure you are excited about your subject
- Be eager to share your talk with your listeners

BE SURE YOU ARE EXCITED ABOUT YOUR SUBJECT

Not all topics that you and I have earned the right to talk about make us excited. For instance, as a do-it-yourself devotee, I certainly am qualified to talk about washing dishes. But somehow or other, I can't get excited about this topic. As a matter of fact, I would rather forget about it altogether. Yet, I have heard housewives – household executives, that is – give superb talks about this same subject. They have somehow aroused within themselves such a fury of indignation about the eternal task of washing dishes, or they have developed such ingenious methods of getting around this disagreeable chore, that they have become really excited about it. As a consequence, they have been able to talk effectively about this subject of washing dishes.

Here is a question that will help you determine the suitability of topics you feel qualified to discuss in public: if someone stood up and directly opposed your point of view, would you be impelled to speak with conviction and earnestness in defence of your position? If you would, you have the right subject for you.

Recently, I came across some notes I had written in 1926 after I had visited the Seventh Session of the League of Nations in Geneva, Switzerland. Here is a paragraph:

'After three or four lifeless speakers read their manuscripts, Sir George Foster of Canada took the floor. With immense satisfaction I noted that he had no papers or notes of any kind. He gestured almost constantly. His heart was in what he was saying. He had something he very much wanted to get across. The fact that he was earnestly trying to convey to the audience certain convictions that he cherished in his own heart was as plain as Lake Geneva outside the windows. Principles I have been advocating in my teaching were beautifully illustrated in that talk.'

I often recall that speech by Sir George. He was sincere; he was earnest. Only by choosing topics which are felt by the heart as well as thought out by the mind will this sincerity be made manifest. Bishop Fulton J. Sheen, one of America's most dynamic speakers, learned this lesson early in life.

'I was chosen for the debating team in college,' he wrote in his book, *Life Is Worth Living*, 'and the night before the Notre Dame debate, our professor of debating called me to his office and scolded me.

"You are absolutely rotten. We have never had anybody in the history of this college who was a worse speaker than yourself."

"Well," I said, trying to justify myself, "if I am so rotten why did you pick me for the team?"

"Because," he answered, "you can think; not because you can

talk. Get over in that corner. Take a paragraph of your speech and go through it." I repeated a paragraph over and over again for an hour, at the end of which he said, "Do you see any mistake in that?" "No." Again an hour and a half, two hours, two and a half hours, at the end of which I was exhausted. He said, "Do you still not see what is wrong?"

Being naturally quick, after two hours and a half, I caught on. I said, "Yes, I am not sincere. I am not myself. I do not talk as if I meant it."'

At this point, Bishop Sheen learned a lesson he always remembered: he put himself into his talk. He became excited about his subject matter. Only then the wise professor said, 'Now, you are ready to speak!'

When a member of one of our classes says, 'I don't get excited about anything, I lead a humdrum sort of life,' our instructors are trained to ask him what he does in his spare time. One goes to the movies, another bowls, and another cultivates roses. One man told his instructor that he collected books of matches. As the instructor continued to question him about this unusual hobby, he gradually became animated. Soon, he was using gestures as he described the cabinets in which he stored his collection. He told his instructor that he had match books from almost every country in the world. When he became excited about his favourite topic, the instructor stopped him. 'Why don't you tell us about this subject? It sounds fascinating to me.' He said that he didn't think anyone would be interested! Here was a man who had spent years in pursuit of a hobby that was almost a passion with him; yet, he was negative about its value as a topic to speak about. This instructor assured this man that the only way to gauge the interest value of a subject was to ask yourself how interested you are in it. He talked that night with all the fervour of the true collector, and I heard later that he gained a certain amount of local recognition by going to various luncheon clubs and talking about match book collecting.

This illustration leads directly to yet another guiding principle for those who want a quick and easy way to learn to speak in public:

BE EAGER TO SHARE YOUR TALK WITH YOUR LISTENERS

There are three factors in every speaking situation: the speaker, the speech or the message, and the audience. The first two rules in this chapter dealt with the interrelationships of the speaker to a speech. Up to this point there is no speaking situation. Only when the speaker relates his talk to a living audience will the speaking situation come to life. The talk may be well prepared; it may concern a topic which the speaker is excited about; but for complete success, another factor must enter into his delivery of the talk. He must make his listeners feel that what he has to say is important to them. He must not only be excited about his topic, but he must be eager to transfer this excitement to his listeners. In every public speaker of note in the history of eloquence, there has been this unmistakable quality of salesmanship, evangelism, call it what you will. The effective speaker earnestly desires his listeners to feel what he feels, to agree with his point of view, to do what he thinks is right for them to do, and to enjoy and relive his experience with him. He is audience-centred and not self-centred. He knows that the success or failure of his talk is not for him to decide – it will be decided in the minds and hearts of his hearers.

I trained a number of men in the New York City Chapter of the American Institute of Banking to speak during a thrift campaign. One of the men in particular wasn't getting across to his audience. The first step in helping that man was to fire up his mind and heart with zeal for his subject. I told him to go off by himself and to think over this subject until he became enthusiastic about it. I asked him to remember that the Probate Court Records in New York show that more than 85 per cent of the people leave nothing at all at death; that only 3.3 per cent leave $10,000 or over. He was to keep constantly in mind that he was not asking people to do him a favour or something that they could not afford to do. He was to say to himself: 'I am preparing these people to have meat and bread and clothes and comfort in their old age, and to leave their wives and children secure.' He had to remember he was going out to perform a great social service. In short, he had to be a crusader.

He thought over these facts. He burned them into his mind. He aroused his own interest, stirred his own enthusiasm, and came to feel that he, indeed, had a mission. Then, when he went out to talk, there was a ring to his words that carried conviction. He sold his listeners on the benefits of thrift because he had an eager desire to help people. He was no longer just a speaker armed with facts; he was a missionary seeking converts to a worthwhile cause.

At one time in my teaching career I relied considerably on the textbook rules of public speaking. In doing this I was merely reflecting some of the bad habits that had been instilled into me by teachers who had not broken away from the stilted mechanics of elocution.

I shall never forget my first lesson in speaking. I was taught to let my arm hang loosely at my side, with the palm turned to the rear, fingers half-closed and thumb touching my leg. I was drilled to bring the arm up in a picturesque curve, to give the wrist a classical turn, and then to unfold the forefinger first, the second finger next, and the little finger last. When the whole aesthetic and ornamental movement had been executed, the arm was to retrace the course of the curve and rest again by the side of the leg. The whole performance was wooden and affected. There was nothing sensible or honest about it.

My instructor made no attempt to get me to put my own individuality into my speaking; no attempt to have me speak like a normal, living human being conversing in an energetic manner with my audience.

Contrast this mechanistic approach to speech training with the three primary rules I have been discussing in this chapter. They are the basis of my entire approach to training in effective speaking. You will come across them again and again in this book.

> A speaker must make his listeners feel that what he has to say is important to them. He must be eager to transfer his excitement to his listeners.

4

Sharing the Talk with the Audience

Russell Conwell's famous lecture, 'Acres of Diamonds', was given nearly 6,000 times. You would think that a talk repeated so often would become set in the speaker's mind, that no word or intonation would vary in delivery. That was not the case. Dr Conwell knew that audiences differ. He recognized that he had to make each successive audience feel that his talk was a personal, living thing created for it, and it alone. How did he succeed in keeping this interrelationship between speaker, speech, and audience alive from one speaking engagement to the next? 'I visit a town or city,' he wrote, 'and try to arrive there early enough to see the postmaster, the barber, the hotel manager, the principal of the schools, some of the ministers, and then go into the stores and talk with people, and see what has been their history and what opportunities they had. Then I give my lecture and talk to those people about the subjects that apply to them locally.'

Dr Conwell was thoroughly aware that successful communication depends upon how well the speaker can make his talk a part of the listeners and the listeners a part of the talk. That is why we have no true copy of 'Acres of Diamonds', one of the most popular talks ever given from a lecture platform. With his clever insight into human nature and his painstaking industry, Dr Conwell did not give the same lecture twice, although he addressed almost six thousand different audiences on the same subject. You can profit from his example by making certain that your talks are always prepared with a specific audience in mind. Here are some simple rules that will help you to build up a strong feeling of rapport with your listeners.

- Talk in terms of your listeners' interests
- Give honest, sincere appreciation
- Identify yourself with the audience
- Make your audience a partner in your talk
- Play yourself down

TALK IN TERMS OF YOUR LISTENERS' INTERESTS

That is exactly what Dr Conwell did. He made a point of working into his lecture plenty of local allusions and examples. His audiences were interested because his talk concerned them, their interests and their problems. This linkage with what your hearers are most interested in, namely, themselves, will ensure attention and guarantee that the lines of communication will remain open. Eric Johnston, former head of the United States Chamber of Commerce and now president of the Motion Picture Association, uses this technique in almost every talk he gives. Note how resourcefully he employed local interests in a commencement address at the University of Oklahoma:

'You Oklahomans are well acquainted with goose-pimple peddlers. You don't have to think back too far to remember when they were writing Oklahoma off the books as a hopeless risk forever.

'Why, in the 1930's, all the ravens of despair were telling the crows to bypass Oklahoma unless they could pack along their own rations.

'They consigned Oklahoma to an everlasting future as part of a new American desert. Nothing would ever bloom again – they said. But in the 1940's Oklahoma was a garden spot, and the toast of Broadway. For, once again, there was "waving wheat that sure smells sweet when the wind comes right behind the rain."

'In one short decade, the dustbowl was smothered with corn stalks as high as the elephant's eye.

'Here was a pay-off for faith – and calculated risk. But it is always possible to see our own times in better perspective against the backdrop of yesterday.

'So, I looked up the files of the *Daily Oklahoman* for the spring of 1901 in preparation for my visit here. I wanted to sample the flavour of life in the territory 50 years ago.

'And what did I discover?

'Why, I found the big accent was all on Oklahoma's future. The big stress was on hope.'

Here is an excellent example of talking in terms of audience interest. Eric Johnston used instances of calculated risk right out of his listeners' backyards. He made them feel that his talk was no mimeographed copy – it was freshly created for them. No audience can withhold attention from a speaker who talks in its interests.

Ask yourself how knowledge of your subject will help the members of your audience solve their problems and achieve their goals. Then proceed to show them that, and you will have their complete attention. If you are an accountant and you start your talk by saying something like this, 'I am going to show you how to save from $50 to a $100 on your tax return,' or you are a lawyer and you tell your listeners how to go about making a will, you will be certain to have an interested audience. Surely, there is some topic in your special fund of knowledge that can be of real help to members of your audience.

When asked what interests people, Lord Northcliffe, the William Randolph Hearst of British journalism, replied, 'Themselves.' He built a newspaper empire on that single truth.

In *Mind in the Making,* James Harvey Robinson describes reverie as 'a spontaneous and favourite kind of thinking'. He goes on to say that, in reverie, we allow our ideas to take their own course, and this course is determined by our hopes and fears, our spontaneous desires, their fulfilment or frustration; by our likes and dislikes, our loves, hates, and resentments. There is nothing so interesting to ourselves as ourselves.

Harold Dwight, of Philadelphia, made an extraordinarily successful talk at a banquet which marked the final session of our course. He talked about each person, in turn, around the entire table – how he had spoken when the course started, how he had improved; he recalled the talks various members had made, the subjects they had discussed; he mimicked some of them, exaggerated their peculiarities, had everyone laughing, had everyone pleased. With such material, he could not possibly have failed. It was absolutely ideal. No other topic under the blue dome of heaven would have so interested that group. Mr Dwight knew how to handle human nature.

Some years ago, I wrote a series of articles for the *American Magazine*, and I had the opportunity of talking with John Siddall, who was then in charge of the Interesting People Department.

'People are selfish,' he said. 'They are interested chiefly in themselves. They are not very much concerned about whether the government should own the railroads; but they do want to know how to get ahead, how to draw more salary, how to keep healthy. If I were editor of this magazine,' he went on, 'I would tell them how to take care of their teeth, how to take baths, how to keep cool in summer, how to get a position, how to handle employees, how to buy homes, how to remember, how to avoid grammatical error, and so on. People are always interested in human interest stories, so I would have some rich man tell how he made a million in real estate. I would get prominent bankers and presidents of various corporations to tell the stories of how they battled their ways up from the ranks to power and wealth.'

Shortly after that, Siddall was made editor. The magazine, then, had a small circulation. Siddall did just what he said he would do. The response? It was overwhelming. The circulation figures climbed up to two hundred thousand, three, four, half a million. Here was something the public wanted. Soon, a million people a month were buying it, then a million and a half, finally two million. It did not stop there, but continued to grow for many years. Siddall appealed to the self-interests of his readers.

Speakers who fail to take the essential egocentricity of their listeners into account are apt to find themselves facing a restless audience, one squirming in boredom, glancing at wristwatches, and looking hopefully toward the exit doors.

> The next time you face an audience, visualize them as eager to hear what you have to say – as long as it applies to them.

GIVE HONEST, SINCERE APPRECIATION

Audiences are composed of individuals, and they react like individuals. Openly criticize an audience and they resent it. Show your appreciation for something they have done that is worthy of praise, and you win a passport into their hearts. This often requires some research on your part. However, fulsome phrases as 'this is the most intelligent audience I have ever addressed', are resented as hollow flattery by most audiences.

In the words of a great speaker, Chauncey M. Depew, you have to 'tell them something about themselves that they didn't think you could possibly know'. For example, a man who spoke before the Baltimore Kiwanis Club recently, could find nothing unusual about that club except that it had in its membership a past international president and an international trustee. This was no news to the members of the club. So, he tried to give it a new twist. He started his talk with this sentence: 'The Baltimore Kiwanis Club is one club in 1,01,898.' The members listened. This speaker was certainly wrong – because there were only 2,897 Kiwanis clubs in the world. The speaker then went on: 'Yes, even if you don't believe it, it is still a feat that your club, mathematically at least, is one in 1,01,898. Not one club in 1,00,000 or one in 2,00,000, but just exactly one in 1,01,898.

'How do I figure that out? Kiwanis International has only 2,897 member clubs. Well, the Baltimore club has a past president of Kiwanis International and an international trustee. Mathematically, the chances that any Kiwanis club will have both a past president and an international trustee at the same time are one in 1,01,898 – and the reason I know it's right is that I got a Johns Hopkins Ph.D in mathematics to figure it out for me.'

Statements like: 'This exceptional gathering of the beauty and chivalry of Ho-Ho-Kus, New Jersey' or 'this highly intelligent audience' or 'I'm glad to be here because I love each one of you' – no, no, no! If you can't show sincere appreciation, don't show any!

> Be exactly 100 per cent sincere. An insincere statement may occasionally fool an individual, but it never fools an audience.

IDENTIFY YOURSELF WITH THE AUDIENCE

As soon as possible, preferably in the first words you utter, indicate some direct relationship with the group you are addressing. If you are honoured by being asked to speak, say so. When Harold Macmillan spoke to the graduating class at DePauw University in Greencastle, Indiana, he opened up the lines of communication in his first sentence:

'I am very grateful for your kind words of welcome,' he said. 'For a prime minister of Great Britain to be invited to your great university is an unusual occasion. But I feel that my present office was not the only nor, indeed, perhaps the main reason for your invitation.'

Then he mentioned that his mother was an American, born in Indiana, and that her father had been one of DePauw's first graduates.

'I can assure you that I am proud to be associated with DePauw University,' he said, 'and to renew an old family tradition.'

You may be sure that Macmillan's reference to an American school and to the American way of life which his mother and her pioneer father knew made friends for him at once.

Another way to open the lines of communication is to use the names of people in the audience. I once sat next to the main speaker at a banquet and I was amazed at his curiosity concerning various people in the hall. All through the meal he kept asking the master of ceremonies who the person in the blue suit at one table was, or what was the name of the lady in the flowered hat. When he arose to speak, it became evident at once why he was curious. He very cleverly wove some of the names he had learned into his talk, and I could see the evident pleasure on the faces of the persons whose names were used, and I sensed the warm friendliness of the audience that this simple technique won for the speaker.

Notice how Frank Pace, Jr, speaking as the president of the General Dynamics Corporation, worked in a few names to advantage. He was speaking at an annual dinner of Religion in American Life, Inc., in New York:

'This has been a delightful and meaningful evening for me in many ways,' he said. 'First, I have my own minister, the Reverend Robert Appleyard, here in the audience. By his words, deeds, and leadership he has been an inspiration to me personally, to my family, and to our entire congregation. Secondly, to sit between Lewis Strauss and Bob Stevens, men whose interest in religion has been amplified by their interest in public service...is again a source of great personal pleasure.'

One word of caution: If you are going to work strange names into your talk, having learned them through inquiries made for the occasion, be sure you have them exactly right; be sure you understand fully the reason for your use of the names; be sure you mention them only in a favourable way; and use them in moderation.

Another method of keeping the audience at peak attentiveness is to use the pronoun 'you' rather than the third-person 'they'. In this way you keep the audience in a state of self-awareness, which I have pointed out earlier, cannot be overlooked by the speaker if he is to hold the interest and attention of his listeners. Here are some excerpts from a talk on sulphuric acid by one of our students in a New York City class:

'Sulphuric acid touches you in your life in a score of ways. If it were not for sulphuric acid, your car would stop, for it is used extensively in the refining of kerosene and gasoline. The electric lights that illuminate your office and your home would not be possible without it.

'When you turn on the water for your bath, you use a nickel-plated faucet, which requires sulphuric acid in its manufacture. The soap you use has possibly been made from greases or oils that have been treated with the acid. The bristles in your hairbrush and your celluloid comb could not have been produced without it. Your razor, no doubt, has been pickled in it after annealing.

'You come down to breakfast. The cup and saucer, if they are other than plain white, could not have come into being without it. Your spoon, knife, and fork have seen a bath of sulphuric acid if they are silver-plated. And so on, through the whole day sulphuric acid affects you at every turn. Go where you will, you cannot escape its influence.'

By skilfully using 'you' and inserting his listeners into the picture, this speaker was able to keep attention alive and glowing. There are times, however, when the pronoun 'you' is dangerous, when it may establish a cleavage between speaker and audience rather than a bridge. This occurs when it might seem as though we were talking down to our audience or lecturing it. Then it is better to say 'we' instead of 'you'.

Dr W.W. Bauer, director of health education of the American Medical Association, often used this technique in his radio and television talks. 'We all want to know how to choose a good doctor, don't we?' he said in one of his talks. 'And if we are going to get the best service from our doctor, don't we all want to know how to be good patients?'

Thus, these are some effective ways of striking a chord with one's audience.

- Identify a direct relationship or association with the audience
- Use the names of some people in the audience
- Rather than the third-person 'they', use the pronoun 'you' in the speech

MAKE YOUR AUDIENCE A PARTNER IN YOUR TALK

Did it ever occur to you that you can keep an audience hanging on every word by using a little showmanship? The moment you choose some member of the audience to help you demonstrate a point or dramatize an idea, you will be rewarded by a noticeable rise in attention. Being aware of themselves as an audience, the members of it are keenly conscious of what happens when one of its own is brought into the act by the speaker. If there is a wall between the man on the platform and the people out there, as many speakers say, the use of audience participation will break that wall down. I remember a speaker who was explaining the distance it takes to stop a car after the brakes have been applied. He asked one of his listeners in the front row to stand and help demonstrate how this distance varied with the speed of the car. The man in the audience took the end of a steel tape measure and carried it 45 feet down the aisle, where he stopped on a signal from the speaker. As I watched this procedure I couldn't help but notice how the whole audience became engrossed in the talk. I said to myself that the tape measure, in addition to being a graphic illustration of the speaker's point, was certainly a line of communication between that speaker and this audience. Without that touch of showmanship the audience might still be concerned with what it was going to have for dinner or what programmes would be on TV that evening.

> Showmanship and questions ensure audience participation and attention

One of my favourite methods of getting audience participation is simply to ask questions and to get responses. I like to get the audience on its feet, repeating a sentence after me, or answering my questions by raising their hands. Percy H. Whiting, whose book, *How to Put Humour in Your Speaking and Writing* contains some valuable advice on the subject of audience participation, suggests having your listeners vote on something, or inviting them to help you solve a problem. 'Get yourself in the right state of mind,' says Mr Whiting, 'a state of mind that recognizes that a speech is unlike a recitation – that it is designed to get audience reaction, to make the audience a partner in the enterprise.' I like that description of the audience as a partner in the enterprise. It is the key to what this chapter is all about. If you use audience participation you confer the rights of partnership on your listeners.

PLAY YOURSELF DOWN

Of course, nothing will take the place of sincerity in this speaker-audience relationship. Norman Vincent Peale once gave some very useful advice to a fellow minister who was having great difficulty keeping the audience intent upon his sermons. He asked this minister to question his feelings about the congregation he addressed each Sunday morning – did he like them, did he want to help them, did he consider them his intellectual inferiors? Dr Peale said that he never ascended the pulpit without feeling a strong sense of affection for the men and women he was about to face. An audience is quick in taking the measure of a speaker who assumes that he is superior in mental accomplishment or in social standing. Indeed, one of the best ways for a speaker to endear himself to an audience is to play himself down.

Edmund S. Muskie, then US senator from Maine, demonstrated this when he spoke to the American Forensic Association in Boston.

'I approach my assignment this morning with many doubts,' he said. 'In the first place, I am conscious of the professional qualifications of this audience, and question the wisdom of exposing my poor talents to your critical view. In the second place, this is a breakfast meeting – an almost impossible time of day for a man to be on guard effectively; and failure in this respect can be fatal to a politician. And thirdly, there is my subject – the influence which debating has had on my career as a public servant. As long as I am active politically, there is likely to be a sharp division of opinion among my constituents as to whether that influence has been good or bad.

'Facing these doubts, I feel very much like the mosquito who found himself unexpectedly in a nudist colony. I don't know where to begin.'

Senator Muskie went on, from there, to make a fine address.

Adlai E. Stevenson played himself down at the beginning of a commencement exercise address at Michigan State University. He said:

'My feeling of inadequacy on these occasions brings to mind Samuel Butler's remark when he was once asked to talk about how to make the most out of life. I think his reply was: "I don't even know how to make the most out of the next 15 minutes." And I feel that way about the next 20 minutes.'

The surest way to antagonize an audience is to indicate that you consider yourself to be above them. When you speak, you are in a showcase and every facet of your personality is on display. The slightest hint of braggadocio is fatal. On the other hand, modesty inspires confidence and good will. You can be modest without being apologetic. Your audience will like and respect you for suggesting your limitations as long as you show you are determined to do your best.

The world of American television is a demanding one, and every season top-rated performers fall under the withering fire of competition. One of the survivors who comes back year after year is Ed Sullivan, who is not a television professional, but a newspaper man. He is an amateur in this fiercely competitive field and he survives because he doesn't presume to be anything but an amateur. Some of his mannerisms on camera would have been handicaps for anyone with less natural appeal. He cups his chin in his hand, hunches his shoulders, tugs at his necktie, and stumbles over words. But these failings are not fatal for Ed Sullivan. He doesn't resent people for criticizing these faults. At least once a season he hires the services of a talented mimic who caricaturizes him to perfection, exaggerating all his faults. Ed Sullivan laughs as unaffectedly as everyone else when this performer holds the mirror up to nature. He welcomes criticism, and audiences love him for it.

> Audiences like humility. They resent the show-off, the egotist.

Henry and Dana Lee Thomas, in their book, *Living Biographies of Religious Leaders*, said of Confucius: 'He never tried to dazzle people with his exclusive knowledge. He merely tried to enlighten them with his inclusive sympathy.' If we have this inclusive sympathy, we have the key that unlocks the door to the audiences' heart.

5

Delivering the Talk

Would you believe it? There are four ways, and only four ways, in which we have contact with the world. We are evaluated and classified by these four contacts: what we do, how we look, what we say, and how we say it. This chapter will deal with the last of these – how we say it.

When I first started to teach public speaking classes, I spent a great deal of time on the use of vocal exercises to develop resonance, increase the range of voice, and enhance inflectional agility. It wasn't long, however, before I began to see the utter futility of teaching adults how to project their tones into the upper sinuses and how to form 'liquid' vowels. This is all very fine for those who can devote three or four years to improving themselves in the art of vocal delivery. I realized that my students would have to settle for the vocal equipment they were born with. I found that if I expended the time and energy I formerly devoted to helping class members to 'breathe diaphragmatically', and worked on the far more important objectives of freeing them from their inhibitions and general reluctance to let themselves go, I would achieve quick and lasting results that were truly amazing. I thank God I had the sense to do this.

CRASH THROUGH YOUR SHELL OF SELF-CONSCIOUSNESS

In my course there are several sessions that have as their purpose the freeing of tightly bound and tense adults. I got down on my knees, literally, to implore my class members to come out of their shells and find out for themselves that the world would treat them with cordiality and welcome when they would do so. It took some doing, I admit, but it was worth it. As Marshal Foch says of the art of war, 'it is simple enough in its conception, but unfortunately, complicated in its execution.' The biggest stumbling block, of course, is stiffness, not only of the physical, but, of the mental as well, a kind of hardening of the categories that comes with growing up.

It is not easy to be natural before an audience. Actors know that. When you were a child, say, four years old, you probably could have mounted a platform and talked naturally to an audience. But when you are 24, or 44, what happens when you mount a platform and start to speak? Do you retain that unconscious naturalness that you possessed at four? You may, but it is dollars to doughnuts that you will become stiff and stilted and mechanical, and draw back into your shell like a snapping turtle.

The problem of teaching or of training adults in delivery is not one of superimposing additional characteristics; it is largely one of removing impediments, of getting them to speak with the same naturalness that they would display if someone were to knock them down.

Hundreds of times I have stopped speakers in the midst of their talks and implored them to talk like a human being. Hundreds of nights I have come home mentally fatigued and nervously exhausted from trying to drill members of my classes to talk naturally. No, believe me, it is not as easy as it sounds.

In one of the sessions of my course I ask the class to act out portions of dialogue, some of which is in dialect. I ask them to throw themselves into these dramatic episodes with abandon. When they do, they discover to their amazement that, though they may have acted like a fool, they didn't feel badly when they were doing it. The class, too, is amazed at the dramatic ability some of the class members display.

> My point is that once you let your hair down before a group you are not likely to hold yourself back when it comes to the normal, everyday expression of your opinions whether to individuals or before groups.

The sudden freedom you feel is like a bird taking wing after being imprisoned in a cage. You see why it is that people flock to the theatre and the movies – because there they see their fellow human beings act with little or no inhibition. There, they see people wearing their emotions prominently displayed on their sleeves.

DON'T TRY TO IMITATE OTHERS: BE YOURSELF

We all admire speakers who can put showmanship into their speaking, who are not afraid to express themselves, not afraid to use the unique, individual, imaginative way of saying what they have to say to the audience.

Shortly after the close of the First World War, I met two brothers in London – Sir Ross and Sir Keith Smith. They had just made the first aeroplane flight from London to Australia to win a fifty-thousand-dollar prize offered by the Australian government. They had created a sensation throughout the British Empire and had been knighted by the King.

Captain Hurley, a well-known scenic photographer, had flown with them over a part of their trip, taking motion pictures. So, I helped them prepare an illustrated travel talk of their flight and trained them in the delivery of it. They gave it twice daily for four months in Philharmonic Hall, London, one speaking in the afternoon, the other at night.

They had had identically the same experience, they had sat side by side as they flew halfway around the world, and they delivered the same talk, almost word for word. Yet, somehow it didn't sound like the same talk at all.

There is something besides the mere words in a talk which counts. It is the flavour with which they are delivered. It is not so much just what you say as how you say it.

Brulloff, the great Russian painter, once corrected a pupil's study. The pupil looked in amazement at the altered drawing, exclaiming: 'Why, you have touched it only a tiny bit, but it is quite another thing.' Brulloff replied, 'Art begins where the tiny bit begins.' That is as true of speaking as it is of painting and of Paderewski's playing.

The same thing holds true when one is touching words. There is an old saying in the English Parliament that everything depends upon the manner in which one speaks and not upon the matter. Quintilian said it long ago, when England was one of the outlying colonies of Rome.

'All Fords are exactly alike,' their maker used to say, but no two men are just alike. Every new life is a new thing under the sun; there has never been anything just like it before, and never will be again. A young man ought to get that idea about himself; he should look for the single spark of individuality that makes him different from other folks, and develop that for all he is worth. Society and schools may try to iron it out of him; their tendency is to put us all in the same mould, but, I say, don't let that spark be lost; it's your only real claim to importance.

All that is doubly true of effective speaking. There is no other human being in the world like you. Hundreds of millions of people have two eyes and a nose and a mouth; but none of them looks precisely like you; and none of them has exactly your traits and methods and cast of mind. Few of them will talk and express themselves just as you do when you are speaking naturally.

In other words, you have an individuality. As a speaker, it is your most precious possession. Cling to it. Cherish it. Develop it. It is the spark that will put force and sincerity into your speaking. It is your only real claim to importance. Please, I beg you, do not attempt to force yourself in a mould and thereby lose your distinctiveness.

CONVERSE WITH YOUR AUDIENCE

Let me give you an illustration that is typical of the fashion in which thousands of persons talk. I happened on one occasion to be stopping in Murren, a summer resort in the Swiss Alps. I was living at a hotel operated by a London company; and they usually sent out from England a couple of lecturers each week to talk to the guests. One of them was a well-known English novelist. Her topic was 'The Future of the Novel'. She admitted that she had not selected the subject herself; and the long and short of it was that she had nothing she cared to say about it to make it worthwhile expressing. She had hurriedly made some rambling notes; and she stood before the audience, ignoring her hearers, not even looking at them, staring sometimes over their heads, sometimes at her notes, sometimes at the floor. She unreeled words into the primeval void with a far-away look in her eyes and a faraway ring in her voice.

That isn't delivering a talk at all. It is a soliloquy. It has no sense of communication.

The first essential of good talking is a sense of communication. The audience must feel that there is a message being delivered straight from the mind and heart of the speaker to their minds and their hearts.

The kind of talk I have just described might as well have been spoken out in the sandy, waterless wastes of the Gobi desert. In fact, it sounded as if it were being delivered in some such spot rather than to a group of living human beings.

An enormous amount of nonsense and twaddle has been written about delivery. It has been shrouded in rules and rites and made mysterious. Old-fashioned elocution has often made it ridiculous. The businessman, going to the library or book shop, has found volumes on oratory that were utterly useless. In spite of progress in other directions, in almost every state in the Union today, schoolboys are still being forced to recite the ornate oratory of orators – a thing that is as useless as a squirrel-headed tire pump, and as out-of-date as a quill pen.

An entirely new school of speaking has sprung up since the twenties. In keeping with the spirit of the times, it is as modern and as practical as the automobile, direct as a telegram, businesslike as a telling advertisement. The verbal fireworks that were once the vogue would no longer be tolerated by an audience today.

A modern audience, regardless of whether it is 15 people at a business conference or 1,000 people under a tent, wants the speaker to talk just as directly as he would in a chat; and in the same general manner he would employ in speaking to one of them in conversation – in the same manner, but with greater force or energy. In order to appear natural, he has to use much more energy in talking to 40 people than he does in talking to one, just as a statue on top of a building has to be of heroic size in order to make it appear of lifelike proportions to an observer on the ground.

At the close of one of Mark Twain's lectures in a Nevada mining camp, an old prospector approached him and inquired: 'Be them your natural tones of eloquence?'

That is what the audience wants: 'your natural tones of eloquence', enlarged a bit.

The only way to acquire the knack of this enlarged naturalness is by practice. And, as you practice, if you find yourself talking in a stilted manner, pause and say sharply to yourself mentally:

'Here! What is wrong? Wake up! Be human.' Then, mentally pick out a person in the audience, someone in the back or the least attentive person you can find, and talk to this person. Forget there is anyone else present at all. Converse with this person. Imagine that he has asked you a question and that you are answering it, and that you are the only one who can answer it. If he were to stand up and talk to you, and you were to talk back to him, that process would immediately and inevitably make your speaking more conversational, more natural, more direct. So, imagine that is precisely what is taking place.

You may go so far as actually to ask questions and answer them. For example, in the midst of your talk, you may say, 'and you ask what proof have I for this assertion? I have adequate proof and here it is…' Then proceed to answer the question. That sort of thing can be done very naturally. It will break up the monotony of one's delivery; it will make it direct and pleasant and conversational.

Speak to the Chamber of Commerce just as you would to John Henry Smith. What is a meeting of the Chamber of Commerce, after all, but a collection of John Henry Smiths? Won't the same methods that are successful with those men individually be successful with them collectively?

Earlier in this chapter was described the delivery of a certain novelist. In the same ballroom in which she had spoken, we had the pleasure, a few nights later, of hearing Sir Oliver Lodge. His subject was 'Atoms and Worlds'. He had devoted to this subject more than half a century of thought, and study, and experiment, and investigation. He had something that was essentially a part of his heart and mind and life, something that he wanted very much to say. He forgot that he was trying to make a speech. That was the least of his worries. He was concerned only with telling the audience about atoms, telling us accurately, lucidly, and feelingly. He was earnestly trying to get us to see what he saw, and to feel what he felt.

And what was the result? He delivered a remarkable talk. It

had both charm and power. It made a deep impression. He was a speaker of unusual ability. Yet, I am sure he didn't regard himself in that light. I am sure that few people who heard him ever thought of him as a public speaker at all.

If you speak in public so that people hearing you will suspect that you have had training in public speaking, you will not be a credit to your instructor, especially an instructor in one of my courses. He desires you to speak with such intensified naturalness that your audience will never dream that you have been formally trained.

> A good window does not call attention to itself. It merely lets in the light. A good speaker is like that. He is so disarmingly natural that his hearers never notice his manner of speaking; they are conscious only of his matter.

PUT YOUR HEART INTO YOUR SPEAKING

Sincerity, enthusiasm, and high earnestness will help you, too. When a man is under the influence of his feelings, his real self comes to the surface. The bars are down. The heat of his emotions has burned all barriers away. He acts spontaneously. He talks spontaneously. He is natural.

So, in the end, even this matter of delivery comes back to the thing which has already been emphasized repeatedly in these pages: namely, put your heart into your talks.

'I shall never forget,' said Dean Brown in his lectures on preaching before the Yale Divinity School, 'the description given by a friend of mine of a church service which he once attended in the city of London. The preacher was George MacDonald; he read for the scripture lesson that morning the eleventh chapter of Hebrews. When the time came for the sermon, he said: "You have all heard about these men of faith. I shall not try to tell you what faith is. There are theological professors who could do that much better than I could do it. I am here to help you believe." Then followed such a simple, heartfelt, and majestic manifestation of the man's own faith in those unseen realities which are eternal, as to beget faith in the minds and hearts of all his hearers. His heart was in his work, and his delivery was effective because it rested upon the genuine beauty of his own inner life.'

His heart was in his work. That is the secret. Yet, I know that advice like this is not popular. It seems vague. It sounds indefinite. The average person wants fool proof rules, something definite, something he can put his hands on, rules as precise as the directions for operating a car.

That is what he wants; that is what I would like to give him. It would be easy for him and it would be easy for me. There are such rules, and there is only one little thing wrong with them – they just don't work. They take all the naturalness, spontaneity, and life and juice out of a man's speaking. I know. In my younger days, I wasted a great deal of energy trying them. They won't appear in these pages for, as Josh Billings observed in one of his lighter moments: 'There ain't no use in knowin' so many things that ain't so.'

Edmund Burke wrote speeches so superb in logic and reasoning and composition that they are today studied as classic models of oratory in the colleges of the land; yet, Burke, as a speaker, was a notorious failure. He didn't have the ability to deliver his gems, to make them interesting and forceful; so, he was called 'the dinner bell' of the House of Commons. When he arose to talk, the other members coughed and shuffled and either went to sleep or went out in droves.

You can throw a steel-jacketed bullet at a man with all your might, and you cannot make even a dent in his clothing. But put powder behind a tallow candle and you can shoot it through a pine board. Many a tallow-candle speech with powder makes, I regret to say, more of an impression than a steel-jacketed talk with no force, no excitement, behind it.

PRACTISE MAKING YOUR VOICE STRONG AND FLEXIBLE

When we are really communicating our ideas to our listeners we are making use of many elements of vocal and physical variety. We shrug our shoulders, move our arms, wrinkle our brows, increase our volume, change pitch and inflection, and talk fast or slow as the occasion and the material may dictate. It is well to remember that all these are effects and not causes. The so-called variables, or modulations of tone, are under the direct influence of our mental and emotional state. That is why it is so important that we have a topic we know and a topic we are excited about when we go before an audience. That is why we must be so eager to share that topic with our listeners.

Since most of us lose the spontaneity and naturalness of youth as we grow older, we tend to dip into a definite mould of physical and vocal communication. We find ourselves less ready to use gestures and animation; we rarely raise or lower our voices from one pitch to another. In short we lose the freshness and spontaneity of true conversation. We may get into the habit of talking too slowly or too rapidly, and our diction, unless carefully watched, tends to become ragged and careless. In this book you have been repeatedly told to act natural, and you may suppose that I, therefore, condone poor diction or monotonous delivery provided it is natural. On the contrary, I say that we should be natural in the sense that we express our ideas and express them with spirit. On the other hand, every good speaker will not accept himself as incapable of improvement in breadth of vocabulary, richness of imagery and diction, and variety and force of expression. These are areas in which everyone interested in self-improvement will seek to improve.

It is an excellent idea to evaluate oneself in terms of volume, pitch variation, and pace. This can be done with the aid of a tape recorder. On the other hand, it would be useful to have friends help you make this evaluation. If it is possible to secure expert advice, so much the better. It should be remembered, however, that these are areas for practice away from the audience. To concern yourself with technique when you are before an audience will prove fatal to effectiveness. Once there, pour yourself into your talk, concentrate your whole being on making a mental and emotional impact on your audience, and nine chances out of ten you will speak with more emphasis and force than you could ever get from books.

> It is very important to evaluate oneself in terms of volume, pitch, and pace. This can be done with the help of a tape recorder, through friends, and even by means of expert advice.

6

Organizing the Long Talk

No sane man would start to build a house without some sort of plan; but why will he begin to deliver a talk without the vaguest notion of what he wishes to accomplish?

A talk is a voyage with a purpose, and it must be charted. The man who starts nowhere, generally gets there.

I wish that I could paint this saying of Napoleon's in flaming letters of red, a foot high over every doorway on the globe where students of effective speaking foregather: 'The art of war is a science in which nothing succeeds which has not been calculated and thought out.'

That is just as true of speaking as of shooting. But do speakers realize it – or, if they do, do they always act on it? They do not. Many a talk has just a trifle more plan and arrangement than a bowl of Irish stew.

What is the best and most effective arrangement for a given set of ideas? No one can say until he has studied them. It is always a new problem, an eternal question that every speaker must ask and answer himself again and again. No infallible rules can be given; but we can, at any rate, indicate the three major phases of the longer talk to get action: the attention step, the body, and conclusion. For each, there are some time-tested methods of developing each phase.

GET ATTENTION IMMEDIATELY

I once asked Dr Lynn Harold Hough, formerly president of Northwestern University, what was the most important fact his long experience as a speaker has taught him. After pondering a moment, he replied, 'To get an arresting opening, something that will seize favourable attention immediately.' Dr Hough struck at the heart of the matter of all persuasive speaking: how to get the audience tuned in right from the speaker's first words. Here are some methods which, if applied, will give high attention value to your opening phrases:

Begin Your Talk with an Incident-example

Lowell Thomas, who has made a world-wide reputation as a news analyst, lecturer, and motion picture producer, began a talk on Lawrence of Arabia with this statement:

'I was going down Christian Street in Jerusalem one day when I met a man clad in the gorgeous robes of an oriental potentate. At his side hung the curved gold sword worn only by the descendants of the prophet Mohammed....'

And he was off – off with a story from his experience. That is what hooks attention. That kind of opening is almost fool proof. It can hardly fail. It moves, it marches. We follow because we identify ourselves as part of a situation and we want to know what is going to happen. I know of no more compelling a method of opening a talk than by the use of a story.

One of my own talks which I have given many times begins with these words:

'Just after I had finished college, I was walking one night down a street in Huron, South Dakota, and I saw a man standing on a box talking to a crowd of people. I was curious, so I became part of the group listening to him. "Do you know", the speaker was saying, "that you never see a bald-headed Indian? Or you never see a bald-headed woman, do you? Now, I'm going to tell you why..."'

> No stalling. No 'warm-up' statements. By launching directly into an incident, you can make it easy to capture an audience's attention.

A speaker who begins a talk with a story from his experience is on safe ground, for there is no groping for words, no loss of ideas. The experience he is relating is his, a re-creation, as it were, of part of his life, the very fibre of his being. The result? A self-assured, relaxed manner which will help a speaker establish himself on a friendly basis with an audience.

Arouse Suspense

Here is the way Mr Powell Healy began a talk at the Penn Athletic Club in Philadelphia:

'82 years ago, there was published in London a little volume, a story, which was destined to become immortal. Many people have called it "the greatest little book in the world". When it first appeared, friends meeting one another on the Strand or Pall Mall asked the question, "Have you read it?" The answer invariably was: "Yes, God bless him, I have."

'The day it was published 1,000 copies were sold. Within a fortnight the demand had consumed 15,000. Since then, it has run into countless thousands of editions and has been translated into every language under heaven. A few years ago, L.P. Morgan purchased the original manuscript for a fabulous sum and it now reposes among the priceless treasures in his magnificent art gallery. What is this world famous book? It is...'

Are you interested? Are you eager to know more? Has the speaker captured the favourable attention of his listeners? Do you feel this opening has held your attention, heightened your interest as it progressed? Why? Because it aroused your curiosity and held you in suspense.

Curiosity! Who is not susceptible to it?

Perhaps, you, too! You are asking just who is the author and what is the book mentioned above? To satisfy your curiosity, here is the answer: The author: Charles Dickens; the book: *A Christmas Carol.*

Creating suspense is a sure-fire method of getting your listeners interested.

Here is how I try to arouse suspense in my lecture on *How to Stop Worrying and Start Living*. I begin like this: 'In the spring of 1871, a young man who was destined to become a world-famous physician, William Osier, picked up a book and read twenty-one words that had a profound effect upon his future.'

What were the twenty-one words? And, how did these words affect his future? These are the questions your listeners will want answered.

State an Arresting Fact

Clifford R. Adams, director of the Marriage Counselling Service of the Pennsylvania State College, began an article in the *Reader's Digest*, entitied, 'How to Pick a Mate,' with these startling facts – facts that make you gasp, facts that make an arresting opener:

- 'Today the chances that our young people will find happiness through marriage are slim indeed. The rise of our divorce rate is frightening. One marriage in five or six landed on the rocks in 1940. By 1946, it is expected to be one in four. And, if long-range trends continue, the rate in 50 years will be one in two.'

Here are two other examples of 'arresting facts' openers:

- 'The war department predicts that, in the first night of an atomic war, 20 million Americans will be killed.'
- 'A few years ago, the *Scripps-Howard* newspapers spent $176,000 on a survey to discover what customers disliked about retail stores. It was the most costly, the most scientific,

> the most thorough survey ever made of retail selling problems. Questionnaires were sent into 54,047 homes in 16 different cities. One of the questions was: "What do you dislike about the stores in this town?" Almost two-fifths of all the answers to that question were the same: Discourteous clerks!'

This method of making startling statements at the beginning of a talk is effective in establishing contact with the listener because it jars the mind. It is a kind of shock technique that enlists attention by using the unexpected to focus attention upon the subject matter of the talk.

One of our class members in Washington, DC, used this method, arousal of curiosity, as effectively as anyone I have ever heard. Her name, Meg Sheil. Here is her opening:

'I was a prisoner for ten years. Not in an ordinary prison, but, in one whose walls were worry about my inferiority and whose bars were the fear of criticism.'

Don't you want to know more about this true-life episode?

A danger of the startling opener must be avoided, that is, the tendency to be over-dramatic or too sensational. I remember one speaker who started his talk by shooting a pistol into the air. He got attention all right, but, he also blasted the eardrums of his listeners.

Make your opening conversational in manner. An efficient way to discover whether you have an opener that is conversational is to try it out across the dinner table. If the way you open your talk isn't conversational enough to be spoken across the dinner table, it probably won't be conversational enough for an audience either.

Frequently, however, the opening of the talk that is supposed to get the listeners' interest is, in reality, the dullest part of the talk. For example, I recently heard a speaker begin like this: 'Trust in the Lord and have faith in your own ability…' A preachy, obvious way to begin a talk! But, note his second sentence; it is interesting; it has heart throb in it: 'My mother was left a widow in 1918 with three children to support, and no money…' Why, oh why, didn't that speaker begin in his first sentence by telling about the struggles of his widowed mother with three little children to support!

> If you want to interest your listeners, don't begin with an introduction. Begin by leaping right into the heart of your story.

That is what Frank Bettger does. He is the author of *How I Raised Myself From Failure to Success in Selling*. He is an artist when it comes to creating suspense in his first sentence. I know, because he and I travelled together all over the United States giving talks on selling under the auspices of the United States Junior Chamber of Commerce. I always admired the superb way he opened his talk on enthusiasm. No preaching. No lecturing. No sermonizing. No general statements. Frank Bettger leaped right into the heart of his subject in his first sentence. He began his talk on enthusiasm like this:

'Shortly after I started out as a professional baseball player. I got one of the biggest shocks of my life.'

What effect did this opening have on his audience? I know, I was there. I saw the reaction. He had everyone's attention instantly. Everyone was eager to hear why and how he was shocked, and what he did about it.

Ask for a Show of Hands

A splendid way to get interested attention is to ask the audience to raise their hands in answer to a question. For example, I have opened my talk on 'How to Prevent Fatigue' with this question:

'Let's see your hands. How many of you get tired more quickly than you feel you ought to?'

Note this point: When you ask for a show of hands, usually give the audience some warning that you are going to do so. Do not open a talk with: 'How many people here believe the income tax should be lowered? Let's see your hands.' Give the audience a chance to be ready for the vote by saying, for instance: 'I am going to ask for a show of hands on a question of importance to you. This is the question: How many of you believe that trading stamps benefit the consumer?'

The technique of asking for a show of hands gets a priceless reaction known as audience participation. When you use it, your talk is no longer a one-sided affair. The audience is participating in it now. When you ask, 'How many of you get tired more quickly than you feel you ought to?' everyone starts thinking of his favourite topic: himself, his aches, and his fatigue. He lifts his hand and possibly looks around to see who else has his hand up. He forgets that he is listening to a talk. He smiles. He nods to a friend sitting next to him. The ice is broken. You, the speaker, are at ease, and so is the audience.

Promise to Tell the Audience How they Can Get Something they Want

An almost unfailing way to get alert attention is to promise to tell your listeners how they can get what they want by doing what you suggest. Following are some illustrations of what I mean:

- 'I am going to tell you how to prevent fatigue. I am going to tell you how to add one hour a day to your waking life.'
- 'I'm going to tell you how you can materially increase your income.'
- 'I promise that, if you will listen to me for ten minutes, I'll tell you one sure way to make yourself more popular.'

> The 'promise' type of opener is sure to get attention because it goes straight to the self-interests of the audience.

All too often, speakers neglect to tie their topics to the vital interests of their hearers. Instead of opening the door to attention, they slam it shut with dull openings that trace the history of the subject matter or laboriously dwell upon the background necessary to an understanding of the topic.

I remember one talk I heard a few years ago on a topic which, in itself, was important to the audience: the necessity of periodic health examinations. How did the speaker begin his talk? Did he add to the natural attractiveness of his subject by an effective opening? No. He started with a colourless recital of the history of his topic and the audience began to lose interest in him and in his subject. An opening built around the 'promise' technique would have been admirably appropriate. For instance:

'Do you know how long you are expected to live? Life insurance companies can predict this by means of life expectancy tables which have been compiled from the lives of millions of persons. You can expect to live two-thirds of the time between your present age and 80. Now, is this long enough for you to live? No, no! We are all passionately eager to live longer and we want to prove that this prediction is wrong. But how, you ask, can this be done? How can I extend my life beyond the shockingly small number of years statisticians say remain for me? Well, there is an answer, a possible way this can be done, and I shall tell you how to do this...'

I leave it to you to decide whether this type of opening captures your interest, if it compels you to listen to the speaker. You must listen to him because he not only is talking about you, about your life, but he has promised to tell you something of the most intense personal value to you. No dull recital of impersonal facts here! Such an opening as this is almost impossible to resist.

Use an Exhibit

Perhaps, the easiest way in the world to gain attention is to hold up something for people to look at. Almost any creature, from the simplest to the most complex, will give heed to that kind of stimulus. It can be used sometimes with effectiveness before the most dignified audience. For example, Mr S.S. Ellis, of Philadelphia opened one of his talks in one of our classes by holding a coin between his thumb and forefinger, and high above his shoulder. Naturally everyone looked. Then he inquired: 'Has anyone here ever found a coin like this on the sidewalk? It announces that the fortunate finder will be given a lot free in such and such a real estate development. He has but to call and present this coin... Mr Ellis then proceeded to condemn the misleading and unethical practices involved.

All of the foregoing methods are commendable. They may be used separately or they may be combined. Recognize that how you open a talk largely determines whether the audience is going to accept you and your message.

AVOID GETTING UNFAVOURABLE ATTENTION

Please, please, I urge you, remember that you must not only capture the attention of your audience, but, you must capture their favourable attention. Please note that I said favourable attention. No rational person would begin a talk by insulting his audience or by making any obnoxious or disagreeable statement that would turn them against him and his message. Yet, how frequently speakers begin talks by attracting attention through the use of one of the following devices:

Do Not Open with an Apology

To begin a talk with an apology does not get you off to a good start, either. How often we all have heard speakers begin by calling the attention of the audience to their lack of preparation or their lack of ability. If you are not prepared, the audience will probably discover it without your assistance. Why insult your audience by suggesting that you did not think them worth preparing for, that just any old thing you had on the fire was good enough to serve them? No, we don't want to hear apologies; we want to be informed and interested – to be interested, remember that. Let your opening sentence capture the interest of your audience. Not the second sentence. Not the third sentence. The first!

Avoid the 'Funny' Story Opening

You may have noticed that there is one method of opening a talk, and one much favoured by speakers, that is not recommended here – the so-called 'funny' story opening. For some lamentable reason, the novice feels that he ought to lighten up his talk by telling a joke; he assumes that the mantel of Mark Twain has descended upon his shoulders. Do not fall into this trap; you will discover to your embarrassment the painful truth that the 'funny' story is more often pathetic than funny – and the story may be known to persons in your audience.

A sense of humour, though, is a prized asset for any speaker. A talk need not begin, nor be, heavy-footed, elephantine, and excessively solemn. Not at all. If you have the ability to tickle the risibility of your audience by some witty reference to a local situation or to something arising out of the occasion or the remarks of a previous speaker, then, by all means, do so. Observe some incongruity. Exaggerate it. That type of humour is more likely to succeed than stale jokes about Pat and Mike, or mothers-in-law, or shaggy dogs, because it is relevant and because it is original.

Perhaps the easiest way to create merriment is to tell a story on yourself. Depict yourself in some ridiculous and embarrassing situation. That gets down to the very essence of humour. Jack Benny has used this device for years. He was one of the first major radio comedians to poke fun at himself. By making himself the butt of jokes concerning his ability to play the violin, his miserliness, and his age, Jack Benny works a rich vein of humour that keeps his ratings high from year to year.

Audiences open their hearts, as well as their minds, to speakers who deliberately deflate themselves by calling attention to some deficiency or failing on their part, in a humorous sense, of course. On the other hand, creating the image of the 'stuffed shirt' or the 'visiting expert with all the answers' leaves an audience cold and unreceptive.

Support Your Main Ideas

In the longer talk to get action you will have several points; the fewer the better – but all of them will require support material. One method of supporting the point of a talk, which is what you want the audience to do, is by illustrating it with a story, or an experience out of your life. This type of example is popular because it appeals to a basic drive in people, summed up by the slogan, 'Everybody Loves a Story'. An incident or happening is the kind of example most often used by the average speaker, but, it is by no means the only way your point can be supported. You might also use statistics, which are nothing more than illustrations scientifically grouped, expert testimony, analogies, exhibits, or demonstrations.

Use Statistics

Statistics are used to show the proportion of instances of a certain kind. They can be impressive and convincing, especially as evidence where an isolated example might not do as well. The effectiveness of the Salk anti-poliomyelitis vaccine programme was measured by statistics gathered in all parts of the country. Isolated cases of ineffectiveness were the exceptions that proved the rule. A talk based on one of these exceptions would not, therefore, convince a parent that the Salk vaccine programme would not protect his child.

Statistics, of themselves, can be boring. They should be judiciously used, and when used they should be clothed in a language that makes them vivid and graphic.

Here is an example of how statistics can be impressive by comparing them with things familiar to us:

In backing up his point that a vast amount of time is lost by New Yorkers' neglecting to answer telephones promptly, an executive said, 'Out of each 100 telephone connections made, seven show a delay of more than a minute before the person called answers. Every day 2,80,000 minutes are lost in this way. In the course of six months, this minute delay in New York is about equal to all the business days that have elapsed since Columbus discovered America.'

Mere numbers and amounts, taken by themselves, are never very impressive. They have to be illustrated; they ought, if possible, to be put in terms of our experiences. I remember listening to a lecture by a guide in the vast power room under Grand Coulee Dam. He could have given us the square-foot figures of the room's size, but that would not have been so convincing as the method he used. He told us that the room was large enough for a crowd of 10,000 people to view a football game on a regulation field and, in addition, there would be room left over for several tennis courts at each end!

Many years ago, a student in my course at the Brooklyn Central YMCA told in a talk the number of houses destroyed by fire during the previous year. He further said that, if these burned buildings had been placed side by side, the line would have reached from New York to Chicago, and that if the people who had been killed in those fires had been placed half a mile apart, that gruesome line would reach back again from Chicago to Brooklyn.

The figures he gave I forgot almost immediately, but, years have passed, and, without any effort on my part, I can still see that line of burning buildings stretching from Manhattan Island to Cook County, Illinois.

Use the Testimony of Experts

Frequently you can effectively back up the points you want to make in the body of your talk by the use of the testimony of an expert. Before using testimony it should be tested by answering these questions:

- Is the quotation I am about to use accurate?
- Is it taken from the area of the man's expert knowledge? To quote Joe Louis on economics would obviously be exploiting his name but not his forte.
- Is the quotation from a man who is known and respected by the audience?
- Are you sure that the statement is based on first-hand knowledge, not personal interest or prejudice?

One of the members of my class at the Brooklyn Chamber of Commerce many years ago, opened a talk on the need for specialization with a quotation from Andrew Carnegie. Did he choose wisely? Yes, because he accurately quoted a man, who was respected by the audience as one who had earned the right to speak on business success. That quotation is still worth repeating today:

'I believe the true road to pre-eminent success in any line is to make yourself master in that line. I have no faith in the policy of scattering one's resources, and in my experience I have rarely, if ever, met a man who achieved pre-eminence in money-making – certainly never one in manufacturing – who was interested in many concerns. The men who have succeeded are the men who have chosen one line and stuck to it.'

Use Analogies

An analogy, according to Webster, is a 'relation of likeness between two things…consisting in the resemblance not of the things themselves but of two or more attributes, circumstances, or effects'.

The use of an analogy is a fine technique for supporting a main idea. Here is an excerpt from a talk on 'The Need for More Electric Power' by C. Girard Davidson when he was assistant secretary of the Interior. Note how he employs a comparison, an analogy, to back up his point:

'A prosperous economy has to keep moving forward or it goes into a tailspin. There is a parallel with the airplane, which is a useless collection of nuts and bolts standing still on the ground. When moving forward in the air, however, it comes into its own and serves as a useful function. To stay up, it has to keep going forward. If it doesn't move, it sinks – and it can't move backward.'

Here is another, perhaps one of the most outstanding analogies in the history of eloquence; it was used by Lincoln in answer to his critics during a crucial period of the Civil War:

'Gentlemen, I want you to suppose a case for a moment. Suppose that all the property you were worth was in gold, and you had put it in the hands of Blondin, the famous rope-walker, to carry across the Niagara Falls on a tightrope. Would you shake the rope while he was passing over it, or keep shouting to him, "Blondin, stoop a little more! Go a little faster!" No, I am sure you would not. You would hold your breath as well as your tongue, and keep your hands off until he was safely over. Now the government is in the same situation. It is carrying an immense weight across a stormy ocean. Untold treasures are in its hands. It is doing the best it can. Don't badger it! Just keep still, and it will get you safely over.'

Use a Demonstration with or without an Exhibit

When executives of the Iron Fireman firm were talking to dealers, they needed some way of dramatizing the fact that fuel should be fed into a furnace from the bottom rather than from the top. So, they hit on this simple but striking demonstration. The speaker lights a candle. Then he says: 'See how clearly the flame burns – how tall it is. Since virtually all the fuel is being converted into heat, it gives off practically no smoke.

'The fuel of the candle is fed in from below, just as the Iron Fireman feeds fuel into a furnace.

'Suppose that this candle was fuelled from above, as hand-stoked furnaces are. (Here, the speaker turns the candle upside down.)

'Notice how the flame dies down. Smell the smoke. Hear it sputter. See how red the flame is because of incomplete combustion. And finally the flame goes out, as a result of inefficient fuelling from above.'

Some years ago, Henry Morton Robinson wrote an interesting article on 'How Lawyers Win Cases' for *Your Life* magazine. In it, he describes how a lawyer named Abe Hummer is credited with a telling dramatic demonstration of showmanship while representing an insurance company in a damage suit. The plaintiff, a Mr Postlethwaite, stated that as a result of falling down an elevator shaft, his shoulder had been so severely injured that he was unable to raise his right arm.

Hummer appeared to be gravely concerned. 'Now Mr Postlethwaite,' he said confidently, 'show the jury how high you can raise your arm.' Gingerly, Postlethwaite brought his arm up to ear level. 'Now show us how high you could raise it before you were injured,' urged Hummer. 'As high as this,' said the plaintiff, shooting his arm at full length over his head.

You may draw your own conclusion regarding the reaction of the jury to this demonstration.

In the longer talk to secure action you might make three, or at most, four points. They could be uttered in less than a minute. To recite them to an audience would be dull and boring. What makes these points come alive? It is the support material you use. This is what gives sparkle and interest to your talk.

> By the use of incidents, comparisons and demonstrations, you make your main ideas clear and vivid; by the use of statistics and testimony you substantiate the truth and emphasize the importance of your main points.

APPEAL FOR ACTION

I dropped in to talk a few minutes one day with George F. Johnson, the industrialist and humanitarian. He was president of the great Endicott-Johnson Corporation at the time. More interesting to me, though, was the knowledge that he was a speaker who could make his hearers laugh, and sometimes cry, and often remember for a long time what he said.

He didn't have a private office. He had a corner of a big, busy factory, and his manner was as unpretentious as his old wooden desk.

'You've come at a good time,' he said as he stood up to greet me. 'I've just got a job out of the way. I've jotted down what I want to say at the end of a talk I'm going to give to the workers tonight.'

'It's always a relief to get a talk ship-shape in your mind from beginning to end,' I told him.

'Oh, I haven't got it all in mind yet,' he said. 'Just the general idea and the specific way I want to finish it.'

He was not a professional speaker. He never went in for ringing words or fine phrases. From experience, however, he had learned one of the secrets of successful communication. He knew that if a talk is to go over well, it has to have a good ending. He realized that the conclusion of a talk is the part toward which all that precedes it must reasonably move if an audience is to be impressed.

The close is really the most strategic point in a talk, what one says last, the final words left ringing in the ears when one ceases – these are likely to be remembered longest. Unlike Mr Johnson, beginners seldom appreciate the importance of this; their endings often leave much to be desired.

What are their most common errors? Let us discuss a few and search for remedies.

First, there is the man who finishes with: 'That is about all I have to say on the matter, so I guess I shall stop.'

This speaker usually throws a smoke screen over his inability to end a talk satisfactorily by lamely saying 'thank you'. That is not an ending. That is a mistake. It reeks of the amateur. That is almost unpardonable. If that is all you have to say, why not round off your talk, and promptly take your seat and stop without talking about stopping. Do that, and the inference that that is all you have to say may, with safety and good taste, be left to the discernment of the audience.

Then, there is the speaker who says all he has to say, but he does not know how to stop.

I believe it was Josh Billings who advised people to take the bull by the tail instead of the horns, since it would be easier to let go. This speaker has the bull by the frontal extremities, and wants to part company with him, but try as hard as he will, he can't get near a friendly fence or tree. So, he finally thrashes about in a circle, covering the same ground, repeating himself, leaving a bad impression.

The remedy? An ending has to be planned sometime, doesn't it? Is it the part of wisdom to try to do it after you are facing an audience, while you are under the strain and stress of talking, while your mind must be intent on what you are saying? Or does common sense suggest the advisability of doing it quietly, calmly, beforehand?

How do you go about bringing your talk to a climactic close? Here are a few suggestions:

Summarize

Here is a good example. The speaker, a traffic manager for one of Chicago's railways, ends his talk with this summary:

'In short, gentlemen, our own back-door yard experience with this block device; the experience in its use in the east, in the west, in the north; the sound operating principles underlying its operation; the actual demonstration in the money saved in one year in wreck prevention – move me most earnestly and unequivocally to recommend its immediate installation on our southern branch.'

You see what he has done? You can see it and feel it without having heard the rest of the talk. He has summed up in a few sentences, in 62 words, practically all the points he had made in the entire talk.

Don't you feel that a summary like that helps? If so, make that technique your own.

Ask for Action

The closing just quoted is also an excellent illustration of the ask-for-action ending. The speaker wanted something done: a block device installed on the southern branch of his road. He based his request for action on the money it would save, on the wrecks it would prevent. The speaker wanted action, and he got it. This was not a mere practice talk. It was delivered before the board of directors of a railway, and it secured the installation of the block device for which it asked.

In your final words of a talk to secure action the time has come to ask for the order. So ask for it! Tell your audience to join, contribute, vote, write, telephone, buy, boycott, enlist, investigate, acquit or whatever it is you want them to do. However, be sure to obey these caution signs.

Ask them to do something specific. Don't say, 'Help the Red Cross.' That's too general. Say, instead, 'Send your enrolment fee of $1 tonight to the American Red Cross, 125 Smith Street in this city.'

Ask the audience for some response that is within their power to give. Don't say, 'Let us cast our ballot against the Demon Rum.' It can't be done. At the moment, we aren't balloting on the Demon Rum. You could, instead, ask them to join a temperance society or to contribute to some organization which is fighting for prohibition.

Make it as easy as you can for your audience to act on your appeal. Don't say, 'Write your congressman to vote against this bill.' 99 per cent of your listeners won't do it. They are not vitally interested; or it is too much trouble; or they will forget. So, make it easy and pleasant to act. How? By writing a letter yourself to your congressman, saying, 'We, the undersigned, urge you to vote against Bill No. 74321.' Pass the letter around with a fountain pen, and you will probably get a lot of signers – and perhaps lose your fountain pen.

HOW TO WIN FRIENDS AND INFLUENCE PEOPLE

PART 1

FUNDAMENTAL TECHNIQUES IN HANDLING PEOPLE

1

'If You Want to Gather Honey, Don't Kick over the Beehive'

On 7 May 1931, the most sensational manhunt New York City had ever known had come to its climax. After weeks of search, 'Two-Gun' Crowley – the killer, the gunman who didn't smoke or drink – was at bay, trapped in his sweetheart's apartment on West End Avenue.

150 policemen and detectives laid siege to his top-floor hideaway. They chopped holes in the roof; they tried to smoke out Crowley, the 'cop killer', with tear gas. Then they mounted their machine guns on surrounding buildings, and for more than an hour one of New York's fine residential areas reverberated with the crack of pistol fire and the rat-tat-tat of machine guns. Crowley, crouching behind an overstuffed chair, fired incessantly at the police. 10,000 excited people watched the battle. Nothing like it had ever been seen before on the sidewalks of New York.

When Crowley was captured, Police Commissioner E.P. Mulrooney declared that the 'Two-Gun' desperado was one of the most dangerous criminals ever encountered in the history of New York. 'He will kill,' said the commissioner, 'at the drop of a feather.'

But how did 'Two-Gun' Crowley regard himself? We know, because while the police were firing into his apartment, he wrote a letter addressed, 'To whom it may concern.' And, as he wrote, the blood flowing from his wounds left a crimson trail on the paper. In this letter Crowley said: 'Under my coat is a weary heart, but a kind one – one that would do nobody any harm.'

A short time before this, Crowley had been having a necking party with his girlfriend on a country road out on Long Island. Suddenly, a policeman walked up to the car and said: 'Let me see your licence.'

Without saying a word, Crowley drew his gun and cut the policeman down with a shower of lead. As the dying officer fell, Crowley leapt out of the car, grabbed the officer's revolver and fired another bullet into the prostrate body. And, that was the killer who said: 'Under my coat is a weary heart, but a kind one – one that would do nobody any harm.'

Crowley was sentenced to the electric chair. When he arrived at the death house in Sing Sing, did he say, 'This is what I get for killing people?' No, he said: 'This is what I get for defending myself'.

The point of the story is this: 'Two-Gun' Crowley didn't blame himself for anything.

Is that an unusual attitude among criminals? If you think so, listen to this:

'I have spent the best years of my life giving people the lighter pleasures, helping them have a good time and all I get is abuse, the existence of a hunted man.'

That's Al Capone speaking. Yes, America's most notorious public enemy – the most sinister gang leader who ever shot up Chicago. Capone didn't condemn himself. He actually regarded himself as a public benefactor – an unappreciated and misunderstood public benefactor.

And, so did Dutch Schultz before he crumpled up under gangster bullets in Newark. Dutch Schultz, one of New York's most notorious rats, said in a newspaper interview that he was a public benefactor. And, he believed it.

I have had some interesting correspondence with Lewis Lawes, who was warden of New York's infamous Sing Sing prison for many years, on this subject, and he declared that, 'Few of the criminals in Sing Sing regard themselves as bad men. They are just as human as you and I. So, they rationalize, they explain. They can tell you why they had to crack a safe or be quick on the trigger finger. Most of them attempt by a form of reasoning, fallacious or logical, to justify their antisocial acts even to themselves, consequently stoutly maintaining that they should never have been imprisoned at all.'

If Al Capone, 'Two-Gun' Crowley, Dutch Schultz and the desperate men and women behind prison walls don't blame themselves for anything – what about the people with whom you and I come in contact?

John Wanamaker, founder of the American stores that bear his name, once confessed: 'I learned 30 years ago that it is foolish to scold. I have enough trouble overcoming my own limitations without fretting over the fact that God has not seen fit to distribute evenly the gift of intelligence.'

Wanamaker learned this lesson early, but I personally had to blunder through this old world for a third of a century before it even began to dawn upon me that 99 times out of a 100, people don't criticize themselves for anything no matter how wrong it may be.

Criticism is futile because it puts a person on the defensive and usually makes him strive to justify himself. Criticism is dangerous, because it wounds a person's precious pride, hurts his sense of importance and arouses resentment.

> B.F. Skinner, the world-famous psychologist, proved through his experiments that an animal rewarded for good behaviour will learn much more rapidly and retain what it learns far more effectively than an animal punished for bad behaviour. Later studies have shown that the same applies to humans. By criticizing, we do not make lasting changes and often incur resentment.

Hans Selye, another great psychologist, said, 'As much as we thirst for approval, we dread condemnation.'

The resentment that criticism engenders can demoralize employees, family members and friends, and still not correct the situation that has been condemned.

George B. Johnston of Enid, Oklahoma, is the safety co-ordinator for an engineering company. One of his responsibilities is to see that employees wear their hard hats whenever they are on the job in the field. He reported that whenever he came across workers who were not wearing hard hats, he would tell them with a lot of authority of the regulation and that they must comply. As a result he would get sullen acceptance, and often after he left, the workers would remove the hats.

He decided to try a different approach. The next time he found some of the workers not wearing their hard hat, he asked if the hats were uncomfortable or did not fit properly. Then he reminded the men in a pleasant tone of voice that the hat was designed to protect them from injury and suggested that it always be worn on the job. The result was increased compliance with the regulation with no resentment or emotional upset.

You will find examples of the futility of criticism bristling on a thousand pages of history. Take, for example, the famous quarrel between Theodore Roosevelt and President Taft – a quarrel that split the Republican party, put Woodrow Wilson in the White House and wrote bold, luminous lines across the First World War and altered the flow of history. Let's review the facts quickly. When Theodore Roosevelt stepped out of the White House in 1908, he supported Taft, who was elected President. Then Theodore Roosevelt went off to Africa to shoot lions. When he returned, he exploded. He denounced Taft for his conservatism, tried to secure the nomination for a third term himself, formed the Bull Moose party, and all but demolished the GOP. In the election that followed, William Howard Taft and the Republican party carried only two states – Vermont and Utah. The most disastrous defeat the party had ever known.

Theodore Roosevelt blamed Taft, but, did President Taft blame himself? Of course, not. With tears in his eyes, Taft said: 'I don't see how I could have done any differently from what I have.'

Who was to blame? Roosevelt or Taft? Frankly, I don't know, and I don't care. The point I am trying to make is that all of Theodore Roosevelt's criticism didn't persuade Taft that he was wrong. It merely made Taft strive to justify himself and to reiterate with tears in his eyes: 'I don't see how I could have done any differently from what I have.'

Or, take the Teapot Dome oil scandal. It kept the newspapers ringing with indignation in the early 1920's. It rocked the nation! Within the memory of living men, nothing like it had ever happened before in American public life. Here are the bare facts of the scandal: Albert B. Fall, secretary of the interior in Harding's cabinet, was entrusted with the leasing of government oil reserves at Elk Hill and Teapot Dome – oil reserves that had been set aside for the future use of the Navy. Did Secretary Fall permit competitive bidding? No, sir. He handed the fat, juicy contract outright to his friend Edward L. Doheny. And what did Doheny do? He gave Secretary Fall what he was pleased to call a 'loan' of $100,000. Then, in a high-handed manner, Secretary Fall ordered United States Marines into the district to drive off competitors whose adjacent wells were sapping oil out of the Elk Hill reserves. These competitors, driven off their ground at the ends of guns and bayonets, rushed into court – and blew the lid off the Teapot Dome scandal. A stench arose so vile that it ruined the Harding administration, nauseated an entire nation, threatened to wreck the Republican party and put Albert B. Fall behind prison bars.

Fall was condemned viciously – condemned as few men in public life have ever been. Did he repent? Never! Years later Herbert Hoover intimated in a public speech that President Harding's death had been due to mental anxiety and worry because a friend had betrayed him. When Mrs Fall heard that, she sprang from her chair, she wept, and she shook her fists at fate and screamed: 'What! Harding betrayed by Fall? No! My husband never betrayed anyone. This whole house full of gold would not tempt my husband to do wrong. He is the one who has been betrayed and led to the slaughter and crucified.'

There you are; human nature in action, wrongdoers, blaming everybody but themselves. We are all like that. So when you and I are tempted to criticize someone tomorrow, let's remember Al Capone, 'Two-Gun' Crowley and Albert Fall.

Let's realize that criticisms are like homing pigeons. They always return home. Let's realize that the person we are going to correct and condemn will probably justify himself or herself, and condemn us in return; or, like the gentle Taft, will say: 'I don't see how I could have done any differently from what I have.'

* * *

On the morning of 15 April 1865, Abraham Lincoln lay on his death-bed in a hall bedroom of a cheap lodging house directly across the street from Ford's Theatre, where John Wilkes Booth had shot him. Lincoln's long body lay stretched diagonally across a sagging bed that was too short for him. A cheap reproduction of Rosa Bonheur's famous painting, 'The Horse Fair' hung above the bed, and a dismal gas jet flickered yellow light.

As Lincoln lay dying, secretary of war, Stanton, said, 'There lies the most perfect ruler of men that the world has ever seen.'

What was the secret of Lincoln's success in dealing with people? I studied the life of Abraham Lincoln for 10 years and devoted all of three years to writing and rewriting a book entitled, *Lincoln the Unknown*. I believe I have made as detailed and exhaustive study of Lincoln's personality and home life as it is possible for any being to make. I made a special study of Lincoln's method of dealing with people. Did he indulge in criticism? Oh, yes. As a young man in the Pigeon Creek Valley of Indiana, he not only criticized but he wrote letters and poems ridiculing people and dropped these letters on the country roads where they were sure to be found. One of these letters aroused resentments that burned for a lifetime.

Even after Lincoln had become a practising lawyer in Springfield, Illinois, he attacked his opponents openly in letters published in the newspapers. But, he did this just once too often.

In the autumn of 1842 he ridiculed a vain, pugnacious politician by the name of James Shields. Lincoln lampooned him through an anonymous letter published in the *Springfield Journal*. The town roared with laughter. Shields, sensitive and proud, boiled with indignation. He found out who wrote the letter, leapt on his horse, started after Lincoln and challenged him to fight a duel. Lincoln didn't want to fight. He was opposed to duelling, but he couldn't get out of it and save his honour. He was given the choice of weapons. Since he had very long arms, he chose cavalry broadswords and took lessons in sword fighting from a West Point graduate; and, on the appointed day, he and Shields met on a sandbar in the Mississippi River, prepared to fight to the death; but, at the last minute, their seconds interrupted and stopped the duel.

That was the most lurid personal incident in Lincoln's life. It taught him an invaluable lesson in the art of dealing with people. Never again did he write an insulting letter. Never again did he ridicule anyone. And from that time on, he almost never criticized anybody for anything.

Time after time, during the Civil War, Lincoln put a new general at the head of the Army of the Potomac, and each one in turn – McClellan, Pope, Burnside, Hooker, Meade – blundered tragically and drove Lincoln to pacing the floor in despair. Half the nation savagely condemned these incompetent generals, but Lincoln, 'with malice toward none, with charity for all', held his peace. One of his favourite quotations was, 'Judge not, that ye be not judged'.

And when Mrs Lincoln and others spoke harshly of the southern people, Lincoln replied: 'Don't criticize them; they are just what we would be under similar circumstances.'

Yet, if any man ever had occasion to criticize, surely it was Lincoln. Let's take just one illustration:

The Battle of Gettysburg was fought during the first three days of July 1863. During the night of 4 July, Lee began to retreat southward while storm clouds deluged the country with rain. When Robert E. Lee reached the Potomac with his defeated army, he found a swollen, impassable river in front of him, and a victorious Union Army behind him. Lee was in a trap. He couldn't escape. Lincoln saw that. Here was a golden, heaven-sent opportunity – the opportunity to capture Lee's army and end the war immediately. So, with a surge of hope, Lincoln ordered Meade not to call a council of war but to attack Lee immediately. Lincoln telegraphed his orders and then sent a special messenger to Meade demanding immediate action.

And what did General Meade do? He did the very opposite of what he was told to do. He called a council of war in direct violation of Lincoln's orders. He hesitated. He procrastinated. He telegraphed all manner of excuses. He refused point-blank to attack Lee. Finally the waters receded and Lee escaped over the Potomac with his forces.

Lincoln was furious. 'What does this mean?' Lincoln cried to his son Robert. 'Great God! What does this mean? We had them within our grasp, and had only to stretch forth our hands and they were ours; yet nothing that I could say or do could make the army move. Under the circumstances, almost any general could have defeated Lee. If I had gone up there, I could have whipped him myself.'

In bitter disappointment, Lincoln sat down and wrote Meade this letter. And remember, at this period of his life Lincoln was extremely conservative and restrained in his phraseology. So, this letter coming from Lincoln in 1863 was tantamount to the severest rebuke.

My dear General,

I do not believe you appreciate the magnitude of the misfortune involved in Lee's escape. He was within our easy grasp, and to have closed upon him would, in connection with our other late successes, have ended the war. As it is, the war will be prolonged indefinitely. If you could not safely attack Lee last Monday, how can you possibly do so south of the river, when you can take with you very few – no more than two-thirds of the force you then had in hand? It would be unreasonable to expect and I do not expect that you can now effect much. Your golden opportunity is gone, and I am distressed immeasurably because of it.

What do you suppose Meade did when he read the letter?

Meade never saw that letter. Lincoln never mailed it. It was found among his papers after his death.

My guess is – and this is only a guess – that after writing that letter, Lincoln looked out of the window and said to himself, 'Just a minute. Maybe I ought not to be so hasty. It is easy enough for me to sit here in the quiet of the White House and order Meade to attack; but if I had been up at Gettysburg, and if I had seen as much blood as Meade has seen during the last week, and if my ears had been pierced with the screams and shrieks of the wounded and dying, maybe I wouldn't be so anxious to attack either. If I had Meade's timid temperament, perhaps, I would have done just what he had done. Anyhow, it is water under the bridge now. If I send this letter, it will relieve my feelings, but it will make Meade try to justify himself. It will make him condemn me. It will arouse hard feelings, impair all his further usefulness as a commander, and perhaps force him to resign from the army.'

So, as I have already said, Lincoln put the letter aside, for he had learned by bitter experience that sharp criticisms and rebukes almost invariably end in futility.

Theodore Roosevelt said that when he, as President, was confronted with a perplexing problem, he used to lean back and look up at a large painting of Lincoln which hung above his desk in the White House and ask himself, 'What would Lincoln do if he were in my shoes? How would he solve this problem?'

Mark Twain lost his temper occasionally and wrote letters that turned the paper brown. For example, he once wrote to a man who had aroused his ire: 'The thing for you is a burial permit. You have only to speak and I will see that you get it.' On another occasion he wrote to an editor about a proofreader's attempts to improve his spelling and punctuation. He ordered: 'Set the matter according to my copy hereafter and see that the proofreader retains his suggestions in the mush of his decayed brain.'

The writing of these stinging letters made Mark Twain feel better. They allowed him to blow off steam, and the letters didn't do any real harm, because Mark's wife secretly lifted them out of the mail. They were never sent.

Do you know someone you would like to change and regulate and improve? Good! That is fine. I am all in favour of it. But, why not begin on yourself? From a purely selfish standpoint, that is a lot more profitable than trying to improve others – yes, and a lot less dangerous. 'Don't complain about the snow on your neighbour's roof,' said Confucius, 'when your own doorstep is unclean.'

When I was still young and trying to impress people, I wrote a foolish letter to Richard Harding Davis, an author who once loomed large on the literary horizon of America. I was preparing a magazine article about authors, and I asked Davis to tell me about his method of work. A few weeks earlier, I had received a letter from someone with this notation at the bottom: 'Dictated but not read.' I was quite impressed. I felt that the writer must be very big and busy and important. I wasn't the slightest bit busy, but, I was eager to make an impression on Richard Harding Davis. So, I ended my short note with the words: 'Dictated but not read'.

He never troubled to answer the letter. He simply returned it to me with this scribbled across the bottom: 'Your bad manners are exceeded only by your bad manners.' True, I had blundered, and perhaps, I deserved this rebuke. But, being human, I resented it. I resented it so sharply that when I read of the death of Richard Harding Davis 10 years later, the one thought that still persisted in my mind – I am ashamed to admit – was the hurt he had given me.

If you and I want to stir up a resentment tomorrow that may rankle across the decades and endure until death, just let us indulge in a little stinging criticism – no matter how certain we are that it is justified.

> When dealing with people, let us remember we are not dealing with creatures of logic. We are dealing with creatures of emotion, creatures bristling with prejudices and motivated by pride and vanity.

Bitter criticism caused the sensitive Thomas Hardy, one of the finest novelists ever to enrich English literature, to give up forever the writing of fiction. Criticism drove Thomas Chatterton, the English poet, to suicide.

Benjamin Franklin, tactless in his youth, became so diplomatic, so adroit at handling people, that he was made American ambassador to France. The secret of his success? 'I will speak ill of no man,' he said, '...and speak all the good I know of everybody.'

Any fool can criticize, condemn and complain – and most fools do.

But it takes character and self-control to be understanding and forgiving.

'A great man shows his greatness,' said Thomas Carlyle, 'by the way he treats little men.'

Bob Hoover, a famous test pilot and frequent performer at air shows, was returning to his home in Los Angeles from an air show in San Diego. As described in the magazine *Flight Operations*, at 300 feet in the air, both engines suddenly stopped. By deft manoeuvring he managed to land the plane, but it was badly damaged although nobody was hurt.

Hoover's first act after the emergency landing was to inspect the aeroplane's fuel. Just as he suspected, the Second World War propeller plane he had been flying had been fuelled with jet fuel rather than gasoline.

Upon returning to the airport, he asked to see the mechanic who had serviced his aeroplane. The young man was sick with the agony of his mistake. Tears streamed down his face as Hoover approached. He had just caused the loss of a very expensive plane and could have caused the loss of three lives as well.

You can imagine Hoover's anger. One could anticipate the tongue-lashing that this proud and precise pilot would unleash for that carelessness. But Hoover didn't scold the mechanic; he didn't even criticize him. Instead, he put his big arm around the man's shoulder and said, 'To show you I'm sure that you'll never do this again, I want you to service my F-51 tomorrow.'

Often parents are tempted to criticize their children. You would expect me to say, 'Don't.' But I will not. I am merely going to say, 'Before you criticize them, read one of the classics of American journalism, "Father Forgets".' It originally appeared as an editorial in the *People's Home Journal*. We are reprinting it here with the author's permission, as condensed in the *Reader's Digest*.

'Father Forgets' is one of those little pieces which, dashed off in a moment of sincere feeling, strikes an echoing chord in so many readers as to become a perennial reprint favourite. 'Since its first appearance, "Father Forgets" has been reproduced', writes the author, W. Livingstone Larned, 'in hundreds of magazines and house organs, and in newspapers the country over. It has been reprinted almost as extensively in many foreign languages. I have given personal permission to thousands who wished to read it from school, church, and lecture platforms. It has been "on the air" on countless occasions and programmemes. Oddly enough, college periodicals have used it, and high school magazines. Sometimes, a little piece seems mysteriously to "click". This one certainly did.'

FATHER FORGETS

W. Livingston Larned

Listen, son: I am saying this as you lie asleep, one little paw crumpled under your cheek and the blonde curls stickily wet on your damp forehead. I have stolen into your room alone. Just a few minutes ago, as I sat reading my paper in the library, a stifling wave of remorse swept over me. Guiltily, I came to your bedside.

There are the things I was thinking, son: I had been cross to you. I scolded you as you were dressing for school because you gave your face merely a dab with a towel. I took you to task for not cleaning your shoes. I called out angrily when you threw some of your things on the floor.

At breakfast I found fault, too. You spilled things. You gulped down your food. You put your elbows on the table. You spread butter too thick on your bread. And as you started off to play and I made for my train, you turned and waved a hand and called, 'Goodbye, Daddy!' and I frowned, and said in reply, 'Hold your shoulders back!'

Then it began all over again in the late afternoon. As I came up the road I spied you, down on your knees, playing marbles. There were holes in your stockings. I humiliated you before your boyfriends by marching you ahead of me to the house. Stockings were expensive – and if you had to buy them you would be more careful! Imagine that, son, from a father!

Do you remember, later, when I was reading in the library, how you came in timidly, with a sort of hurt look in your eyes? When I glanced up over my paper, impatient at the interruption, you hesitated at the door. 'What is it you want?' I snapped.

You said nothing, but ran across in one tempestuous plunge, and threw your arms around my neck and kissed me, and your small arms tightened with an affection that God had set blooming in your heart and which even neglect could not wither. And then, you were gone, pattering up the stairs.

Well, son, it was shortly afterwards that my paper slipped from my hands and a terrible sickening fear came over me. What has habit been doing to me? The habit of finding fault, of reprimanding – this was my reward to you for being a boy. It was not that I did not love you; it was that I expected too much of youth. I was measuring you by the yardstick of my own years.

And there was so much that was good and fine and true in your character. The little heart of you was as big as the dawn itself over the wide hills. This was shown by your spontaneous impulse to rush in and kiss me good night. Nothing else matters tonight, son. I have come to your bedside in the darkness, and I have knelt there, ashamed!

It is a feeble atonement; I know you would not understand these things if I told them to you during your waking hours. But tomorrow I will be a real daddy! I will chum with you, and suffer when you suffer, and laugh when you laugh. I will bite my tongue when impatient words come. I will keep saying as if it were a ritual: 'He is nothing but a boy – a little boy!'

I am afraid I have visualized you as a man. Yet, as I see you now, son, crumpled and weary in your cot, I see that you are still a baby. Yesterday you were in your mother's arms, your head on her shoulder. I have asked too much, too much.

* * *

Instead of condemning people, let's try to understand them. Let's try to figure out why they do what they do. That's a lot more profitable and intriguing than criticism; and it breeds sympathy, tolerance and kindness. 'To know all is to forgive all.'

As Dr Johnson said: 'God himself, sir, does not propose to judge man until the end of his days.' Why should you and I?

2

'He Who Can Do This Has the Whole World with Him. He Who Cannot Walks a Lonely Way'

I often went fishing up in Maine during the summer. Personally, I am very fond of strawberries and cream, but I have found that for some strange reason, fish prefer worms. So, when I went fishing, I didn't think about what I wanted. I didn't bait the hook with strawberries and cream. Rather, I dangled a worm or a grasshopper in front of the fish and said: 'Wouldn't you like to have that?'

Why not use the same common sense when fishing for people?

That is what Lloyd George, Great Britain's prime minister during First World War, did. When someone asked him how he managed to stay in power after the other wartime leaders – Wilson, Orlando and Clemenceau – had been forgotten, he replied that if his staying on top might be attributed to any one thing, it would be to his having learned that it was necessary to bait the hook to suit the fish.

Why talk about what we want? That is childish. Absurd. Of course, you are interested in what you want. You are eternally interested in it. But no one else is. The rest of us are just like you: we are interested in what we want.

So, the only way on earth to influence other people is to talk about what they want and show them how to get it.

Remember that tomorrow when you are trying to get somebody to do something. If, for example, you don't want your children to smoke, don't preach at them, and don't talk about what you want; show them that cigarettes may keep them from making the basketball team or winning the hundred-yard dash.

This is a good thing to remember regardless of whether you are dealing with children or calves or chimpanzees. For example: one day Ralph Waldo Emerson and his son tried to get a calf into the barn. But they made the common mistake of thinking only of what they wanted: Emerson pushed and his son pulled. But the calf was doing just what they were doing: he was thinking only of what he wanted; so he stiffened his legs and stubbornly refused to leave the pasture. The Irish housemaid saw their predicament. She couldn't write essays and books; but, on this occasion at least, she had more horse sense, or calf sense, than Emerson had. She thought of what the calf wanted; so she put her maternal finger in the calf's mouth and let the calf suck her finger as she gently led him into the barn.

Every act you have ever performed since the day you were born was performed because you wanted something. How about the time you gave a large contribution to the Red Cross? Yes, that is no exception to the rule. You gave the Red Cross the donation because you wanted to lend a helping hand; you wanted to do a beautiful, unselfish, divine act. 'In as much as ye have done it unto one of the least of these my brethren, ye have done it unto me.'

If you hadn't wanted that feeling more than you wanted your money, you would not have made the contribution. Of course, you might have made the contribution because you were ashamed to refuse or because a customer asked you to do it. But one thing is certain. You made the contribution because you wanted something.

Harry A. Overstreet, in his illuminating book, *Influencing Human Behaviour* said, 'Action springs out of what we fundamentally desire...and the best piece of advice which can be given to would-be persuaders, whether in business, in the home, in the school, in politics, is – first, arouse in the other person an eager want. He who can do this has the whole world with him. He who cannot walks a lonely way.'

Andrew Carnegie, the poverty-stricken Scotch lad who started to work at two cents an hour and finally gave away $365 million, learned early in life that the only way to influence people is to talk in terms of what the other person wants. He attended school only four years; yet he learned how to handle people.

To illustrate: His sister-in-law was worried sick over her two boys. They were at Yale, and they were so busy with their own affairs that they neglected to write home and paid no attention whatever to their mother's frantic letters.

Then Carnegie offered to wager a $100 that he could get an answer by return mail, without even asking for it. Someone called his bet; so he wrote his nephews a chatty letter, mentioning casually in a postscript that he was sending each one a five-dollar bill.

He neglected, however, to enclose the money.

Back came replies by return mail thanking 'Dear Uncle Andrew' for his kind note and – you can finish the sentence yourself.

Another example of persuading comes from Stan Novak of Cleveland, Ohio, a participant in our course. Stan came home from work one evening to find his youngest son, Tim, kicking and screaming on the living room floor. He was to start kindergarten the next day and was protesting that he would not go. Stan's normal reaction would have been to banish the child to his room and tell him he'd better make up his mind to go. He had no choice. But tonight, recognizing that this would not really help Tim start kindergarten in the best frame of mind, Stan sat down and thought, 'If I were Tim, why would I be excited about going to kindergarten?' He and his wife made a list of all the fun things Tim would do such as finger painting, singing songs, making new friends. Then they put them into action.

'We all started finger painting on the kitchen table – my wife,

Lil, my other son, Bob, and myself, all having fun. Soon, Tim was peeping around the corner. Next, he was begging to participate. "Oh, no! You have to go to kindergarten first to learn how to finger paint." With all the enthusiasm I could muster I went through the list talking in terms he could understand – telling him all the fun he would have in kindergarten. The next morning, I thought I was the first one up. I went downstairs and found Tim sitting sound asleep in the living room chair.

'"What are you doing here?" I asked. "I'm waiting to go to kindergarten. I don't want to be late." The enthusiasm of our entire family had aroused in Tim an eager want that no amount of discussion or threat could have possibly accomplished.'

Tomorrow you may want to persuade somebody to do something. Before you speak, pause and ask yourself: 'How can I make this person want to do it?'

That question will stop us from rushing into a situation heedlessly, with futile chatter about our desires.

At one time I rented the grand ballroom of a certain New York hotel for 20 nights in each season in order to hold a series of lectures.

At the beginning of one season, I was suddenly informed that I should have to pay almost three times as much rent as formerly. This news reached me after the tickets had been printed and distributed and all the announcements had been made.

Naturally, I didn't want to pay the increase, but what was the use of talking to the hotel about what I wanted? They were only interested in what they wanted. So, a couple of days later I went to see the manager.

'I was a bit shocked when I got your letter,' I said, 'but I don't blame you at all. If I had been in your position, I should probably have written a similar letter myself. Your duty as the manager of the hotel is to make all the profit possible. If you don't do that you will be fired and you ought to be fired. Now, let's take a piece of paper and write down the advantages and the disadvantages that will accrue to you, if you insist on this increase in rent.'

Then I took a letterhead and ran a line through the centre and headed one column 'Advantages' and the other column 'Disadvantages'.

I wrote down under the head 'Advantages' these words: 'Ballroom free'. Then I went on to say: 'You will have the advantage of having the ballroom free to rent for dances and conventions. That is a big advantage, for affairs like that will pay you much more than you can get for a series of lectures. If I tie your ballroom up for twenty nights during the course of the season, it is sure to mean a loss of some very profitable business to you.

'Now, let's consider the "Disadvantages". First, instead of increasing your income from me, you are going to decrease it. In fact, you are going to wipe it out because I cannot pay the rent you are asking. I shall be forced to hold these lectures at some other place.

'There's another disadvantage to you, also. These lectures attract crowds of educated and cultured people to your hotel. That is good advertising for you, isn't it? In fact, if you spent $5,000 advertising in the newspapers, you couldn't bring as many people to look at your hotel as I can bring by these lectures. That is worth a lot to a hotel, isn't it?'

As I talked, I wrote these two disadvantages under the proper heading, and handed the sheet of paper to the manager, saying: 'I wish you would carefully consider both the advantages and disadvantages that are going to accrue to you and then give me your final decision.'

I received a letter the next day, informing me that my rent would be increased only 50 per cent instead of 300 per cent.

Mind you, I got this reduction without saying a word about what I wanted. I talked all the time about what the other person wanted and how he could get it.

Suppose, I had done the human, natural thing; suppose, I had stormed into his office and said, 'What do you mean by raising my rent 300 per cent when you know the tickets have been printed and the announcements made? 300 per cent! Ridiculous! Absurd! I won't pay it!'

What would have happened then? An argument would have begun to steam and boil and sputter – and you know how arguments end. Even if I had convinced him that he was wrong, his pride would have made it difficult for him to back down and give in.

Here is one of the best bits of advice ever given about the fine art of human relationships. 'If there is any one secret of success,' said Henry Ford, 'it lies in the ability to get the other person's point of view and see things from that person's angle as well as from your own.'

That is so good, I want to repeat it: 'If there is any one secret of success, it lies in the ability to get the other persons point of view and see things from that person's angle as well as from your own.'

That is so simple, so obvious, that anyone ought to see the truth of it at a glance; yet 90 per cent of the people on this earth ignore it 90 per cent of the time.

An example? Look at the letters that come across your desk tomorrow morning, and you will find that most of them violate this important canon of common sense. Take this one, a letter written by the head of the radio department of an advertising agency with offices scattered across the continent. This letter was sent to the managers of local radio stations throughout the country. (I have set down, in brackets, my reactions to each paragraph.)

> Mr John Blank,
> Blankville,
> Indiana
>
> Dear Mr Blank:
>
> The — company desires to retain its position in advertising agency leadership in the radio field.

[Who cares about what your company desires? I am worried about my own problems. The bank is foreclosing the mortgage on my house, the bugs are destroying the hollyhocks, the stock market tumbled yesterday. I missed the 8.15 this morning. I wasn't invited to the Jones's dance last night, the doctor tells me I have high blood pressure and neuritis and dandruff. And then what happens? I come down to the office this morning worried, open my mail and here is some little whippersnapper off in New York yapping about what his company wants. Bah! If he only realized what sort of impression his letter makes, he would get out of the advertising business and start manufacturing sheep dip.]

> This agency's national advertising accounts were the bulwark of the network. Our subsequent clearances of station time have kept us at the top of agencies year after year.

[You are big and rich and right at the top, are you? So what? I don't give two whoops in Hades if you are as big as General Motors and General Electric and the General Staff of the US Army all combined. If you had as much sense as a half-witted hummingbird, you would realize that I am interested in how big I am – not how big you are. All this talk about your enormous success makes me feel small and unimportant.]

> We desire to service our accounts with the last word on radio station information.

[You desire! You desire. You unmitigated ass. I'm not interested in what you desire or what the President of the United States desires. Let me tell you, once and for all, that I am interested in what I desire – and you haven't said a word about that yet in this absurd letter of yours.]

> Will you, therefore, put the company on your preferred list for weekly station information – every single detail that will be useful to an agency in intelligently booking time.

['Preferred list'. You have your nerve! You make me feel insignificant by your big talk about your company and then, you ask me to put you on a 'preferred' list, and you don't even say 'please' when you ask it.]

> A prompt acknowledgement of this letter, giving us your latest 'doings' will be mutually helpful.

[You fool! You mail me a cheap form letter – a letter scattered far and wide like the autumn leaves – and you have the gall to ask me, when I am worried about the mortgage and the hollyhocks and my blood pressure, to sit down and dictate a personal note acknowledging your form letter – and you ask me to do it 'promptly'. What do you mean, 'promptly'? Don't you know I am just as busy as you are – or, at least, I like to think I am. And while we are on the subject, who gave you the lordly right to order me around? You say it will be 'mutually helpful'. At last, at last, you have begun to see my viewpoint. But you are vague about how it will be to my advantage.]

> Very truly yours,
> John Doe
> Manager. Radio Department
>
> PS: The enclosed reprint from the 'Blankville Journal' will be of interest to you, and you may want to broadcast it over your station.

[Finally, down here in the postscript, you mention something that may help me solve one of my problems. Why didn't you begin your letter with – but, what's the use? Any advertising man who is guilty of perpetrating such drivel as you have sent me has something wrong with his medulla oblongata. You don't need a letter giving our latest doings. What you need is a quart of iodine in your thyroid gland.]

Now, if people who devote their lives to advertising and who pose as experts in the art of influencing people to buy – if they write a letter like that, what can we expect from the butcher and baker or the auto mechanic?

Here is another letter, written by the superintendent of a large freight terminal to a student of this course, Edward Vermylen. What effect did this letter have on the man to whom it was addressed? Read it and then I'll tell you.

A. Zerega's Sons, Inc.
28 Front St
Brooklyn, NY 11201

Attention: Mr Edward Vermylen

Gentlemen:

The operations at our outbound-rail-receiving station are handicapped because a material percentage of the total business is delivered to us in the late afternoon. This condition results in congestion, overtime on the part of our forces, delays to trucks, and in some cases delays to freight. On November 10, we received from your company a lot of 510 pieces, which reached here at 4.20 p.m.

We solicit your cooperation toward overcoming the undesirable effects arising from late receipt of freight. May we ask that, on days on which you ship the volume which was received on the above date, effort be made either to get the truck here earlier or to deliver us part of the freight during the morning?

The advantage that would accrue to you under such an arrangement would be that of more expeditious discharge of your trucks and the assurance that your business would go forward on the date of its receipt.

Very truly yours,
J— B—, Supt.

After reading this letter, Mr Vermylen, sales manager for A. Zerega's Sons, Inc., sent it to me with the following comment:

'This letter had the reverse effect from that which was intended. The letter begins by describing the terminal's difficulties, in which we are not interested, generally speaking. Our cooperation is then requested without any thought as to whether it would inconvenience us, and then finally, in the last paragraph, the fact is mentioned that if we do cooperate it will mean more expeditious discharge of our trucks with the assurance that our freight will go forward on the date of its receipt.'

In other words, that in which we are most interested is mentioned last, and the whole effect is one of raising a spirit of antagonism rather than of cooperation.

Let's see if we can't rewrite and improve this letter. Let's not waste any time talking about our problems. As Henry Ford admonishes, let's, 'Get the other person's point of view and see things from his or her angle, as well as from our own.' Here is one way of revising the letter. It may not be the best way, but isn't it an improvement?

> Mr Edward Vermylen
> c/o A Zerega's Sons, Inc.
> 28 Front St.
> Brooklyn, NY 11201
>
> Dear Mr Vermylen:
>
> Your company has been one of our good customers for 14 years. Naturally, we are very grateful for your patronage and are eager to give you the speedy, efficient service you deserve. However, we regret to say that it isn't possible for us to do that when your trucks bring us a large shipment late in the afternoon, as they did on November 10. Why? Because many other customers make late afternoon deliveries, also. Naturally, that causes congestion. That means your trucks are held up unavoidably at the pier and sometimes even your freight is delayed.
>
> That's bad, but it can be avoided. If you make your deliveries at the pier in the morning when possible, your trucks will be able to keep moving, your freight will get immediate attention, and our workers will get home early at night to enjoy a dinner of the delicious macaroni and noodles that you manufacture.

Regardless of when your shipments arrive, we shall always cheerfully do all in our power to serve you promptly.

You are busy. Please don't trouble to answer this note.

Yours truly,
J— B—, Supt.

Barbara Anderson, who worked in a bank in New York, desired to move to Phoenix, Arizona, because of the health of her son. Using the principles she had learned in our course, she wrote the following letter to 12 banks in Phoenix:

Dear Sir:

My 10 years of bank experience should be of interest to a rapidly growing bank like yours.

In various capacities in bank operations with the Bankers Trust Company in New York, leading to my present assignment as Branch Manager, I have acquired skills in all phases of banking including depositor relations, credits, loans and administration.

I will be relocating to Phoenix in May and I am sure I can contribute to your growth and profit. I will be in Phoenix the week of 3 April and would appreciate the opportunity to show you how I can help your bank meet its goals.

Sincerely,
Barbara L. Anderson

Do you think Mrs Anderson received any response from that letter? 11 of the 12 banks invited her to be interviewed, and she had a choice of which bank's offer to accept. Why? Mrs Anderson did not state what she wanted, but wrote in the letter how she could help them, and focused on their wants, not her own.

Thousands of salespeople are pounding the pavements today, tired, discouraged and underpaid. Why? Because they are always thinking only of what they want. They don't realize that neither you nor I want to buy anything. If we did, we would go out and buy it. But both of us are eternally interested in solving our problems. And if salespeople can show us how their services or merchandise will help us solve our problems, they won't need to sell us. We'll buy. Customers like to feel that they are buying – not being sold.

Yet, many salespeople spend a lifetime in selling without seeing things from the customer's angle. For example, for many years I lived in Forest Hills, a little community of private homes in the centre of Greater New York. One day as I was rushing to the station, I chanced to meet a real estate operator who had bought and sold property in that area for many years. He knew Forest Hills well, so I hurriedly asked him whether or not my stucco house was built with metal lath or hollow tile. He said he didn't know and told me what I already knew – that I could find out by calling the Forest Hills Garden Association. The following morning, I received a letter from him. Did he give me the information I wanted? He could have got it in 60 seconds by a telephone call. But, he didn't. He told me again that I could get it by telephoning, and then asked me to let him handle my insurance.

He was not interested in helping me. He was interested only in helping himself.

J. Howard Lucas of Birmingham, Alabama, tells how two salespeople from the same company handled the same type of situation. He reported:

'Several years ago I was on the management team of a small company. Headquartered near us was the district office of a large insurance company. Their agents were assigned territories, and our company was assigned to two agents, whom I shall refer to as Carl and John.

'One morning, Carl dropped by our office and casually mentioned that his company had just introduced a new life insurance policy for executives and thought we might be interested later on, and he would get back to us when he had more information on it.

'The same day, John saw us on the sidewalk while returning from a coffee break, and he shouted: "Hey Luke, hold up, I have some great news for you fellows." He hurried over and very excitedly told us about an executive life insurance policy his company had introduced that very day. (It was the same policy that Carl had casually mentioned.) He wanted us to have one of the first issued. He gave us a few important facts about the coverage and ended saying, "The policy is so new, I'm going to have someone from the home office come out tomorrow and explain it. Now, in the meantime, let's get the applications signed and on the way so he can have more information to work with." His enthusiasm aroused in us an eager want for this policy even though we still did not have details. When they were made available to us, they confirmed John's initial understanding of the policy, and he not only sold each of us a policy but, later doubled our coverage.

'Carl could have had those sales, but he made no effort to arouse in us any desire for the policies.'

The world is full of people who are grabbing and self-seeking. So, the rare individual who unselfishly tries to serve others has an enormous advantage. He has little competition. Owen D. Young, a noted lawyer and one of America's great business leaders, once said: 'People who can put themselves in the place of other people, who can understand the workings of their minds, need never worry about what the future has in store for them.'

> If out of reading this book you get just one thing – an increased tendency to think always in terms of other people's point of view, and see things from their angle – if you get that one thing out of this book, it may easily prove to be one of the building blocks of your career.

Looking at the other person's point of view and arousing in him an eager want for something is not to be construed as manipulating that person so that he will do something that is only for your benefit and his detriment. Each party should gain from the negotiation. In the letters to Mr Vermylen, both the sender and the receiver of the correspondence gained by implementing what was suggested. Both the bank and Mrs Anderson won by her letter in that the bank obtained a valuable employee and Mrs Anderson a suitable job. And in the example of John's sale of insurance to Mr Lucas, both gained through this transaction.

Another example in which everybody gains through this principle of arousing an eager want comes from Michael E. Whidden of Warwick, Rhode Island, who is a territory salesman for the Shell Oil Company. Mike wanted to become the Number One salesperson in his district, but one service station was holding him back. It was run by an older man who could not be motivated to clean up his station. It was in such poor shape that sales were declining significantly.

This manager would not listen to any of Mike's pleas to upgrade the station. After many exhortations and heart-to-heart talks – all of which had no impact – Mike decided to invite the manager to visit the newest Shell station in his territory.

The manager was so impressed by the facilities at the new station that when Mike visited him the next time, his station was cleaned up and had recorded a sales increase. This enabled Mike to reach the Number One spot in his district. All his talking and discussion hadn't helped, but by arousing an eager want in the manager, by showing him the modern station, he had accomplished his goal, and both the manager and Mike benefited.

Most people go through college and learn to read Virgil and master the mysteries of calculus without ever discovering how their own minds function. For instance, I once gave a course in effective speaking for the young college graduates who were entering the employ of the Carrier Corporation, the large air conditioner manufacturer. One of the participants wanted to persuade the others to play basketball in their free time, and this is about what he said: 'I want you to come out and play basketball. I like to play basketball, but the last few times I've been to the gymnasium there haven't been enough people to get up a game. Two or three of us got by throwing the ball around the other night – and I got a black eye. I wish all of you would come down tomorrow night. I want to play basketball.'

Did he talk about anything you want? You don't want to go to a gymnasium that no one else goes to, do you? You don't care about what he wants. You don't want to get a black eye.

Could he have shown you how to get the things you want by using the gymnasium? Surely. More pep. Keener edge to the appetite. Clearer brain. Fun. Games. Basketball.

To repeat Professor Overstreet's wise advice: First, arouse in the other person an eager want. He who can do this has the whole world with him. He who cannot walks a lonely way.

One of the students in the author's training course was worried about his little boy. The child was underweight and refused to eat properly. His parents used the usual method. They scolded and nagged. 'Mother wants you to eat this and that. Father wants you to grow up to be a big man.'

Did the boy pay any attention to these pleas? Just about as much as you pay to one fleck of sand on a sandy beach.

No one with a trace of horse sense would expect a child three years old, to react to the viewpoint of a father, 30 years old. Yet, that was precisely what that father had expected. It was absurd. He finally saw that. So, he said to himself: 'What does that boy want? How can I tie up what I want to what he wants?'

It was easy for the father when he started thinking about it. His boy had a tricycle that he loved to ride up and down the sidewalk in front of the house in Brooklyn. A few doors down the street lived a bully – a bigger boy who would pull the little boy off his tricycle and ride it himself.

Naturally, the little boy would run screaming to his mother, and she would have to come out and take the bully off the tricycle and put her little boy on again. This happened almost every day.

What did the little boy want? It didn't take a Sherlock Holmes to answer that one. His pride, his anger, his desire for a feeling of importance – all the strongest emotions in his makeup – goaded him to get revenge, to smash the bully in the nose. And when his father explained that the boy would be able to wallop the daylights out of the bigger kid someday if he would only eat the things his mother wanted him to eat – when his father promised him that – there was no longer any problem of dietetics. That boy would have eaten spinach, sauerkraut, salt mackerel – anything in order to be big enough to whip the bully who had humiliated him so often.

After solving that problem, the parents tackled another: The little boy had the unholy habit of wetting his bed.

He slept with his grandmother. In the morning, his grandmother would wake up and feel the sheet and say: 'Look, Johnny, what you did again last night.'

He would say: 'No, I didn't do it. You did it.'

Scolding, spanking, shaming him, reiterating that the parents didn't want him to do it – none of these things kept the bed dry. So, the parents asked: 'How can we make this boy want to stop wetting his bed?'

What were his wants? First, he wanted to wear pyjamas like Daddy instead of wearing a nightgown like Grandmother. Grandmother was getting fed up with his nocturnal inequities, so, she gladly offered to buy him a pair of pyjamas if he would reform. Second, he wanted a bed of his own. Grandmother didn't object.

His mother took him to a department store in Brooklyn, winked at the salesgirl, and said: 'Here is a little gentleman who would like to do some shopping.'

The salesgirl made him feel important by saying: 'Young man, what can I show you?'

He stood a couple of inches taller and said: 'I want to buy a bed for myself.'

When he was shown the one his mother wanted him to buy, she winked at the salesgirl and the boy was persuaded to buy it.

The bed was delivered the next day; and that night, when Father came home, the little boy ran to the door shouting: 'Daddy! Daddy! Come upstairs and see my bed that I bought!'

The father, looking at the bed, obeyed Charles Schwab's injunction: he was 'hearty in his approbation and lavish in his praise.'

'You are not going to wet this bed, are you?' the father said.

'Oh no, no! I am not going to wet this bed.' The boy kept his promise, for his pride was involved. That was his bed. He and he alone had bought it. And he was wearing pyjamas now like a little man. He wanted to act like a man. And he did.

Another father, K.T. Dutschmann, a telephone engineer, and a student of this course, couldn't get his three-year-old daughter to eat breakfast food. The usual scolding, pleading, coaxing methods had all ended in futility. So, the parents asked themselves: 'How can we make her want to do it?'

The little girl loved to imitate her mother, to feel big and grown up; so one morning they put her on a chair and let her make the breakfast food. At just the psychological moment, the father drifted into the kitchen while she was stirring the cereal and she said: 'Oh, look, Daddy, I am making the cereal this morning.'

She ate two helpings of the cereal without any coaxing, because she was interested in it. She had achieved a feeling of importance; she had found in making the cereal an avenue of self-expression.

William Winter once remarked that 'self-expression is the dominant necessity of human nature.' Why can't we adapt this same psychology to business dealings? When we have a brilliant idea, instead of making others think it is ours, why not let them cook and stir the idea themselves. They will then regard it as their own; they will like it and maybe eat a couple of helpings of it.

Remember: 'First, arouse in the other person an eager want. He who can do this has the whole world with him. He who cannot walks a lonely way.'

FUNDAMENTAL TECHNIQUES IN HANDLING PEOPLE

PRINCIPLE 1

Don't criticize, condemn or complain

PRINCIPLE 2

Give honest and sincere appreciation

PRINCIPLE 3

Arouse in the other person an eager want

PART 2

HOW TO MAKE PEOPLE LIKE YOU

3

An Easy Way to Become a Good Conversationalist

Some time ago, I attended a bridge party. I don't play bridge – and there was a woman there who didn't play bridge either. She had discovered that I had once been Lowell Thomas's manager before he went on the radio and that I had travelled in Europe a great deal while helping him prepare the illustrated travel talks he was then delivering. So, she said: 'Oh, Mr Carnegie, I do want you to tell me about all the wonderful places you have visited and the sights you have seen.'

As we sat down on the sofa, she remarked that she and her husband had recently returned from a trip to Africa. 'Africa!' I exclaimed. 'How interesting! I've always wanted to see Africa, but I never got there except for a twenty-four-hour stay once in Algiers. Tell me, did you visit the big-game country? Yes? How fortunate. I envy you. Do tell me about Africa.'

That kept her talking for 45 minutes. She never again asked me where I had been or what I had seen. She didn't want to hear me talk about my travels. All she wanted was an interested listener, so she could expand her ego and tell about where she had been.

Was she unusual? No. Many people are like that.

For example, I met a distinguished botanist at a dinner party given by a New York book publisher. I had never talked with a botanist before, and I found him fascinating. I literally sat on the edge of my chair and listened while he spoke of exotic plants and experiments in developing new forms of plant life and indoor gardens (and even told me astonishing facts about the humble potato). I had a small indoor garden of my own – and he was good enough to tell me how to solve some of my problems.

As I said, we were at a dinner party. There must have been a dozen other guests, but I violated all the canons of courtesy, ignored everyone else and talked for hours to the botanist.

Midnight came. I said good night to everyone and departed. The botanist then turned to our host and paid me several flattering compliments. I was 'most stimulating.' I was this and I was that, and he ended by saying I was a 'most interesting conversationalist.'

An interesting conversationalist? Why, I had said hardly anything at all. I couldn't have said anything if I had wanted to without changing the subject, for I didn't know any more about botany than I knew about the anatomy of a penguin. But I had done this: I had listened intently. I had listened because I was genuinely interested. And he felt it. Naturally, that pleased him. That kind of listening is one of the highest compliments we can pay anyone. 'Few human beings,' wrote Jack Woodford in *Strangers in Love*, 'few human beings are proof against the implied flattery of rapt attention.' I went even further than giving him rapt attention. I was 'hearty in my approbation and lavish in my praise.'

I told him that I had been immensely entertained and instructed – and I had. I told him I wished I had his knowledge – and I did. I told him that I should love to wander the fields with him – and I have. I told him I must see him again – and I did.

And so, I had him thinking of me as a good conversationalist when, in reality, I had been merely a good listener and had encouraged him to talk.

What is the secret, the mystery, of a successful business interview? Well, according to former Harvard president Charles W.

Eliot, 'There is no mystery about successful business intercourse... Exclusive attention to the person who is speaking to you is very important. Nothing else is so flattering as that.'

Eliot himself was a past master of the art of listening. Henry James, one of America's first great novelists, recalled: 'Dr Eliot's listening was not mere silence, but a form of activity. Sitting very erect on the end of his spine with hands joined in his lap, making no movement except that he revolved his thumbs around each other faster or slower, he faced his interlocutor and seemed to be hearing with his eyes as well as his ears. He listened with his mind and attentively considered what you had to say while you said it... At the end of an interview the person who had talked to him felt that he had had his say.'

Self-evident, isn't it? You don't have to study for four years in Harvard to discover that. Yet, I know and you know department store owners who will rent expensive space, buy their goods economically, dress their windows appealingly, spend thousands of dollars in advertising and then hire clerks who haven't the sense to be good listeners – clerks who interrupt customers, contradict them, irritate them and all but drive them from the store.

A department store in Chicago almost lost a regular customer who spent several thousand dollars each year in that store because a sales clerk wouldn't listen. Mrs Henrietta Douglas, who took our course in Chicago, had purchased a coat at a special sale. After she had brought it home she noticed that there was a tear in the lining. She came back the next day and asked the sales clerk to exchange it. The clerk refused even to listen to her complaint. 'You bought this at a special sale,' she said. She pointed to a sign on the wall. 'Read that,' she exclaimed. 'All sales are final.' Once you bought it, you have to keep it. Sew up the lining yourself.'

'But this was damaged merchandise,' Mrs Douglas complained.

'Makes no difference,' the clerk interrupted. 'Final's final.'

Mrs Douglas was about to walk out indignantly, swearing never to return to that store ever, when she was greeted by the department manager, who knew her from her many years of patronage. Mrs Douglas told her what had happened.

The manager listened attentively to the whole story, examined the coat and then said: 'Special sales are "final" so we can dispose of merchandise at the end of the season. But this "no return" policy does not apply to damaged goods. We will certainly repair or replace the lining, or if you prefer, give you your money back.'

What a difference in treatment! If that manager had not come along and listened to the customer, a long-term patron of that store could have been lost forever.

Listening is just as important in one's home life, as in the world of business. Millie Esposito of Croton-on-Hudson, New York, made it her business to listen carefully when one of her children wanted to speak with her. One evening she was sitting in the kitchen with her son, Robert, and after a brief discussion of something that was on his mind, Robert said: 'Mom, I know that you love me very much.'

Mrs Esposito was touched and said: 'Of course I love you very much. Did you doubt it?'

Robert responded: 'No, but I really know you love me because whenever I want to talk to you about something you stop whatever you are doing and listen to me.'

The chronic kicker, even the most violent critic, will frequently soften and be subdued in the presence of a patient, sympathetic listener – a listener who will be silent while the irate fault-finder dilates like a king cobra and spews the poison out of his system. To illustrate: The New York Telephone Company discovered a few years ago that it had to deal with one of the most vicious customers who ever cursed a customer service representative. And he did curse. He raved. He threatened to tear the phone out by its roots. He refused to pay certain charges that he declared were false. He wrote letters to the newspapers. He filed innumerable complaints with the Public Service Commission, and he started several suits against the telephone company.

At last, one of the company's most skilful 'trouble shooters' was sent to interview this stormy petrel. This 'trouble shooter' listened and let the cantankerous customer enjoy himself pouring out his tirade. The telephone representative listened and said 'yes' and sympathized with his grievance.

'He raved on and I listened for nearly three hours,' the 'troubleshooter' said as he related his experiences before one of my classes. 'Then I went back and listened some more. I interviewed him four times, and before the fourth visit was over I had become a charter member of an organization he was starting. He called it the "Telephone Subscribers Protective Association". I am still a member of this organization, and, so far as I know, I'm the only member in the world today besides Mr—.

'I listened and sympathized with him on every point that he had made during these interviews. He had never had a telephone representative talk with him that way before, and he became almost friendly. The point on which I went to see him was not even mentioned on the first visit, nor was it mentioned on the second or third, but upon the fourth interview, I closed the case completely – he paid all his bills in full, and for the first time in the history of his difficulties with the telephone company, he voluntarily withdrew his complaints from the Public Service Commission.'

Doubtless, Mr— had considered himself a holy crusader, defending the public rights against callous exploitation. But in reality, what he had really wanted was a feeling of importance. He got this feeling of importance at first by kicking and complaining. But as soon as he got his feeling of importance from a representative of the company, his imagined grievances vanished into thin air.

One morning years ago, an angry customer stormed into the office of Julian F. Detmer, founder of the Detmer Woollen Company, which later became the world's largest distributor of woollens to the tailoring trade.

'This man owed us a small sum of money,' Mr Detmer explained to me. 'The customer denied it, but we knew he was wrong. So, our credit department had insisted that he pay. After getting a number of letters from our credit department, he packed his grip, made a trip to Chicago, and hurried into my office to inform me not only that he was not going to pay that bill, but that he was never going to buy another dollar's worth of goods from the Detmer Woollen Company.

'I listened patiently to all he had to say. I was tempted to interrupt, but I realized that would be bad policy. So, I let him talk himself out. When he finally simmered down and got in a receptive mood, I said quietly: "I want to thank you for coming to Chicago to tell me about this. You have done me a great favour, for if our credit department has annoyed you, it may annoy other good customers, and that would be just too bad. Believe me, I am far more eager to hear this than you are to tell it."

'That was the last thing in the world he expected me to say. I think he was a trifle disappointed, because he had come to Chicago to tell me a thing or two, but here I was, thanking him instead of scrapping with him. I assured him we would wipe the charge off the books and forget it, because he was a very careful man with only one account to look after, while our clerks had to look after thousands. Therefore, he was less likely to be wrong than we were.

'I told him that I understood exactly how he felt and that, if I were in his shoes, I should undoubtedly feel precisely as he did. Since he wasn't going to buy from us anymore, I recommended some other woollen houses.

'In the past, we had usually lunched together when he came to Chicago, so I invited him to have lunch with me this day as well. He accepted reluctantly, but when we came back to the office he placed a larger order than ever before. He returned home in a softened mood and, wanting to be just as fair with us as we had been with him, looked over his bills, found one had been mislaid, and sent us a cheque with his apologies.

'Later, when his wife presented him with a baby boy, he gave his son the middle name of Detmer, and he remained a friend and customer of the house until his death twenty-two years afterwards.'

Years ago, a poor Dutch immigrant boy washed the windows of a bakery shop after school to help support his family. His people were so poor that in addition he used to go out in the street with a basket every day and collect stray bits of coal that had fallen in the gutter where the coal wagons had delivered fuel. That boy, Edward Bok, never got more than six years of schooling in his life; yet, eventually he made himself one of the most successful magazine editors in the history of American journalism. How did he do it? That is a long story, but how he got his start can be told briefly. He got his start by using the principles in this chapter.

He left school when he was 13, and became an office boy for Western Union, but he didn't for one moment give up the idea of an education. Instead, he started to educate himself. He saved his car fares and went without lunch until he had enough money to buy an encyclopaedia of American biography – and then he did an unheard-of thing. He read the lives of famous people and wrote to them asking for additional information about their childhoods. He was a good listener. He asked famous people to tell him more about themselves. He wrote to General James A. Garfield, who was then running for President, and asked if it was true that he was once a tow boy on a canal; and Garfield replied. He wrote to General Grant asking about a certain battle, and Grant drew a map for him and invited this 14-year-old boy to dinner and spent the evening talking to him.

Soon our Western Union messenger boy was corresponding with many of the most famous people in the nation: Ralph Waldo Emerson, Oliver Wendell Holmes, Longfellow, Mrs Abraham Lincoln, Louisa May Alcott, General Sherman, and Jefferson Davis. Not only did he correspond with these distinguished people, but as soon as he got a vacation, he visited many of them as a welcome guest in their homes. This experience imbued him with a confidence that was invaluable. These men and women fired him with a vision and ambition that shaped his life. And all this, let me repeat, was made possible solely by the application of the principles we are discussing here.

Isaac F. Marcosson, a journalist who interviewed hundreds of celebrities, declared that many people fail to make a favourable impression because they don't listen attentively. 'They have been so much concerned with what they are going to say next that they do not keep their ears open. Very important people have told me that they prefer good listeners to good talkers, but the ability to listen seems rarer than almost any other good trait.'

And not only important personages crave a good listener, but ordinary folk do, too. As the *Reader's Digest* once said: 'Many persons call a doctor when all they want is an audience.'

During the darkest hours of the Civil War, Lincoln wrote to an old friend in Springfield, Illinois, asking him to come to Washington. Lincoln said he had some problems he wanted to discuss with him. The old neighbour called at the White House, and Lincoln talked to him for hours about the advisability of issuing a proclamation freeing the slaves. Lincoln went over all the arguments for and against such a move, and then read letters and newspaper articles, some denouncing him for not freeing the slaves and others denouncing him for fear he was going to free them. After talking for hours, Lincoln shook hands with his old neighbour, said good night, and sent him back to Illinois without even asking for his opinion. Lincoln had done all the talking himself. That seemed to clarify his mind. 'He seemed to feel easier after that talk,' the old friend said. Lincoln hadn't wanted advice. He had wanted merely a friendly, sympathetic listener to whom he could unburden himself. That's what we all want when we are in trouble. That is frequently all the irritated customer wants, and the dissatisfied employee or the hurt friend.

One of the great listeners of modern times was Sigmund Freud. A man who met Freud described his manner of listening: 'It struck me so forcibly that I shall never forget him. He had qualities which I had never seen in any other man. Never had I seen such concentrated attention. There was none of the piercing "soul penetrating gaze" business. His eyes were mild and genial. His voice was low and kind. His gestures were few. But the attention he gave me, his appreciation of what I said, even when I said it badly, was extraordinary. You've no idea what it meant to be listened to like that.'

If you want to know how to make people shun you and laugh at you behind your back and even despise you, here is the recipe: Never listen to anyone for long. Talk incessantly about yourself. If you have an idea while the other person is talking, don't wait for him or her to finish, butt right in and interrupt in the middle of a sentence.

Do you know people like that? I do, unfortunately; and the astonishing part of it is that some of them are prominent.

Bores, that is all they are – bores intoxicated with their own egos, drunk with a sense of their own importance.

People who talk only of themselves think only of themselves. And, 'Those people who think only of themselves,' Dr Nicholas Murray Butler, long-time president of Columbia University, said, 'are hopelessly uneducated no matter how instructed they may be.'

> If you aspire to be a good conversationalist, be an attentive listener; to be interesting, be interested. Ask questions that other persons will enjoy answering, encourage them to talk about themselves and their accomplishments.

Remember that the people you are talking to are a hundred times more interested in themselves and their wants and problems than they are in you and your problems. A person's toothache means more to that person than a famine in China which kills a million people. A boil on one's neck interests one more than 40 earthquakes in Africa. Think of that the next time you start a conversation.

4

How to Interest People

Everyone who was ever a guest of Theodore Roosevelt was astonished at the range and diversity of his knowledge. Whether his visitor was a cowboy or a Rough Rider, a New York politician or a diplomat, Roosevelt knew what to say. And how was it done? The answer was simple. Whenever Roosevelt expected a visitor, he sat up late the night before, reading up on the subject in which he knew his guest was particularly interested.

For Roosevelt knew, as all leaders know, that the royal road to a person's heart is to talk about the things he or she treasures most.

The genial William Lyon Phelps, essayist and professor of literature at Yale, learned this lesson early in life.

'When I was eight years old and was spending a weekend visiting my Aunt Libby Linsley at her home in Stratford-on-the-Housatonic,' he wrote in his essay on human nature, 'a middle-aged man called one evening, and after a polite skirmish with my aunt, he devoted his attention to me. At that time, I happened to be excited about boats, and the visitor discussed the subject in a way that seemed particularly interesting. After he left, I spoke of him with enthusiasm. What a man! My aunt informed me he was a New York lawyer, that he cared nothing whatever about boats – that he took not the slightest interest in the subject. "But why then did he talk all the time about boats?"

"Because he is a gentleman. He saw you were interested in boats, and he talked about the things he knew would interest and please you. He made himself agreeable."

And William Lyon Phelps added: 'I never forgot my aunt's remark.'

As I write this chapter, I have before me a letter from Edward L. Chalif, who was active in Boy Scout work.

'One day I found I needed a favour,' wrote Mr Chalif. 'A big Scout jamboree was coming off in Europe, and I wanted the president of one of the largest corporations in America to pay the expenses of one of my boys for the trip.

'Fortunately, just before I went to see this man, I heard that he had drawn a cheque for a million dollars, and that after it was cancelled, he had it framed.

'So, the first thing I did when I entered his office was to ask to see the cheque. A cheque for a million dollars! I told him I never knew that anybody had ever written such a cheque, and that I wanted to tell my boys that I had actually seen a cheque for a million dollars. He gladly showed it to me; I admired it and asked him to tell me all about how it happened to be drawn.

You notice, don't you, that Mr Chalif didn't begin by talking about the Boy Scouts, or the jamboree in Europe, or what it was he wanted? He talked in terms of what interested the other man. Here's the result:

'Presently, the man I was interviewing said: "Oh, by the way, what was it you wanted to see me about?" To my vast surprise,' Mr Chalif continues, 'he not only granted immediately what I asked for, but much more. I had asked him to send only one boy to Europe, but he sent five boys and myself, gave me a letter of credit for $1,000 and told us to stay in Europe for seven weeks. He also gave me letters of introduction to his branch presidents, putting them at our service, and he himself met us in Paris and showed us the town. Since then, he has given jobs to some of the boys whose parents were in want, and he is still active in our group.

'Yet I know if I hadn't found out what he was interested in, and got him warmed up first, I wouldn't have found him one-tenth as easy to approach.'

Is this a valuable technique to use in business? Is it? Let's see. Take Henry G. Duvernoy of Duvernoy and Sons, a wholesale baking firm in New York.

Mr Duvernoy had been trying to sell bread to a certain New York hotel. He had called on the manager every week for four years. He went to the same social affairs the manager attended. He even took rooms in the hotel and lived there in order to get the business. But he failed.

'Then,' said Mr Duvernoy, 'after studying human relations, I resolved to change my tactics. I decided to find out what interested this man – what caught his enthusiasm.

'I discovered he belonged to a society of hotel executives called the Hotel Greeters of America. He not only belonged, but his bubbling enthusiasm had made him president of the organization, and the president of the International Greeters. No matter where its conventions were held, he would be there.

'So when I saw him the next day, I began talking about the Greeters. What a response I got. What a response! He talked to me for half an hour about the Greeters, his tones vibrant with enthusiasm. I could plainly see that this society was not only his hobby, it was the passion of his life. Before I left his office, he had "sold" me a membership in his organization.

'In the meantime, I had said nothing about bread. But a few days later, the steward of his hotel phoned me to come over with samples and prices.

"I don't know what you did to the old boy," the steward greeted me, "but he sure is sold on you!"

'Think of it! I had been drumming at that man for four years – trying to get his business – and I'd still be drumming at him if I hadn't finally taken the trouble to find out what he was interested in, and what he enjoyed talking about.'

Edward E. Harriman of Hagerstown, Maryland, chose to live in the beautiful Cumberland valley of Maryland after he completed his military service. Unfortunately, at that time there were few jobs available in the area. A little research uncovered the fact that a number of companies in the area were either owned or controlled by an unusual business maverick, R.J. Funkhouser, whose rise from poverty to riches intrigued Mr Harriman. However, he was known for being inaccessible to job seekers. Mr Harriman wrote:

'I interviewed a number of people and found that his major interest was anchored in his drive for power and money. Since he protected himself from people like me by use of a dedicated and stern secretary, I studied her interests and goals and only then I paid an unannounced visit at her office. She had been Mr Funkhouser's orbiting satellite for about 15 years. When I told her I had a proposition for him which might translate itself into financial and political success for him, she became enthused. I also conversed with her about her constructive participation in his success. After this conversation she arranged for me to meet Mr Funkhouser.

'I entered his huge and impressive office determined not to ask directly for a job. He was seated behind a large carved desk and thundered at me, "How about it, young man?" I said, "Mr Funkhouser, I believe I can make money for you." He immediately rose and invited me to sit in one of the large upholstered chairs. I enumerated my ideas and the qualifications I had to realize these ideas, as well as how they would contribute to his personal success and that of his businesses.

"R.J.", as he became known to me, hired me at once and for over 20 years I have grown in his enterprises and we both have prospered.'

Talking in terms of the other person's interests pays off for both parties. Howard Z. Herzig, a leader in the field of employee communications, has always followed this principle. When asked what reward he got from it, Mr Herzig responded that he not only received a different reward from each person but that in general the reward had been an enlargement of his life each time he spoke to someone.

5

How to Make People Like You Instantly

I was waiting in line to register a letter in the post office at 33rd Street and 8th Avenue in New York. I noticed that the clerk appeared to be bored with the job – weighing envelopes, handing out stamps, making change, issuing receipts – the same monotonous grind year after year. So, I said to myself: 'I am going to try to make that clerk like me. Obviously, to make him like me, I must say something nice, not about myself, but about him. So, I asked myself, 'What is there about him that I can honestly admire?' That is sometimes a hard question to answer, especially with strangers; but, in this case, it happened to be easy. I instantly saw something I admired no end.

While he was weighing my envelope, I remarked with enthusiasm: 'I wish I had your head of hair!'

He looked up, half-startled, his face beaming with smiles!

'Well, it isn't as good as it used to be,' he said modestly. I assured him that although it might have lost some of its pristine glory, nevertheless it was still magnificent. He was immensely pleased. We carried on a pleasant little conversation and the last thing he said to me was: 'Many people have admired my hair.'

I'll bet that person went to lunch that day walking on air. I'll bet he went home that night and told his wife about it. I'll bet he looked in the mirror and said: 'It is a beautiful head of hair.'

I told this story once in public and a man asked me afterwards: 'What did you want to get out of him?'

What was I trying to get out of him??? What was I trying to get out of him???

If we are so contemptibly selfish that we can't radiate a little happiness and pass on a bit of honest appreciation without trying to get something out of the other person in return – if our souls are no bigger than sour crab apples, we shall meet with the failure we so richly deserve.

Oh yes, I did want something out of that chap. I wanted something priceless. And I got it. I got the feeling that I had done something for him without his being able to do anything whatever in return for me. That is a feeling that flows and sings in your memory long after the incident is past.

There is one all-important law of human conduct. If we obey that law, we shall almost never get into trouble. In fact, that law, if obeyed, will bring us countless friends and constant happiness. But the very instant we break the law, we shall get into endless trouble. The law is this:

> Always make the other person feel important.

John Dewey, as we have already noted, said that the desire to be important is the deepest urge in human nature; and William James said: 'The deepest principle in human nature is the craving to be appreciated.' As I have already pointed out, it is this urge that differentiates us from the animals. It is this urge that has been responsible for civilization itself.

Philosophers have been speculating on the rules of human relationships for thousands of years, and out of all that speculation, there has evolved only one important precept. It is not new. It is as old as history. Zoroaster taught it to his followers in Persia 2,500 years ago. Confucius preached it in China twenty-four centuries ago. Lao-tse, the founder of Taoism, taught it to his disciples in the Valley of the Han. Buddha preached it on the bank of the Holy Ganges 500 years before Christ. The sacred books of Hinduism taught it among the stony hills of Judea nineteen centuries ago. Jesus summed it up in one thought – probably the most important rule in the world: 'Do unto others as you would have others do unto you.'

You want the approval of those with whom you come in contact. You want recognition of your true worth. You want a feeling that you are important in your little world. You don't want to listen to cheap, insincere flattery, but you do crave sincere appreciation. You want your friends and associates to be, as Charles Schwab put it, 'hearty in their approbation and lavish in their praise'. All of us want that.

So, let's obey the golden rule, and give unto others what we would have others give unto us.

How? When? Where? The answer is: All the time, everywhere.

David G. Smith of Eau Claire, Wisconsin, told one of our classes how he handled a delicate situation when he was asked to take charge of the refreshment booth at a charity concert.

'The night of the concert I arrived at the park and found two elderly ladies in a very bad humour standing next to the refreshment stand. Apparently, each thought that she was in charge of this project. As I stood there pondering what to do, one of the members of the sponsoring committee appeared and handed me a cash box and thanked me for taking over the project. She introduced Rose and Jane as my helpers and then ran off.

'A great silence ensued. Realizing that the cash box was a symbol of authority (of sorts), I gave the box to Rose and explained that I might not be able to keep the money straight and that if she took care of it I would feel better. I then suggested to Jane that she show two teenagers who had been assigned to refreshments how to operate the soda machine, and asked her to be responsible for that part of the project.

'The whole evening was very enjoyable with Rose happily counting the money, Jane supervising the teenagers, and me enjoying the concert.'

You don't have to wait until you are ambassador to France or chairman of the Clambake Committee of your lodge before you use this philosophy of appreciation. You can work magic with it almost every day.

If, for example, the waitress brings us mashed potatoes when we have ordered French fries, let's say, 'I'm sorry to trouble you, but I prefer the French fries.' She'll probably reply, 'No trouble at all,' and will be glad to change the potatoes, because we have shown respect for her.

Little phrases such as 'I'm sorry to trouble you', 'Would you be so kind as to?', 'Won't you please?', 'Would you mind?', 'Thank you' – little courtesies like these oil the cogs of the monotonous grind of everyday life – and incidentally, they are the hallmark of good breeding.

Let's take another illustration. Hall Caine's novels – *The Christian*, *The Deemster*, *The Manxman* – were all best sellers in the early part of this century (twentieth century). Millions of people read his novels, countless millions. He was the son of a blacksmith. He never had more than eight years' schooling in his life; yet when he died he was the richest literary man of his time.

The story goes like this: Hall Caine loved sonnets and ballads; so he devoured all of Dante Gabriel Rossetti's poetry. He even wrote a lecture chanting the praises of Rossetti's artistic achievement – and sent a copy to Rossetti himself. Rossetti was delighted. 'Any young man who has such an exalted opinion of my ability,' Rossetti probably said to himself, 'must be brilliant.' So, Rossetti invited this blacksmith's son to come to London and act as his secretary. That was the turning point in Hall Caine's life; for, in his new position, he met the literary artists of the day. Profiting by their advice and inspired by their encouragement, he launched upon a career that emblazoned his name across the sky.

His home, Greeba Castle, on the Isle of Man, became a Mecca for tourists from the far corners of the world, and he left a multi-million dollar estate. Yet, who knows, he might have died poor and unknown had he not written an essay expressing his admiration for a famous man.

Such is the power, the stupendous power, of sincere heartfelt appreciation.

Rossetti considered himself important. That is not strange. Almost everyone considers himself important, very important.

The life of many a person could probably be changed if only someone would make him feel important. Ronald J. Rowland, who is one of the instructors of our course in California, is also a teacher of arts and crafts. He wrote to us about a student named Chris in his beginning-crafts class:

'Chris was a very quiet, shy boy lacking in self-confidence, the kind of student that often does not receive the attention he deserves. I also teach an advanced class that had grown to be somewhat of a status symbol and a privilege for a student to have earned the right to be in it.

'On Wednesday, Chris was diligently working at his desk. I really felt there was a hidden fire deep inside him. I asked Chris if he would like to be in the advanced class. How I wish I could express the look in Chris's face, the emotions in that shy 14-year-old boy, trying to hold back his tears.

"Who me, Mr Rowland? Am I good enough?"

"Yes, Chris, you are good enough."

'I had to leave at that point because tears were coming to my eyes. As Chris walked out of class that day, seemingly two inches taller, he looked at me with bright blue eyes and said in a positive voice, "Thank you, Mr Rowland."

'Chris taught me a lesson I will never forget – our deep desire to feel important. To help me never forget this rule, I made a sign which reads "YOU ARE IMPORTANT". This sign hangs in the front of the classroom for all to see and to remind me that each student I face is equally important.'

The unvarnished truth is that almost all the people you meet feel themselves superior to you in some way, and a sure way to their hearts is to let them realize in some subtle way that you realize their importance, and recognize it sincerely.

Remember what Emerson said: 'Every man I meet is my superior in some way. In that, I learn of him.'

And the pathetic part of it is that frequently those who have the least justification for a feeling of achievement bolster up their egos by a show of tumult and conceit which is truly nauseating. As Shakespeare put it: '...man, proud man, /Drest in a little brief authority, /...Plays such fantastic tricks before high heaven /As make the angels weep.'

I am going to tell you how business people in my own courses have applied these principles with remarkable results. Let's take the case of a Connecticut attorney (because of his relatives he prefers not to have his name mentioned).

Shortly after joining the course, Mr R— drove to Long Island with his wife to visit some of her relatives. She left him to chat with an old aunt of hers and then rushed off by herself to visit some of the younger relatives. Since he soon had to give a speech professionally on how he applied the principles of appreciation, he thought he would gain some worthwhile experience talking with the elderly lady. So, he looked around the house to see what he could honestly admire.

'This house was built about 1890, wasn't it?' he enquired.

'Yes,' she replied, 'that is precisely the year it was built.'

'It reminds me of the house I was born in,' he said. 'It's beautiful. Well built. Roomy. You know, they don't build houses like this any more.'

'You're right,' the old lady agreed. 'The young folks nowadays don't care for beautiful homes. All they want is a small apartment, and then they go gadding about in their automobiles.

'This is a dream house,' she said in a voice vibrating with tender memories. 'This house was built with love. My husband and I dreamed about it for years before we built it. We didn't have an architect. We planned it all ourselves.'

She showed Mr R— about the house, and he expressed his hearty admiration for the beautiful treasures she had picked up in her travels and cherished over a lifetime – paisley shawls, an old English tea set, Wedgwood china, French beds and chairs, Italian paintings and silk draperies that had once hung in a French chateau.

After showing Mr R— through the house, she took him out to the garage. There, jacked up on blocks, was a Packard car – in mint condition.

'My husband bought that car for me shortly before he passed on,' she said softly. I have never ridden in it since his death...You appreciate nice things, and I'm going to give this car to you.'

'Why, aunty,' he said, 'you overwhelm me. I appreciate your generosity, of course; but I couldn't possibly accept it. I'm not even a relative of yours. I have a new car, and you have many relatives that would like to have that Packard.'

'Relatives!' she exclaimed. 'Yes, I have relatives who are just waiting till I die so they can get that car. But they are not going to get it.'

'If you don't want to give it to them, you can very easily sell it to a second-hand dealer,' he told her.

'Sell it!' she cried. 'Do you think I would sell this car? Do you think I could stand to see strangers riding up and down the street in that car – that car that my husband bought for me? I wouldn't dream of selling it. I'm going to give it to you. You appreciate beautiful things.'

He tried to get out of accepting the car, but he couldn't without hurting her feelings.

This lady, left all alone in a big house with her paisley shawls, her French antiques and her memories, was starving for a little recognition. She had once been young and beautiful and sought after. She had once built a house warm with love and had collected things from all over Europe to make it beautiful. Now, in the isolated loneliness of old age, she craved a little human warmth, a little genuine appreciation – and no one gave it to her. And when she found it, like a spring in the desert, her gratitude couldn't adequately express itself with anything less than the gift of her cherished Packard.

Let's take another case: Donald M. McMahon, who was superintendent of Lewis and Valentine, nurserymen and landscape architects in Rye, New York, related this incident:

'Shortly after I attended the talk on *How to Win Friends and Influence People*, I was landscaping the estate of a famous attorney. The owner came out to give me a few instructions about where he wished to plant a mass of rhododendrons and azaleas.

'I said, "Judge, you have a lovely hobby. I've been admiring your beautiful dogs. I understand you win a lot of blue ribbons every year at the show in Madison Square Garden."

'The effect of this little expression of appreciation was striking. "Yes," the judge replied, "I do have a lot of fun with my dogs. Would you like to see my kennel?"

'He spent almost an hour showing me his dogs and the prizes they had won. He even brought out their pedigrees and explained about the bloodlines responsible for such beauty and intelligence.

'Finally, turning to me, he asked: "Do you have any small children?"

"Yes, I do," I replied, "I have a son."

"Well, wouldn't he like a puppy?" the judge enquired.

"Oh, yes, he'd be tickled pink."

"All right, I'm going to give him one," the judge announced.

'He started to tell me how to feed the puppy. Then he paused. "You'll forget it if I tell you. I'll write it out." So, the judge went in the house, typed out the pedigree and feeding instructions, and gave me a puppy worth several hundred dollars and one hour and 15 minutes of his valuable time largely because I had expressed my honest admiration for his hobby and achievements.'

George Eastman, of Kodak fame, invented the transparent film that made motion pictures possible, amassed a fortune of a hundred million dollars, and made himself one of the most famous businessmen on earth. Yet, in spite of all these tremendous accomplishments, he craved little recognitions even as you and I.

To illustrate: When Eastman was building the Eastman School of Music and also Kilbourn Hall in Rochester, James Adamson, then president of the Superior Seating Company of New York, wanted to get the order to supply the theatre chairs for these buildings. Phoning the architect, Mr Adamson made an appointment to see Mr Eastman in Rochester.

When Adamson arrived, the architect said: 'I know you want to get this order, but I can tell you right now that you won't stand a ghost of a show if you take more than five minutes of George Eastman's time. He is a strict disciplinarian. He is very busy. So, tell your story quickly and get out.'

Adamson was prepared to do just that.

When he was ushered into the room he saw Mr Eastman bending over a pile of papers at his desk. Presently, Mr Eastman looked up, removed his glasses and walked toward the architect and Mr Adamson, saying: 'Good morning, gentlemen, what can I do for you?'

The architect introduced them, and then Mr Adamson said: 'While we've been waiting for you, Mr Eastman, I've been admiring your office. I wouldn't mind working in a room like this myself. I'm in the interior-woodworking business, and I never saw a more beautiful office in all my life.'

George Eastman replied: 'You remind me of something I had almost forgotten. It is beautiful, isn't it? I enjoyed it a great deal when it was first built. But I come down here now with a lot of other things on my mind and sometimes don't even see the room for weeks at a time.'

Adamson walked over and rubbed his hand across a panel. 'This is English oak, isn't it? A little different texture from the Italian oak.'

'Yes,' Eastman replied. 'Imported English oak. It was selected for me by a friend who specializes in fine woods.'

Then Eastman showed him about the room, commenting on the proportions, the colouring, the hand carving and other effects he had helped to plan and execute.

While drifting about the room, admiring the woodwork, they paused before a window, and George Eastman, in his modest, soft-spoken way, pointed out some of the institutions through which he was trying to help humanity: the University of Rochester, the General Hospital, the Homoeopathic Hospital, the Friendly Home, the Children's Hospital. Mr Adamson congratulated him warmly on the idealistic way he was using his wealth to alleviate the sufferings of humanity. Presently, George Eastman unlocked a glass case and pulled out the first camera he had ever owned – an invention he had bought from an Englishman.

Adamson questioned him at length about his early struggles to get started in business, and Mr Eastman spoke with real feeling about the poverty of his childhood, telling how his widowed mother had kept a boarding house while he clerked in an insurance office. The terror of poverty haunted him day and night, and he resolved to make enough money so that his mother wouldn't have to work. Mr Adamson drew him out with further questions and listened, absorbed, while he related the story of his experiments with dry photographic plates. He told how he had worked in an office all day, and sometimes experimented all night, taking only brief naps while the chemicals were working, some-times working and sleeping in his clothes for 72 hours at a stretch.

James Adamson had been ushered into Eastman's office at 10.15 a.m. and had been warned that he must not take more than five minutes; but an hour had passed, then two hours passed. And they were still talking.

Finally, George Eastman turned to Adamson and said, 'The last time I was in Japan I bought some chairs, brought them home, and put them in my sun porch. But the sun peeled the paint, so I went downtown the other day and bought some paint and painted the chairs myself. Would you like to see what sort of job I can do painting chairs? All right. Come up to my home and have lunch with me and I'll show you.'

After lunch, Mr Eastman showed Adamson the chairs he had brought from Japan. They weren't worth more than a few dollars, but George Eastman, now a multimillionaire, was proud of them because he himself had painted them.

The order for the seats amounted to $90,000. Who do you suppose got the order – James Adamson or one of his competitors?

From the time of this story until Mr Eastman's death, he and James Adamson were close friends.

Claude Marais, a restaurant owner in Rouen, France, used this principle and saved his restaurant the loss of a key employee. This woman had been in his employ for five years and was a vital link between M Marais and his staff of twenty-one people. He was shocked to receive a registered letter from her advising him of her resignation.

M Marais reported: 'I was very surprised and, even more, disappointed, because I was under the impression that I had been fair to her and receptive to her needs. In as much as she was a friend as well as an employee, I probably had taken her too much for granted and maybe was even more demanding of her than of other employees.

'I could not, of course, accept this resignation without some explanation. I took her aside and said, "Paulette, you must understand that I cannot accept your resignation. You mean a great deal to me and to this company, and you are as important to the success of this restaurant as I am." I repeated this in front of the entire staff, and I invited her to my home and reiterated my confidence in her with my family present.

'Paulette withdrew her resignation, and today I can rely on her as never before. I frequently reinforce this by expressing my appreciation for what she does and showing her how important she is to me and to the restaurant.'

'Talk to people about themselves,' said Disraeli, one of the shrewdest men who ever ruled the British Empire. 'Talk to people about themselves and they will listen for hours.'

SIX WAYS TO MAKE PEOPLE LIKE YOU

PRINCIPLE 1

Become genuinely interested in other people

PRINCIPLE 2

Smile

PRINCIPLE 3

Remember that a person's name is to that person the sweetest and most important sound in any language

PRINCIPLE 4

Be a good listener. Encourage others to talk about themselves

PRINCIPLE 5

Talk in terms of the other person's interests

PRINCIPLE 6

Make the other person feel important – and do it sincerely

Part 3

How To Win People To Your Way of Thinking

6

If You're Wrong, Admit It

Within a minute's walk of my house there was a wild stretch of virgin timber, where the blackberry thickets foamed white in the springtime, where the squirrels nested and reared their young, and the horse weeds grew as tall as a horse's head. This unspoiled woodland was called Forest Park – and it was a forest, probably not much different in appearance from what it was when Columbus discovered America. I frequently walked in this park with Rex, my little Boston bulldog. He was a friendly, harmless little hound; and since we rarely met anyone in the park, I took Rex along without a leash or a muzzle.

One day we encountered a mounted policeman in the park, a policeman itching to show his authority.

'What do you mean by letting that dog run loose in the park without a muzzle and leash?' he reprimanded me. 'Don't you know it's against the law?'

'Yes, I know it is,' I replied softly, 'but I didn't think he would do any harm out here.'

'You didn't think! You didn't think! The law doesn't give a tinker's damn about what you think. That dog might kill a squirrel or bite a child. Now, I'm going to let you off this time; but if I catch this dog out here again without a muzzle and a leash, you'll have to tell it to the judge.'

If you're wrong, admit it. I meekly promised to obey.

And I did obey – for a few times. But Rex didn't like the muzzle, and neither did I; so we decided to take a chance. Everything was lovely for a while, and then we struck a snag. Rex and I raced over the brow of a hill one afternoon and there, suddenly – to my dismay – I saw the majesty of the law, astride a bay horse. Rex was out in front, heading straight for the officer.

I was in for it. I knew it. So, I didn't wait until the policeman started talking. I beat him to it. I said: 'Officer, you've caught me red-handed. I'm guilty. I have no alibis, no excuses. You warned me last week that if I brought the dog out here again without a muzzle you would fine me.'

'Well, now,' the policeman responded in a soft tone. 'I know it's a temptation to let a little dog like that have a run out here when nobody is around.'

'Sure it's a temptation,' I replied, 'but it is against the law.'

'Well, a little dog like that isn't going to harm anybody,' the policeman remonstrated.

'No, but he may kill squirrels,' I said.

'Well now, I think you are taking this a bit too seriously,' he told me. 'I'll tell you what you do. You just let him run over the hill there where I can't see him – and we'll forget all about it.'

That policeman, being human, wanted a feeling of importance; so when I began to condemn myself, the only way he could nourish his self-esteem was to take the magnanimous attitude of showing mercy.

But suppose I had tried to defend myself – well, did you ever argue with a policeman?

Instead of breaking lances with him, I admitted that he was absolutely right and I was absolutely wrong; I admitted it quickly, openly and with enthusiasm. The affair terminated graciously in my taking his side and his taking my side. Lord Chesterfield himself could hardly have been more gracious than this mounted policeman, who, only a week previously, had threatened to have the law on me.

> If we know we are going to be rebuked anyhow, isn't it far better to beat the other person to it and do it ourselves? Isn't it much easier to listen to self-criticism than to bear condemnation from alien lips?

Say about yourself all the derogatory things you know the other person is thinking or wants to say or intends to say, and say them before that person has a chance to say them. The chances are a hundred to one that a generous, forgiving attitude will be taken and your mistakes will be minimized just as the mounted policeman did with me and Rex.

Ferdinand E. Warren, a commercial artist, used this technique to win the goodwill of a petulant, scolding buyer of art.

'It is important, in making drawings for advertising and publishing purposes, to be precise and very exact,' Mr Warren said as he told the story.

'Some art editors demand that their commissions be executed immediately; and in these cases, some slight error is liable to occur. I knew one art director in particular who was always delighted to find fault with some little thing. I have often left his office in disgust, not because of the criticism, but because of his method of attack. Recently I delivered a rush job to this editor, and he phoned me to call at his office immediately. He said something was wrong. When I arrived, I found just what I had anticipated – and dreaded. He was hostile, gloating over his chance to criticize. He demanded with heat why I had done so and so. My opportunity had come to apply the self-criticism I had been studying about. So I said: "Mr So-and-so, if what you say is true, I am at fault and there is absolutely no excuse for my blunder. I have been doing drawings for you long enough to know better. I'm ashamed of myself."

'Immediately he started to defend me. "Yes, you're right, but after all, this isn't a serious mistake. It is only..."

'I interrupted him. "Any mistake," I said, "may be costly and they are all irritating."

'He started to break in, but I wouldn't let him. I was having a grand time. For the first time in my life, I was criticizing myself – and I loved it.

'"I should have been more careful," I continued. "You give me a lot of work, and you deserve the best; so I'm going to do this drawing all over."

'"No! No!" he protested. "I wouldn't think of putting you to all that trouble." He praised my work, assured me that he wanted only a minor change and that my slight error hadn't cost his firm any money; and, after all, it was a mere detail – not worth worrying about.

'My eagerness to criticize myself took all the fight out of him. He ended up taking me to lunch; and before we parted, he gave me a cheque and another commission.'

There is a certain degree of satisfaction in having the courage to admit one's errors. It not only clears the air of guilt and defensiveness, but often helps solve the problem created by the error.

Bruce Harvey of Albuquerque, New Mexico, had incorrectly authorized payment of full wages to an employee on sick leave. When he discovered his error, he brought it to the attention of the employee and explained that to correct the mistake he would have to reduce his next pay cheque by the entire amount of the overpayment. The employee pleaded that as that would cause him a serious financial problem, could the money be repaid over a period of time? In order to do this, Harvey explained, he would have to obtain his supervisor's approval. 'And this I knew,' reported Harvey, 'would result in a boss-type explosion. While trying to decide how to handle this situation better, I realized that the whole mess was my fault and I would have to admit it to my boss.

'I walked into his office, told him that I had made a mistake and then informed him of the complete facts. He replied in an explosive manner that it was the fault of the personnel department. I repeated that it was my fault. He exploded again about carelessness in the accounting department. Again I explained it was my fault. He blamed two other people in the office. But each time I reiterated it was my fault. Finally, he looked at me and said, "Okay, it was your fault. Now straighten it out." The error was corrected and nobody got into trouble. I felt great because I was able to handle a tense situation and had the courage not to seek alibis. My boss has had more respect for me ever since.'

Any fool can try to defend his or her mistakes – and most fools do – but it raises one above the herd and gives one a feeling of nobility and exultation to admit one's mistakes. For example, one of the most beautiful things that history records about Robert E. Lee is the way he blamed himself and only himself for the failure of Pickett's charge at Gettysburg.

Pickett's charge was undoubtedly the most brilliant and picturesque attack that ever occurred in the Western world. General George E. Pickett himself was picturesque. He wore his hair so long that his auburn locks almost touched his shoulders; and, like Napoleon in his Italian campaigns, he wrote ardent love letters almost daily while on the battlefield. His devoted troops cheered him that tragic July afternoon as he rode off jauntily toward the Union lines, his cap set at a rakish angle over his right ear. They cheered and they followed him, man touching man, rank pressing rank, with banners flying and bayonets gleaming in the sun. It was a gallant sight. Daring. Magnificent. A murmur of admiration ran through the Union lines as they beheld it.

Pickett's troops swept forward at an easy trot, through orchard and cornfield, across a meadow and over a ravine. All the time, the enemy's cannon was tearing ghastly holes in their ranks. But on they pressed, grim, irresistible.

Suddenly the Union infantry rose from behind the stone wall on Cemetery Ridge where they had been hiding and fired volley after volley into Pickett's onrushing troops. The crest of the hill was a sheet of flame, a slaughterhouse, a blazing volcano. In a few minutes, all of Pickett's brigade commanders except one were down, and four-fifths of his 5,000 men had fallen.

General Lewis A. Armistead, leading the troops in the final plunge, ran forward, vaulted over the stone wall, and, waving his cap on the top of his sword, shouted:

'Give 'em the steel, boys!'

They did. They leapt over the wall, bayoneted their enemies, smashed skulls with clubbed muskets and planted the battle flags of the South on Cemetery Ridge.

The banners waved there only for a moment. But that moment, brief as it was, recorded the high-water mark of the Confederacy.

Pickett's charge – brilliant and heroic – was nevertheless the beginning of the end. Lee had failed. He could not penetrate the North. And he knew it.

The South was doomed.

Lee was so saddened, so shocked, that he sent in his resignation and asked Jefferson Davis, the president of the Confederacy, to appoint 'a younger and abler man'. If Lee had wanted to blame the disastrous failure of Pickett's charge on someone else, he could have found a score of alibis. Some of his division commanders had failed him. The cavalry hadn't arrived in time to support the infantry attack. This had gone wrong and that had gone awry.

But Lee was far too noble to blame others. As Pickett's beaten and bloody troops struggled back to the Confederate lines, Robert E. Lee rode out to meet them all alone and greeted them with a self-condemnation that was little short of sublime. 'All this has been my fault,' he confessed. 'I and I alone have lost this battle.'

Few generals in all of history have had the courage and character to admit that.

Michael Cheung, who teaches our course in Hong Kong, told of how the Chinese culture presents some special problems and how sometimes it is necessary to recognize that the benefit of applying a principle may be more advantageous than maintaining an old tradition. He had one middle-aged class member who had been estranged from his son for many years. The father had been an opium addict, but was now cured. In Chinese tradition an older person cannot take the first step. The father felt that it was up to his son to take the initiative toward a reconciliation. In an early session, he told the class about the grandchildren he had never seen and how much he desired to be reunited with his son. His classmates, all Chinese, understood his conflict between his desire and long-established tradition. The father felt that young people should have respect for their elders and that he was right in not giving in to his desire, but to wait for his son to come to him.

Toward the end of the course the father again addressed his class. 'I have pondered this problem,' he said. 'Dale Carnegie says, "If you are wrong, admit it quickly and emphatically." It is too late for me to admit it quickly, but I can admit it emphatically. I wronged my son. He was right in not wanting to see me and to expel me from his life. I may lose face by asking a younger person's forgiveness, but I was at fault and it is my responsibility to admit this.' The class applauded and gave him their full support. At the next class he told how he went to his son's house, asked for and received forgiveness and was now embarked on a new relationship with his son, his daughter-in-law and the grandchildren he had at last met.

Elbert Hubbard was one of the most original authors who ever stirred up a nation, and his stinging sentences often aroused fierce resentment. But Hubbard with his rare skill for handling people frequently turned his enemies into friends.

For example, when some irritated reader wrote in to say that he didn't agree with such and such an article and ended by calling Hubbard this and that, Elbert Hubbard would answer like this:

'Come to think it over, I don't entirely agree with it myself. Not everything I wrote yesterday appeals to me today. I am glad to learn what you think on the subject. The next time you are in the neighbourhood you must visit us and we'll get this subject threshed out for all time. So here is a handclasp over the miles, and I am,

Yours sincerely,

What could you say to a man who treated you like that?

When we are right, let's try to win people gently and tactfully to our way of thinking, and when we are wrong – and that will be surprisingly often, if we are honest with ourselves – let's admit our mistakes quickly and with enthusiasm. Not only will that technique produce astonishing results; but, believe it or not, it is a lot more fun, under the circumstances, than trying to defend oneself.

Remember the old proverb: 'By fighting you never get enough, but by yielding you get more than you expected.'

7

A Drop of Honey

If your temper is aroused and you tell 'em a thing or two, you will have a fine time unloading your feelings. But what about the other person? Will he share your pleasure? Will your belligerent tones, your hostile attitude, make it easy for him to agree with you?

'If you come at me with your fists doubled,' said Woodrow Wilson, 'I think I can promise you that mine will double as fast as yours; but if you come to me and say, "Let us sit down and take counsel together, and, if we differ from each other, understand why it is that we differ, just what the points at issue are," we will presently find that we are not so far apart after all, that the points on which we differ are few and the points on which we agree are many, and that if we only have the patience and the candour and the desire to get together, we will get together.'

Nobody appreciated the truth of Woodrow Wilson's statement more than John D. Rockefeller, Jr. Back in 1915, Rockefeller was the most fiercely despised man in Colorado. One of the bloodiest strikes in the history of American industry had been shocking the state for two terrible years. Irate, belligerent miners were demanding higher wages from the Colorado Fuel and Iron Company; Rockefeller controlled that company. Property had been destroyed, troops had been called out. Blood had been shed. Strikers had been shot, their bodies riddled with bullets.

At a time like that, with the air seething with hatred, Rockefeller wanted to win the strikers to his way of thinking. And he did it. How? Here's the story. After weeks spent in making friends, Rockefeller addressed the representatives of the strikers. This speech, in its entirety, is a masterpiece. It produced astonishing results. It calmed the tempestuous waves of hate that threatened to engulf Rockefeller. It won him a host of admirers. It presented facts in such a friendly manner that the strikers went back to work without saying another word about the increase in wages for which they had fought so violently.

The opening of that remarkable speech follows. Note how it fairly glows with friendliness. Rockefeller, remember, was talking to men who, a few days previously, had wanted to hang him by the neck to a sour apple tree; yet, he couldn't have been more gracious, more friendly if he had addressed a group of medical missionaries. His speech was radiant with such phrases as 'I am proud to be here', 'having visited in your homes', 'met many of your wives and children', 'we meet here not as strangers, but as friends'...'spirit of mutual friendship', 'our common interests', 'it is only by your courtesy that I am here'.

'This is a red-letter day in my life,' Rockefeller began. 'It is the first time I have ever had the good fortune to meet the representatives of the employees of this great company, its officers and superintendents, together, and I can assure you that I am proud to be here, and that I shall remember this gathering as long as I live. Had this meeting been held two weeks ago, I should have stood here a stranger to most of you, recognizing a few faces. Having had the opportunity last week of visiting all the camps in the southern coal field and of talking individually with practically all of the representatives, except those who were away; having visited in your homes, met many of your wives and children, we meet here not as strangers, but as friends, and it is in that spirit of mutual friendship that I am glad to have this opportunity to discuss with you our common interests.

'Since this is a meeting of the officers of the company and the representatives of the employees, it is only by your courtesy that I am here, for I am not so fortunate as to be either one or the other; and yet, I feel that I am intimately associated with you men, for, in a sense, I represent both the stockholders and the directors.'

Isn't that a superb example of the fine art of making friends out of enemies?

Suppose Rockefeller had taken a different tack. Suppose he had argued with those miners and hurled devastating facts in their faces. Suppose he had told them by his tones and insinuations that they were wrong. Suppose that, by all the rules of logic, he had proved that they were wrong. What would have happened? More anger would have been stirred up, more hatred, more revolt.

If a man's heart is rankling with discord and ill will toward you, you can't win him to your way of thinking with all the logic in Christendom. Scolding parents and domineering bosses and husbands and nagging wives ought to realize that people don't want to change their minds. They can't be forced or driven to agree with you or me. But they may possibly be led to, if we are gentle and friendly.

Lincoln said that, in effect, over a hundred years ago. Here are his words:

'It is an old and true maxim that "a drop of honey catches more flies than a gallon of gall". So with men, if you would win a man to your cause, first convince him that you are his sincere friend. Therein is a drop of honey that catches his heart; which, say what you will, is the great high road to his reason.'

Business executives have learnt that it pays to be friendly to strikers. For example, when 2,500 employees in the White Motor Company's plant struck for higher wages and a union shop, Robert F. Black, then president of the company, didn't lose his temper and condemn and threaten and talk of tyranny and communists. He actually praised the strikers. He published an advertisement in the

Cleveland papers, complimenting them on 'the peaceful way in which they laid down their tools'. Finding the strike pickets idle, he bought them a couple of dozen baseball bats and gloves and invited them to play ball on vacant lots. For those who preferred bowling, he rented a bowling alley.

This friendliness on Mr Black's part did what friendliness always does: it begot friendliness. So the strikers borrowed brooms, shovels and rubbish carts, and began picking up matches, papers, cigarette stubs and cigar butts around the factory. Imagine it! Imagine strikers tidying up the factory grounds while battling for higher wages and recognition of the union. Such an event had never been heard of before in the long, tempestuous history of American labour wars. That strike ended with a compromise settlement within a week – ended without any ill feeling or rancour.

Daniel Webster, who looked like a god and talked like Jehovah, was one of the most successful advocates who ever pleaded a case; yet he ushered in his most powerful arguments with such friendly remarks as: 'It will be for the jury to consider' or 'This may, perhaps, be worth thinking of' or 'Here are some facts that I trust you will not lose sight of,' or 'You, with your knowledge of human nature, will easily see the significance of these facts'.

> No bulldozing. No high-pressure methods. No attempt to force his opinions on others. Webster used the soft-spoken, quiet, friendly approach, and it helped to make him famous.

You may never be called upon to settle a strike or address a jury, but you may want to get your rent reduced. Will the friendly approach help you then? Let's see.

O.L. Straub, an engineer, wanted to get his rent reduced. And he knew his landlord was hard-boiled. 'I wrote him,' Mr Straub said in a speech before the class, 'notifying him that I was vacating my apartment as soon as my lease expired. The truth was, I didn't want to move. I wanted to stay if I could get my rent reduced. But the situation seemed hopeless. Other tenants had tried – and failed. Everyone told me that the landlord was extremely difficult to deal with. But I said to myself, "I am studying a course in how to deal with people, so I'll try it on him – and see how it works."

'He and his secretary came to see me as soon as he got my letter. I met him at the door with a friendly greeting. I fairly bubbled with good will and enthusiasm. I didn't begin talking about how high the rent was. I began talking about how much I liked his apartment house. Believe me, I was "hearty in my approbation and lavish in my praise". I complimented him on the way he ran the building and told him I should like so much to stay for another year but I couldn't afford it.

'He had evidently never had such a reception from a tenant. He hardly knew what to make of it.

'Then he started to tell me his troubles. Complaining tenants. One had written him 14 letters, some of them positively insulting. Another threatened to break his lease unless the landlord kept the man on the floor above from snoring. "What a relief it is," he said, "to have a satisfied tenant like you." And then, without my even asking him to do it, he offered to reduce my rent a little. I wanted more, so I named the figure I could afford to pay, and he accepted without a word.

'As he was leaving, he turned to me and asked, "What decorating can I do for you?"

'If I had tried to get the rent reduced by the methods the other tenants were using, I am positive I should have met with the same failure they encountered. It was the friendly, sympathetic, appreciative approach that won.'

Dean Woodcock of Pittsburgh, Pennsylvania, is the superintendent of a department of the local electric company. His staff was called upon to repair some equipment on top of a pole. This type of work had formerly been performed by a different department and had only recently been transferred to Woodcock's section. Although his people had been trained in the work, this was the first time they had ever actually been called upon to do it. Everybody in the organization was interested in seeing if and how they could handle it. Mr Woodcock, several of his subordinate managers, and members of other departments of the utility went to see the operation. Many cars and trucks were there, and a number of people were standing around watching the two lone men on top of the pole.

Glancing around, Woodcock noticed a man up the street getting out of his car with a camera. He began taking pictures of the scene. Utility people are extremely conscious of public relations, and suddenly Woodcock realized what this setup looked like to the man with the camera – overkill, dozens of people being called out to do a two-person job. He strolled up the street to the photographer.

'I see you're interested in our operation.'

'Yes, and my mother will be more than interested. She owns stock in your company. This will be an eye-opener for her. She may even decide her investment was unwise. I've been telling her for years there's a lot of waste motion in companies like yours. This proves it. The newspapers might like these pictures, too.'

'It does look like it, doesn't it? I'd think the same thing in your position. But this is a unique situation…' and Dean Woodcock went on to explain how this was the first job of this type for his department and how everybody from executives down was interested. He assured the man that under normal conditions two people could handle the job. The photographer put away his camera, shook Woodcock's hand, and thanked him for taking the time to explain the situation to him.

Dean Woodcock's friendly approach saved his company much embarrassment and bad publicity.

Another member of one of our classes, Gerald H. Winn of Littleton, New Hampshire, reported how, by using a friendly approach, he obtained a very satisfactory settlement on a damage claim.

'Early in the spring,' he stated, 'before the ground had thawed from the winter freezing, there was an unusually heavy rainstorm and the water, which normally would have run off to nearby ditches and storm drains along the road, took a new course onto a building lot where I had just built a new home.

'Not being able to run off, the water pressure built up around the foundation of the house. The water forced itself under the concrete basement floor, causing it to explode, and the basement filled with water. This ruined the furnace and the hot-water heater. The cost to repair this damage was in excess of $2,000. I had no insurance to cover this type of damage.

'However, I soon found out that the owner of the subdivision had neglected to put in a storm drain near the house which could have prevented this problem. I made an appointment to see him. During the 25 mile trip to his office, I carefully reviewed the situation and, remembering the principles I learned in this course, I decided that showing my anger would not serve any worthwhile purpose. When I arrived, I kept very calm and started by talking about his recent vacation to the West Indies; then, when I felt the timing was right, I mentioned the "little" problem of water damage. He quickly agreed to do his share in helping to correct the problem.

'A few days later he called and said he would pay for the damage and also put in a storm drain to prevent the same thing from happening in the future.

'Even though it was the fault of the owner of the subdivision, if I had not begun in a friendly way, there would have been a great deal of difficulty in getting him to agree to the total liability.'

Years ago, when I was a barefoot boy walking through the woods to a country school out in northwest Missouri, I read a fable about the sun and the wind. They quarrelled about which was the stronger, and the wind said, 'I'll prove I am. See the old man down there with a coat? I bet I can get his coat off him quicker than you can.'

So, the sun went behind a cloud, and the wind blew until it was almost a tornado, but the harder it blew, the tighter the old man clutched his coat to him.

Finally, the wind calmed down and gave up, and then the sun came out from behind the clouds and smiled kindly on the old man. Presently, he mopped his brow and pulled off his coat. The sun then told the wind that gentleness and friendliness were always stronger than fury and force.

> The use of gentleness and friendliness is demonstrated day after day by people who have learned that a drop of honey catches more flies than a gallon of gall.

F. Gale Connor of Lutherville, Maryland, proved this when he had to take his four-month-old car to the service department of the car dealer for the third time. He told our class: 'It was apparent that talking to, reasoning with or shouting at the service manager was not going to lead to a satisfactory resolution of my problems.

'I walked over to the showroom and asked to see the agency owner, Mr White. After a short wait, I was ushered into Mr White's office. I introduced myself and explained to him that I had bought my car from his dealership because of the recommendations of friends who had had previous dealings with him. I was told that his prices were very competitive and his service was outstanding. He smiled with satisfaction as he listened to me. I then explained the problem I was having with the service department. "I thought you might want to be aware of any situation that might tarnish your fine reputation," I added. He thanked me for calling this to his attention and assured me that my problem would be taken care of. Not only did he personally get involved, but he also lent me his car to use while mine was being repaired.'

Aesop was a Greek slave who lived at the court of Croesus and spun immortal fables 600 years before Christ. Yet, the truths he taught about human nature are just as true in Boston and Birmingham now, as they were twenty-six centuries ago in Athens. The sun can make you take off your coat more quickly than the wind; and kindliness, the friendly approach and appreciation can make people change their minds more readily than all the bluster and storming in the world.

Remember what Lincoln said: 'A drop of honey catches more flies than a gallon of gall.'

8

A Formula That Will Work Wonders for You

Remember that other people may be totally wrong. But they don't think so. Don't condemn them. Any fool can do that. Try to understand them. Only wise, tolerant, exceptional people even try to do that.

There is a reason why the other man thinks and acts as he does. Ferret out that reason – and you have the key to his actions, perhaps to his personality.

Try honestly to put yourself in his place.

If you say to yourself, 'How would I feel, how would I react if I were in his shoes?' you will save yourself time and irritation, for, 'by becoming interested in the cause, we are less likely to dislike the effect'. And, in addition, you will sharply increase your skill in human relationships.

'Stop a minute,' says Kenneth M. Goode in his book *How to Turn People Into Gold*, 'stop a minute to contrast your keen interest in your own affairs with your mild concern about anything else. Realize then, that everybody else in the world feels exactly the same way! Then, along with Lincoln and Roosevelt, you will have grasped the only solid foundation for interpersonal relationships; namely, that success in dealing with people depends on a sympathetic grasp of the other person's viewpoint.'

Sam Douglas of Hempstead, New York, used to tell his wife that she spent too much time working on their lawn, pulling weeds, fertilizing, cutting the grass twice a week when the lawn didn't look any better than it had when they moved into their home four years earlier. Naturally, she was distressed by his remarks, and each time he made such remarks the balance of the evening was ruined.

After taking our course, Mr Douglas realized how foolish he had been all those years. It never occurred to him that she enjoyed doing that work and she might really appreciate a compliment on her diligence.

One evening after dinner, his wife said she wanted to pull some weeds and invited him to keep her company. He first declined, but then thought better of it and went out after her and began to help her pull weeds. She was visibly pleased, and together they spent an hour in hard work and pleasant conversation.

After that he often helped her with the gardening and complimented her on how fine the lawn looked, what a fantastic job she was doing with a yard where the soil was like concrete. Result: a happier life for both because he had learned to look at things from her point of view – even if the subject was only weeds.

In his book, *Getting Through to People**, Dr Gerald S. Nirenberg commented: 'Cooperativeness in conversation is achieved when you show that you consider the other person's ideas and feelings as important as your own. Starting your conversation by giving the other person the purpose or direction of your conversation, governing what you say by what you would want to hear if you were the listener, and accepting his or her viewpoint will encourage the listener to have an open mind to your ideas.'

I have always enjoyed walking and riding in a park near my home. Like the Druids of ancient Gaul, I all but worship an oak tree, so I was distressed season after season to see the young trees

---

*Dr Gerald S. Nirenberg, *Getting Through to People* (Englewood Cliffs, N.J. Prentice-Hall, 1963), p. 31.

and shrubs killed off by needless fires. These fires weren't caused by careless smokers. They were almost all caused by youngsters who went out to the park to go native and cook a frankfurter or an egg under the trees. Sometimes, these fires raged so fiercely that the fire department had to be called out to fight the conflagration.

There was a sign on the edge of the park saying that anyone who started a fire was liable to fine and imprisonment, but the sign stood in an unfrequented part of the park, and few of the culprits ever saw it. A mounted policeman was supposed to look after the park; but he didn't take his duties too seriously, and the fires continued to spread. On one occasion, I rushed up to a policeman and told him about a fire spreading rapidly through the park and wanted him to notify the fire department, and he nonchalantly replied that it was none of his business because it wasn't in his precinct! I was desperate, so after that when I went riding, I acted as a self-appointed committee-of-one to protect the public domain. In the beginning, I am afraid I didn't even attempt to see the other people's point of view. When I saw a fire blazing under the trees, I was so unhappy about it, so eager to do the right thing, that I did the wrong thing. I would ride up to the boys, warn them that they could be jailed for starting a fire, order with a tone of authority that it be put out; and, if they refused, I would threaten to have them arrested. I was merely unloading my feelings without thinking of their point of view.

The result? They obeyed – obeyed sullenly and with resentment. After I rode on over the hill, they probably rebuilt the fire and longed to burn up the whole park.

With the passing of the years, I acquired a trifle more knowledge of human relations, a little more tact, a somewhat greater tendency to see things from the other person's standpoint. Then, instead of giving orders, I would ride up to a blazing fire and begin something like this:

'Having a good time, boys? What are you going to cook for

supper? I loved to build fires myself when I was a boy – and I still love to. But you know they are dangerous here in the park. I know you boys don't mean to do any harm, but other boys aren't so careful. They come along and see that you have built a fire; so they build one and don't put it out when they go home and it spreads among the dry leaves and kills the trees. We won't have any trees here at all if we aren't more careful. You could be put in jail for building this fire. But I don't want to be bossy and interfere with your pleasure. I like to see you enjoy yourselves; but won't you please rake all the leaves away from the fire right now – and you'll be careful to cover it with dirt, a lot of dirt, before you leave, won't you? And the next time you want to have some fun, won't you please build your fire over the hill there in the sandpit? It can't do any harm there. Thanks so much, boys. Have a good time.'

What a difference that kind of talk made! It made the boys want to cooperate. No sullenness, no resentment. They hadn't been forced to obey orders. They had saved their faces. They felt better and I felt better because I had handled the situation with consideration for their point of view.

> Seeing things through another person's eyes may ease tensions when personal problems become overwhelming.

Elizabeth Novak of New South Wales, Australia, was six weeks late with her car payment. 'On a Friday,' she reported, 'I received a nasty phone call from the man who was handling my account informing me that if I did not come up with $122 by Monday morning I could anticipate further action from the company. I had no way of raising the money over the weekend, so when I received his phone call first thing on Monday morning I expected the worst. Instead of becoming upset, I looked at the situation from his point of view. I apologized most sincerely for causing him so much inconvenience and remarked that I must be his most troublesome customer as this was not the first time I was behind in my payments. His tone of voice changed immediately, and he reassured me that I was far from being one of his really troublesome customers. He went on to tell me several examples of how rude his customers sometimes were, how they lied to him and often tried to avoid talking to him at all. I said nothing. I listened and let him pour out his troubles to me. Then, without any suggestion from me, he said it did not matter if I couldn't pay all the money immediately. It would be all right if I paid him $20 by the end of the month and made up the balance whenever it was convenient for me to do so.'

Tomorrow, before asking anyone to put out a fire or buy your product or contribute to your favourite charity, why not pause and close your eyes and try to think the whole thing through from another person's point of view? Ask yourself: 'Why should he or she want to do it?' True, this will take time, but it will avoid making enemies and will get better results – and with less friction and less shoe leather.

'I would rather walk the sidewalk in front of a person's office for two hours before an interview,' said Dean Donham of the Harvard business school, 'than step into that office without a perfectly clear idea of what I was going to say and what that person – from my knowledge of his or her interests and motives – was likely to answer.'

That is so important that I am going to repeat it in italics for the sake of emphasis.

I would rather walk the sidewalk in front of a person's office for two hours before an interview than step into that office without a perfectly clear idea of what I was going to say and what that person – from my knowledge of his or her interests and motives – was likely to answer.

If, as a result of reading this book, you get only one thing – an increased tendency to think always in terms of the other person's point of view, and see things from that person's angle, as well as your own – if you get only one thing from this book, it may easily prove to be one of the stepping stones of your career.

9

The Movies Do It. TV Does It. Why Don't You Do It?

Many years ago, the *Philadelphia Evening Bulletin* was being maligned by a dangerous whispering campaign. A malicious rumour was being circulated. Advertisers were being told that the newspaper was no longer attractive to readers because it carried too much advertising and too little news. Immediate action was necessary. The gossip had to be squelched. But how?

This is the way it was done.

The *Bulletin* clipped from its regular edition all reading matter of all kinds on one average day, classified it and published it as a book. The book was called *One Day*. It contained 307 pages – as many as a hard-covered book; yet the *Bulletin* had printed all this news and feature material on one day and sold it, not for several dollars, but for a few cents.

The printing of that book dramatized the fact that the *Bulletin* carried an enormous amount of interesting reading matter. It conveyed the facts more vividly, more interestingly, more impressively, than pages of figures and mere talk could have done.

> This is the day of dramatization. Merely stating a truth isn't enough. The truth has to be made vivid, interesting, dramatic. You have to use showmanship. The movies do it. Television does it. And you will have to do it if you want attention.

Experts in window display know the power of dramatization. For example, the manufacturers of a new rat poison gave dealers a window display that included two live rats. The week the rats were shown, sales zoomed to five times their normal rate.

Television commercials abound with examples of the use of dramatic techniques in selling products. Sit down one evening in front of your television set and analyse what the advertisers do in each of their presentations. You will note how an antacid medicine changes the colour of the acid in a test tube while its competitor doesn't, how one brand of soap or detergent gets a greasy shirt clean when the other brand leaves it grey. You'll see a car manoeuvre around a series of turns and curves – far better than just being told about it. Happy faces will show contentment with a variety of products. All of these dramatize for the viewer the advantages offered by whatever is being sold – and they do get people to buy them.

You can dramatize your ideas in business or in any other aspect of your life. It's easy. Jim Yeamans, who sells for the NCR company (National Cash Register) in Richmond, Virginia, told how he made a sale by dramatic demonstration.

'Last week I called on a neighbourhood grocer and saw that the cash registers he was using at his checkout counters were very old-fashioned. I approached the owner and told him: "You are literally throwing away pennies every time a customer goes through your line." With that I threw a handful of pennies on the floor. He quickly became more attentive. The mere words should have been of interest to him, but the sound of pennies hitting the floor really stopped him. I was able to get an order from him to replace all of his old machines.'

It works in home life as well. When the old-time lover proposed to his sweetheart, did he just use words of love? No! He went down on his knees. That really showed he meant what he said. We don't propose on our knees any more, but many suitors still set up a romantic atmosphere before they pop the question.

Dramatizing what you want works with children as well. Joe B. Fant, Jr, of Birmingham, Alabama, was having difficulty getting his five-year-old boy and three-year-old daughter to pick up their toys, so he invented a 'train'. Joey (Captain Casey Jones) was the engineer on his tricycle. Janet's wagon was attached, and in the evening she loaded all the 'coal' on the caboose (her wagon) and then jumped in while her brother drove her around the room. In this way the room was cleaned up – without lectures, arguments or threats.

Mary Catherine Wolf of Mishawaka, Indiana, was having some problems at work and decided that she had to discuss them with the boss. On Monday morning she requested an appointment with him but was told he was very busy and she should arrange with his secretary for an appointment later in the week. The secretary indicated that his schedule was very tight, but she would try to fit her in.

Ms Wolf described what happened next:

'I did not get a reply from her all week long. Whenever I questioned her, she would give me a reason why the boss could not see me. Friday morning came and I had heard nothing definite. I really wanted to see him and discuss my problems before the weekend, so I asked myself how I could get him to see me.

'What I finally did was this: I wrote him a formal letter. I indicated in the letter that I fully understood how extremely busy he was all week, but it was important that I speak with him. I enclosed a form letter and a self-addressed envelope and asked him to please fill it out or ask his secretary to do it and return it to me. The form letter read as follows:

> Ms Wolf, I will be able to see you on — at — a.m./p.m. I will give you — minutes of my time.

'I put this letter in his in-basket at 11 a.m., at 2 p.m. I checked my mailbox. There was my self-addressed envelope. He had answered my form letter himself and indicated he could see me that afternoon and could give me 10 minutes of his time. I met with him, and we talked for over an hour and resolved my problems.

'If I had not dramatized to him the fact that I really wanted to see him. I would probably be still waiting for an appointment.'

James B. Boynton had to present a lengthy market report. His firm had just finished an exhaustive study for a leading brand of cold cream. Data were needed immediately about the competition in this market; the prospective customer was one of the biggest – and most formidable – men in the advertising business.

And his first approach failed almost before he began.

'The first time I went in,' Mr Boynton explains, 'I found myself sidetracked into a futile discussion of the methods used in the investigation. He argued and I argued. He told me I was wrong, and I tried to prove that I was right.

'I finally won my point, to my own satisfaction – but my time was up, the interview was over, and I still hadn't produced results.

'The second time, I didn't bother with tabulations of figures and data. I went to see this man, I dramatized my facts.

'As I entered his office, he was busy on the phone. While he finished his conversation, I opened a suitcase and dumped thirty-two jars of cold cream on top of his desk – all products he knew – all competitors of his cream.

'On each jar, I had a tag itemizing the results of the trade investigation. And each tag told its story briefly, dramatically.

'What happened?

'There was no longer an argument. Here was something new, something different. He picked up first one then another of the jars of cold cream and read the information on the tag. A friendly conversation developed. He asked additional questions. He was intensely interested. He had originally given me only ten minutes to present my facts, but ten minutes passed, twenty minutes, forty minutes and at the end of an hour we were still talking.

'I was presenting the same facts this time that I had presented previously. But this time I was using dramatization, showmanship – and what a difference it made.'

WIN PEOPLE TO YOUR WAY OF THINKING

PRINCIPLE 1

The only way to get the best of an argument is to avoid it

PRINCIPLE 2

Show respect for the other person's opinions. Never say, 'You're wrong.'

PRINCIPLE 3

If you are wrong, admit it quickly and emphatically

PRINCIPLE 4

Begin in a friendly way

PRINCIPLE 5

Get the other person saying 'Yes, yes' immediately

PRINCIPLE 6

Let the other person do a great deal of the talking

PRINCIPLE 7

Let the other person feel that the idea is his or hers

PRINCIPLE 8

Try honestly to see things from the other person's point of view

PRINCIPLE 9

Be sympathetic with the other person's ideas and desires

PRINCIPLE 10

Appeal to the nobler motives

PRINCIPLE 11

Dramatize your ideas

PRINCIPLE 12

Throw down a challenge

PART 4

HOW TO BE A GOOD LEADER

10

Talk about Your Own Mistakes First

My niece, Josephine Carnegie, had come to New York to be my secretary. She was nineteen, had graduated from high school three years previously, and her business experience was a trifle more than zero. She became one of the most proficient secretaries west of Suez, but in the beginning, she was – well, susceptible to improvement. One day when I started to criticize her, I said to myself: 'Just a minute, Dale Carnegie; just a minute. You are twice as old as Josephine. You have had ten thousand times as much business experience. How can you possibly expect her to have your viewpoint, your judgement, your initiative – mediocre though they may be? And just a minute, Dale, what were you doing at nineteen? Remember the asinine mistakes and blunders you made? Remember the time you did this...and that...?'

After thinking the matter over, honestly and impartially, I concluded that Josephine's batting average at nineteen was better than mine had been – and that, I'm sorry to confess, isn't paying Josephine much of a compliment.

So after that, when I wanted to call Josephine's attention to a mistake, I used to begin by saying, 'You have made a mistake, Josephine, but the Lord knows, it's no worse than many I have made. You were not born with judgement. That comes only with experience, and you are better than I was at your age. I have been guilty of so many stupid, silly things myself, I have very little inclination to criticize you or anyone. But don't you think it would have been wiser if you had done so and so?'

It isn't nearly so difficult to listen to a recital of your faults if the person criticizing begins by humbly admitting that he, too, is far from impeccable.

E.G. Dillistone, an engineer in Brandon, Manitoba, Canada, was having problems with his new secretary. Letters he dictated were coming to his desk for signature with two or three spelling mistakes per page. Mr Dillistone reported how he handled this:

'Like many engineers, I have not been noted for my excellent English or spelling. For years I have kept a little black thumb-index book for words I had trouble spelling. When it became apparent that merely pointing out the errors was not going to cause my secretary to do more proofreading and dictionary work, I resolved to take another approach. When the next letter came to my attention that had errors in it, I sat down with the typist and said:

'"Somehow this word doesn't look right. It's one of the words I always have had trouble with. That's the reason I started this spelling book of mine. (I opened the book to the appropriate page.) Yes, here it is. I'm very conscious of my spelling now because people do judge us by our letters and misspellings make us look less professional."

'I don't know whether she copied my system or not, but since that conversation, her frequency of spelling errors has been significantly reduced.'

The polished Prince Bernhard von Biilow learned the sharp necessity of doing this back in 1909. Von Biilow was then the Imperial Chancellor of Germany, and on the throne sat Wilhelm II – Wilhelm, the haughty; Wilhelm, the arrogant; Wilhelm, the last of the German Kaisers, building an army and navy that he boasted could whip their weight in wild cats.

Then an astonishing thing happened. The Kaiser said things, incredible things, things that rocked the continent and started a series of explosions heard around the world. To make matters infinitely worse, the Kaiser made silly, egotistical, absurd announcements in public, he made them while he was a guest in England, and he gave his royal permission to have them printed in the *Daily Telegraph*. For example, he declared that he was the only German who felt friendly toward the English; that he was constructing a navy against the menace of Japan; that he, and he alone, had saved England from being humbled in the dust by Russia and France; that it had been his campaign plan that enabled England's Lord Roberts to defeat the Boers in South Africa; and so on and on.

No other such amazing words had ever fallen from the lips of a European king in peacetime within a hundred years. The entire continent buzzed with the fury of a hornet's nest. England was incensed. German statesmen were aghast. And in the midst of all this consternation, the Kaiser became panicky and suggested to Prince von Biilow, the Imperial Chancellor, that he take the blame. Yes, he wanted von Biilow to announce that it was all his responsibility, that he had advised his monarch to say these incredible things.

'But Your Majesty,' von Biilow protested, 'it seems to me utterly impossible that anybody either in Germany or England could suppose me capable of having advised Your Majesty to say any such thing.'

The moment those words were out of von Biilow's mouth, he realized he had made a grave mistake. The Kaiser blew up.

'You consider me a donkey,' he shouted, 'capable of blunders you yourself could never have committed!'

Von Biilow knew that he ought to have praised before he condemned; but since that was too late, he did the next best thing. He praised after he had criticized. And it worked a miracle.

'I'm far from suggesting that,' he answered respectfully. 'Your Majesty surpasses me in many respects; not only, of course, in naval and military knowledge, but above all, in natural science. I have often listened in admiration when Your Majesty explained the barometer, or wireless telegraphy, or the Roentgen rays. I am shamefully ignorant of all branches of natural science, have no notion of chemistry or physics, and am quite incapable of explaining the simplest of natural phenomena. But,' Von Biilow continued, 'in compensation, I possess some historical knowledge and perhaps certain qualities useful in politics, especially in diplomacy.'

The Kaiser beamed. Von Biilow had praised him. Von Biilow had exalted him and humbled himself. The Kaiser could forgive anything after that. 'Haven't I always told you,' he exclaimed with enthusiasm, 'that we complete one another famously? We should stick together, and we will!'

He shook hands with von Biilow, not once, but several times. And later in the day he was so enthusiastic that he exclaimed with doubled fists, 'If anyone says anything to me against Prince von Biilow, I shall punch him in the nose.'

Von Biilow saved himself in time – but, canny diplomat that he was, he nevertheless had made one error: he should have begun by talking about his own shortcomings and Wilhelm's superiority – not by intimating that the Kaiser was a half-wit in need of a guardian.

If a few sentences humbling oneself and praising the other party can turn a haughty, insulted Kaiser into a staunch friend, imagine what humility and praise can do for you and me in our daily contacts. Rightfully used, they will work veritable miracles in human relations.

Admitting one's own mistakes – even when one hasn't corrected them – can help convince somebody to change his behaviour. This was illustrated more recently by Clarence Zerhusen of Timonium, Maryland, when he discovered his 15-year-old son was experimenting with cigarettes.

'Naturally, I didn't want David to smoke,' Mr Zerhusen told us, 'but his mother and I smoked cigarettes; we were giving him a bad example all the time. I explained to Dave how I started smoking at about his age and how the nicotine had got the best of me and now it was nearly impossible for me to stop. I reminded him how irritating my cough was and how he had been after me to give up cigarettes not many years before.

'I didn't exhort him to stop or make threats or warn him about their dangers. All I did was point out how I was hooked on cigarettes and what it had meant to me.

'He thought about it for a while and decided he wouldn't smoke until he had graduated from high school. As the years went by David never did start smoking and has no intention of ever doing so.

'As a result of that conversation I made the decision to stop smoking cigarettes myself, and with the support of my family, I have succeeded.'

11

No One Likes to Take Orders

I once had the pleasure of dining with Miss Ida Tarbell, the dean of American biographers. When I told her I was writing this book, we began discussing this all-important subject of getting along with people, and she told me that while she was writing her biography of Owen D. Young, she interviewed a man who had sat for three years in the same office with Mr Young. This man declared that during all that time he had never heard Owen D. Young give a direct order to anyone. He always gave suggestions, not orders. Owen D. Young never said, for example, 'Do this or do that,' or 'Don't do this or don't do that.' He would say, 'You might consider this,' or 'Do you think that would work?' Frequently he would say, after he had dictated a letter, 'What do you think of this?' In looking over a letter of one of his assistants, he would say, 'Maybe if we were to phrase it this way it would be better.' He always gave people the opportunity to do things themselves; he never told his assistants to do things; he let them do them, let them learn from their mistakes.

A technique like that makes it easy for a person to correct errors. A technique like that saves a person's pride and gives him or her a feeling of importance. It encourages cooperation instead of rebellion.

Resentment caused by a brash order may last a long time – even if the order was given to correct an obviously bad situation.

Dan Santarelli, a teacher at a vocational school in Wyoming, Pennsylvania, told one of our classes how one of his students had blocked the entrance way to one of the school's shops by illegally parking his car in it. One of the other instructors stormed into the classroom and asked in an arrogant tone, 'Whose car is blocking the driveway?' When the student who owned the car responded, the instructor screamed: 'Move that car and move it right now, or I'll wrap a chain around it and drag it out of there.'

Now, that student was wrong. The car should not have been parked there. But from that day on, not only did that student resent the instructor's action, but all the students in the class did everything they could to give the instructor a hard time and make his job unpleasant.

How could he have handled it differently? If he had asked in a friendly way, 'Whose car is in the driveway?' and then suggested that if it were moved, other cars could get in and out, the student would have gladly moved it and neither he nor his classmates would have been upset and resentful.

> Asking questions not only makes an order more palatable; it often stimulates the creativity of the persons whom you ask. People are more likely to accept an order if they have had a part in the decision that caused the order to be issued.

When Ian Macdonald of Johannesburg, South Africa, the general manager of a small manufacturing plant specializing in precision machine parts, had the opportunity to accept a very large order, he was convinced that he would not meet the promised delivery date. The work already scheduled in the shop and the short completion time needed for this order made it seem impossible for him to accept the order.

Instead of pushing his people to accelerate their work and rush the order through, he called everybody together, explained the situation to them and told them how much it would mean to the company and to them if they could make it possible to produce the order on time. Then he started asking questions:

'Is there anything we can do to handle this order?'

'Can anyone think of different ways to process it through the shop that will make it possible to take the order?'

'Is there any way to adjust our hours or personnel assignments that would help?'

The employees came up with many ideas and insisted that he take the order. They approached it with a 'We can do it' attitude, and the order was accepted, produced and delivered on time.

12

How to Spur People on to Success

Pete Barlow was an old friend of mine. He had a dog-and-pony act and spent his life travelling with circuses and vaudeville shows. I loved to watch Pete train new dogs for his act. I noticed that the moment a dog showed the slightest improvement, Pete patted and praised him and gave him meat and made a great deal about it.

That's nothing new. Animal trainers have been using that same technique for centuries.

Why, I wonder, don't we use the same common sense when trying to change people that we use when trying to change dogs? Why don't we use meat instead of a whip? Why don't we use praise instead of condemnation? Let us praise even the slightest improvement. That inspires the other person to keep on improving.

In his book, *I Ain't Much, Baby – But I'm All I Got**, the psychologist Jess Lair comments: 'Praise is like sunlight to the warm human spirit; we cannot flower and grow without it. And yet, while most of us are only too ready to apply to others the cold wind of criticism, we are somehow reluctant to give our fellow the warm sunshine of praise.'

I can look back at my own life and see where a few words of praise have sharply changed my entire future. Can't you say the same

---

*Jess Lair, *I Ain't Much, Baby – But I'm All I Got* (Greenwich, Conn.: Fawcett, 1976), p. 248.

thing about your life? History is replete with striking illustrations of the sheer witchery of praise.

For example, many years ago a boy of 10 was working in a factory in Naples. He longed to be a singer, but his first teacher discouraged him. 'You can't sing.' he said. 'You haven't any voice at all. It sounds like the wind in the shutters.'

But his mother, a poor peasant woman, put her arms about him and praised him and told him she knew he could sing, she could already see an improvement, and she went barefoot in order to save money to pay for his music lessons. That peasant mother's praise and encouragement changed that boy's life. His name was Enrico Caruso, and he became the greatest and most famous opera singer of his age.

In the early nineteenth century, a young man in London aspired to be a writer. But everything seemed to be against him. He had never been able to attend school more than four years. His father had been flung in jail because he couldn't pay his debts, and this young man often knew the pangs of hunger. Finally, he got a job pasting labels on bottles of blacking in a rat-infested warehouse, and he slept at night in a dismal attic room with two other boys – guttersnipes from the slums of London. He had so little confidence in his ability to write that he sneaked out and mailed his first manuscript in the dead of night so nobody would laugh at him. Story after story was refused. Finally the great day came when one was accepted. True, he wasn't paid a shilling for it, but one editor had praised him. One editor had given him recognition. He was so thrilled that he wandered aimlessly around the streets with tears rolling down his cheeks.

The praise, the recognition, that he received through getting one story in print, changed his whole life, for if it hadn't been for that encouragement, he might have spent his entire life working in rat-infested factories. You may have heard of that boy. His name was Charles Dickens.

Another boy in London made his living as a clerk in a dry-goods store. He had to get up at 5 o' clock, sweep out the store and slave for 14 hours a day. It was sheer drudgery and he despised it. After two years, he could stand it no longer, so he got up one morning and, without waiting for breakfast, tramped 15 miles to talk to his mother, who was working as a housekeeper.

He was frantic. He pleaded with her. He wept. He swore he would kill himself if he had to remain in the shop any longer. Then he wrote a long, pathetic letter to his old schoolmaster, declaring that he was heartbroken, that he no longer wanted to live. His old schoolmaster gave him a little praise and assured him that he really was very intelligent and fitted for finer things and offered him a job as a teacher.

That praise changed the future of that boy and made a lasting impression on the history of English literature. For that boy went on to write innumerable best-selling books and made over a million dollars with his pen. You've probably heard of him. His name: H.G. Wells.

> Use of praise instead of criticism is the basic concept of B.F. Skinner's teachings. This great contemporary psychologist has shown by experiments with animals and with humans that when criticism is minimized and praise emphasized, the good things people do will be reinforced and the poorer things will atrophy for lack of attention.

John Ringelspaugh of Rocky Mount, North Carolina, used this in dealing with his children. It seemed that, as in so many families, parents' chief form of communication with the children was yelling at them. And, as in so many cases, the children became a little worse rather than better after each such session – and so did the parents. There seemed to be no end in sight for this problem.

Mr Ringelspaugh determined to use some of the principles he was learning in our course to solve this situation. He reported: 'We decided to try praise instead of harping on their faults. It wasn't easy when all we could see were the negative things they were doing; it was really tough to find things to praise. We managed to find something, and within the first day or two some of the really upsetting things they were doing quit happening. Then some of their other faults began to disappear. They began capitalizing on the praise we were giving them. They even began going out of their way to do things right. Neither of us could believe it. Of course, it didn't last forever, but the norm reached after things levelled off was so much better. It was no longer necessary to react the way we used to. The children were doing far more right things than wrong ones.' All of this was a result of praising the slightest improvement in the children rather than condemning everything they did wrong.

This works on the job too. Keith Roper of Woodland Hills, California, applied this principle to a situation in his company. Some material came to him in his print shop which was of exceptionally high quality. The printer who had done this job was a new employee who had been having difficulty adjusting to the job. His supervisor was upset about what he considered a negative attitude and was seriously thinking of terminating his services.

When Mr Roper was informed of this situation, he personally went over to the print shop and had a talk with the young man. He told him how pleased he was with the work he had just received and pointed out it was the best work he had seen produced in that shop for some time. He pointed out exactly why it was superior and how important the young man's contribution was to the company.

Do you think this affected that young printer's attitude toward the company? Within days there was a complete turn-about. He told several of his co-workers about the conversation and how someone in the company really appreciated good work. And from that day on, he was a loyal and dedicated worker.

What Mr Roper did was not just flatter the young printer and say 'You're good.' He specifically pointed out how his work was superior.

Because he had singled out a specific accomplishment, rather than just making general flattering remarks, his praise became much more meaningful to the person to whom it was given. Everybody likes to be praised, but when praise is specific, it comes across as sincere – not something the other person may be saying just to make one feel good.

Remember, we all crave appreciation and recognition, and will do almost anything to get it. But nobody wants insincerity. Nobody wants flattery.

Let me repeat: The principles taught in this book will work only when they come from the heart. I am not advocating a bag of tricks. I am talking about a new way of life.

Talking about changing people. If you and I will inspire the people with whom we come in contact to a realization of the hidden treasures they possess, we can do far more than change people. We can literally transform them.

Exaggeration? Then listen to these sage words from William James, one of the most distinguished psychologists and philosophers America has ever produced:

'Compared with what we ought to be, we are only half awake. We are making use of only a small part of our physical and mental resources. Stating the thing broadly, the human individual thus lives far within his limits. He possesses powers of various sorts which he habitually fails to use.'

Yes, you who are reading these lines possess powers of various sorts which you habitually fail to use; and one of these powers you are probably not using to the fullest extent is your magic ability to praise people and inspire them with a realization of their latent possibilities.

Abilities wither under criticism; they blossom under encouragement.

13

Give a Dog a Good Name

What do you do when a person who has been a good worker begins to turn in shoddy work? You can fire him or her, but that really doesn't solve anything. You can berate the worker, but this usually causes resentment. Henry Henke, a service manager for a large truck dealership in Lowell, Indiana, had a mechanic whose work had become less than satisfactory. Instead of bawling him out or threatening him, Mr Henke called him into his office and had a heart-to-heart talk with him.

'Bill,' he said, 'you are a fine mechanic. You have been in this line of work for a good number of years. You have repaired many vehicles to the customers' satisfaction. In fact, we've had a number of compliments about the good work you have done. Yet, of late, the time you take to complete each job has been increasing and your work has not been up to your own old standards. Because you have been such an outstanding mechanic in the past, I felt sure you would want to know that I am not happy with this situation, and perhaps jointly we could find some way to correct the problem.'

Bill responded that he hadn't realized he had been falling down in his duties and assured his boss that the work he was getting was not out of his range of expertise and he would try to improve in the future.

Did he do it? You can be sure he did. He once again became a fast and thorough mechanic. With that reputation Mr Henke had given him to live up to, how could he do anything else but turn out work comparable to that which he had done in the past.

'The average person,' said Samuel Vauclain, then president of the Baldwin Locomotive Works, 'can be led readily if you have his or her respect and if you show that you respect that person for some kind of ability.'

> In short, if you want to improve a person in a certain respect, act as though that particular trait were already one of his or her outstanding characteristics.

Shakespeare said, 'Assume a virtue, if you have it not.' And it might be well to assume and state openly that other people have the virtue you want them to develop. Give them a fine reputation to live up to, and they will make prodigious efforts rather than see you disillusioned.

Georgette Leblanc, in her book, *Souvenirs, My Life With Maeterlinck*, describes the startling transformation of a humble Belgian Cinderella:

'A servant girl from a neighbouring hotel brought my meals,' she wrote. 'She was called "Marie the Dishwasher" because she had started her career as a scullery assistant. She was a kind of monster, cross-eyed, bandy-legged, and poor in flesh and spirit.

'One day, while she was holding my plate of macaroni in her red hand, I said to her point-blank, "Marie, you do not know what treasures are within you."

'Accustomed to holding back her emotion, Marie waited for a few moments, not daring to risk the slightest gesture for fear of a catastrophe. Then she put the dish on the table, sighed and said ingenuously, "Madame, I would never have believed it." She did not doubt, she did not ask a question. She simply went back to the kitchen and repeated what I had said, and such is the force of faith that no one made fun of her. From that day on, she was even given a certain consideration. But the most curious change of all occurred in the humble Marie herself. Believing she was the tabernacle of unseen marvels, she began taking care of her face and body so carefully that her starved youth seemed to bloom and modestly hide her plainness.

'Two months later, she announced her coming marriage with the nephew of the chef. "I'm going to be a lady," she said, and thanked me. A small phrase had changed her entire life.'

Georgette Leblanc had given 'Marie the Dishwasher' a reputation to live up to – and that reputation had transformed her.

Bill Parker, a sales representative for a food company in Daytona Beach, Florida, was very excited about the new line of products his company was introducing and was upset when the manager of a large independent food market turned down the opportunity to carry it in his store. Bill brooded all day over this rejection and decided to return to the store before he went home that evening and try again.

'Jack,' he said, 'since I left this morning I realized I hadn't given you the entire picture of our new line, and I would appreciate some of your time to tell you about the points I omitted. I have respected the fact that you are always willing to listen and are big enough to change your mind when the facts warrant a change.'

Could Jack refuse to give him another hearing? Not with that reputation to live up to.

One morning Dr Martin Fitzhugh, a dentist in Dublin, Ireland, was shocked when one of his patients pointed out to him that the metal cup holder which she was using to rinse her mouth was not very clean. True, the patient drank from the paper cup, not the holder, but it certainly was not professional to use tarnished equipment.

When the patient left, Dr Fitzhugh retreated to his private office to write a note to Bridgit, the charwoman, who came twice a week to clean his office. He wrote:

> My dear Bridgit,
>
> I see you so seldom, I thought I'd take the time to thank you for the fine job of cleaning you've been doing. By the way, I thought I'd mention that since two hours, twice a week, is a very limited amount of time, please feel free to work an extra half hour from time to time if you feel you need to do those "once-in-a-while" things like polishing the cup holders and the like. I, of course, will pay you for the extra time.

'The next day, when I walked into my office,' Dr Fitzhugh reported, 'my desk had been polished to a mirror-like finish, as had my chair, which I nearly slid out of. When I went into the treatment room I found the shiniest, cleanest chrome-plated cup holder I had ever seen nestled in its receptacle. I had given my charwoman a fine reputation to live up to, and because of this small gesture she outperformed all her past efforts. How much additional time did she spend on this? That's right – none at all.'

There is an old saying: 'Give a dog a bad name and you may as well hang him'. But give him a good name – and see what happens!

When Mrs Ruth Hopkins, a fourth-grade teacher in Brooklyn, New York, looked at her class roster the first day of school, her excitement and joy of starting a new term was tinged with anxiety. In her class this year she would have Tommy, the school's most notorious 'bad boy'. His third-grade teacher had constantly complained about Tommy to colleagues, the principal and anyone else who would listen. He was not just mischievous; he caused serious discipline problems in the class, picked fights with the boys, teased the girls, was fresh to the teacher and seemed to get worse as he grew older. His only redeeming feature was his ability to learn rapidly and master the school work easily.

Mrs Hopkins decided to face the 'Tommy problem' immediately. When she greeted her new students, she made little comments to each of them: 'Rose, that's a pretty dress you are wearing,' or 'Alicia, I hear you draw beautifully.' When she came to Tommy, she looked him straight in the eyes and said, 'Tommy, I understand you are a natural leader. I'm going to depend on you to help me make this class the best class in the fourth grade this year.' She reinforced this over the first few days by complimenting Tommy on everything he did and commenting on how this showed what a good student he was. With that reputation to live up to, even a nine-year-old couldn't let her down – and he didn't.

14

Make the Fault Seem Easy to Correct

A bachelor friend of mine, about forty years old, became engaged, and his fiancée persuaded him to take some belated dancing lessons. 'The Lord knows I needed dancing lessons,' he confessed as he told me the story, 'for I danced just as I did when I first started twenty years ago. The first teacher I engaged probably told me the truth. She said I was all wrong; I would just have to forget everything and begin all over again. But that took the heart out of me. I had no incentive to go on. So I quit her.

'The next teacher may have been lying, but I liked it. She said nonchalantly that my dancing was a bit old-fashioned perhaps, but the fundamentals were all right, and she assured me I wouldn't have any trouble learning a few new steps. The first teacher had discouraged me by emphasizing my mistakes. This new teacher did the opposite. She kept praising the things I did right and minimizing my errors. "You have a natural sense of rhythm," she assured me. "You really are a natural-born dancer." Now my common sense tells me that I always have been and always will be a fourth-rate dancer; yet, deep in my heart, I still like to think that maybe she meant it. To be sure, I was paying her to say it; but why bring that up?

'At any rate, I know I am a better dancer than I would have been if she hadn't told me I had a natural sense of rhythm. That encouraged me. That gave me hope. That made me want to improve.'

Tell your child, your spouse or your employee that he or she is stupid or dumb at a certain thing, has no gift for it and is doing it all wrong, and you have destroyed almost every incentive to try to improve. But use the opposite technique:

> Be liberal with your encouragement, make the thing seem easy to do, let the other person know that you have faith in his ability to do it, that he has an undeveloped flair for it – and he will practise until the dawn comes in the window in order to excel.

Lowell Thomas, a superb artist in human relations, used this technique. He gave you confidence, inspired you with courage and faith. For example, I spent a weekend with Mr and Mrs Thomas; and on Saturday night, I was asked to sit in on a friendly bridge game before a roaring fire. Bridge? Oh, no! No! Not me. I knew nothing about it. The game had always been a black mystery to me. No! No! Impossible!

'Why, Dale, it is no trick at all,' Lowell replied. 'There is nothing to bridge except memory and judgement. You've written articles on memory. Bridge will be a cinch for you. It's right up your alley.'

And presto, almost before I realized what I was doing, I found myself for the first time at a bridge table. All because I was told I had a natural flair for it and the game was made to seem easy.

Speaking of bridge reminds me of Ely Culbertson, whose books on bridge have been translated into a dozen languages and have sold more than a million copies. Yet, he told me he never would have made a profession out of the game if a certain young woman hadn't assured him he had a flair for it.

When he came to America in 1922, he tried to get a job teaching in philosophy and sociology, but he couldn't.

Then he tried selling coal, and he failed at that.

Then he tried selling coffee, and he failed at that, too.

He had played some bridge, but it had never occurred to him in those days that someday he would teach it. He was not only a poor card player, but he was also very stubborn. He asked so many questions and held so many post mortem examinations that no one wanted to play with him.

Then he met a pretty bridge teacher, Josephine Dillon, fell in love, and married her. She noticed how carefully he analysed his cards and persuaded him that he was a potential genius at the card table. It was that encouragement and that alone, Culbertson told me, that caused him to make a profession of bridge.

Clarence M. Jones, one of the instructors of our course in Cincinnati, Ohio, told how encouragement and making faults seem easy to correct completely changed the life of his son.

'In 1970 my son David, who was then fifteen years old, came to live with me in Cincinnati. He had led a rough life. In 1958 his head was cut open in a car accident, leaving a very bad scar on his forehead. In 1960 his mother and I were divorced and he moved to Dallas, Texas, with his mother. Until he was fifteen he had spent most of his school years in special classes for slow learners in the Dallas school system. Possibly because of the scar, school administrators had decided he was brain-injured and could not function at a normal level. He was two years behind his age group, so he was only in the seventh grade. Yet, he did not know his multiplication tables, added on his fingers and could barely read.

'There was one positive point. He loved to work on radio and TV sets. He wanted to become a TV technician. I encouraged this and pointed out that he needed maths to qualify for the training. I decided to help him become proficient in this subject. We obtained four sets of flash cards: multiplication, division, addition, and subtraction. As we went through the cards, we put the correct answers in a discard stack. When David missed one, I gave him the correct answer and then put the card in the repeat stack until there were no cards left. I made a big deal out of each card he got right, particularly if he had missed it previously. Each night we would go through the repeat stack until there were no cards left. Each night we timed the exercise with a stop watch. I promised him that when he could get all the cards correct in eight minutes with no incorrect answers, we would quit doing it every night. This seemed an impossible goal to David. The first night it took 52 minutes, the second night, 48, then 45, 44, 41, then under 40 minutes. We celebrated each reduction. I'd call in my wife, and we would both hug him and we'd all dance a jig. At the end of the month he was doing all the cards perfectly in less than eight minutes. When he made a small improvement he would ask to do it again. He had made the fantastic discovery that learning was easy and fun.

'Naturally his grades in algebra took a jump. It is amazing how much easier algebra is when you can multiply. He astonished himself by bringing home a B in maths. That had never happened before. Other changes came with almost unbelievable rapidity. His reading improved rapidly, and he began to use his natural talents in drawing. Later in the school year his science teacher assigned him to develop an exhibit. He chose to develop a highly complex series of models to demonstrate the effect of levers. It required skill not only in drawing and model making but in applied mathematics. The exhibit took first prize in his school's science fair and was entered in the city competition and won third prize for the entire city of Cincinnati.

'That did it. Here was a kid who had flunked two grades, who had been told he was "brain-damaged", who had been called "Frankenstein" by his classmates and told his brains must have leaked out of the cut on his head. Suddenly he discovered he could really learn and accomplish things. The result? From the last quarter of the eighth grade all the way through high school, he never failed to make the honour roll; in high school he was elected to the national honour society. Once he found learning was easy, his whole life changed.'

SIX WAYS TO MAKE PEOPLE LIKE YOU

PRINCIPLE 1

Begin with praise and honest appreciation

PRINCIPLE 2

Call attention to other people's mistakes indirectly

PRINCIPLE 3

Talk about your own mistakes before criticizing the other person

PRINCIPLE 4

Ask questions instead of giving direct orders

PRINCIPLE 5

Let the other person save face

PRINCIPLE 6

Praise the slightest improvement and praise every improvement. Be hearty in your approbation and lavish in your praise

PRINCIPLE 7

Give the other person a fine reputation to live up to

PRINCIPLE 8

Use encouragement. Make the fault seem easy to correct

PRINCIPLE 9

Make the other person happy about doing the thing you suggest.

HOW TO STOP WORRYING AND START LIVING

1

Live in 'Day-tight Compartments'

In the spring of 1871, a young man picked up a book and read twenty-one words that had a profound effect on his future. A medical student at the Montreal General Hospital, he was worried about passing the final examination, worried about what to do, where to go, how to build up a practice, how to make a living.

The twenty-one words that this young medical student read in 1871 helped him to become the most famous physician of his generation. He organized the world-famous Johns Hopkins School of Medicine. He became Regius Professor of Medicine at Oxford – the highest honour that can be bestowed upon any medical man in the British Empire. He was knighted by the King of England. When he died, two huge volumes containing 1466 pages were required to tell the story of his life.

His name was Sir William Osier. Here are the twenty-one words that he read in the spring of 1871 – twenty-one words from Thomas Carlyle that helped him lead a life free from worry: 'Our main business is not to see what lies dimly at a distance, but to do what lies clearly at hand.'

* * *

Forty-two years later, on a soft spring night when the tulips were blooming on the campus, this man, Sir William Osier, addressed the students of Yale University. He told those Yale students that a man like himself who had been a professor in four universities and had written a popular book was supposed to have 'brains of a special quality'. He declared that that was untrue. He said that his intimate friends knew that his brains were 'of the most mediocre character'.

What, then, was the secret of his success? He stated that it was owing to what he called living in 'day-tight compartments'. What did he mean by that? A few months before he spoke at Yale, Sir William Osier had crossed the Atlantic on a great ocean liner where the captain, standing on the bridge, could press a button and – presto! – there was a clanging of machinery and various parts of the ship were immediately shut off from one another – shut off into watertight compartments. 'Now each one of you,' Dr Osier said to those Yale students, 'is a much more marvellous organization than the great liner, and bound on a longer voyage. What I urge is that you so learn to control the machinery as to live with "day-tight compartments" as the most certain way to ensure safety on the voyage. Get on the fridge, and see that at least the great bulkheads are in working order. Touch a button and hear, at every level of your life, the iron doors shutting out the past – the dead yesterdays. Touch another and shut off, with a metal curtain, the future – the unborn tomorrows. Then you are safe – safe for today! Shut off the past! Let the dead past bury its dead. Shut out the yesterdays which have lighted fools the way to dusty death. The load of tomorrow, added to that of yesterday, carried today, makes the strongest falter. Shut off the future as tightly as the past. The future is today. There is no tomorrow. The day of man's salvation is now. Waste of energy, mental distress, nervous worries dog the steps of a man who is anxious about the future. Shut close, then, the great fore and aft bulkheads, and prepare to cultivate the habit of a life of "day-tight compartments".'

Did Dr Osier mean to say that we should not make any effort to prepare for tomorrow? No. Not at all. But he did go on in that address to say that the best possible way to prepare for tomorrow is to concentrate with all your intelligence, all your enthusiasm, on doing today's work superbly today. That is the only possible way you can prepare for the future.

Sir William Osier urged the students at Yale to begin the day with Christ's prayer: 'Give us this day our daily bread'.

Remember that that prayer asks only for today's bread. It doesn't complain about the stale bread we had to eat yesterday; and it doesn't say: 'Oh, God, it has been pretty dry out in the wheat belt lately and we may have another drought – and then how will I get bread to eat next fall – or suppose I lose my job – oh, God, how could I get bread then?'

No, this prayer teaches us to ask for today's bread only. Today's bread is the only kind of bread you can possibly eat.

Years ago, a penniless philosopher was wandering through a stony country where the people had a hard time making a living. One day a crowd gathered about him on a hill, and he gave what is probably the most-quoted speech ever delivered anywhere at any time. This speech contains twenty-six words that have gone ringing down across the centuries: 'Take, therefore, no thought for the morrow; for the morrow shall take thought for the things of itself. Sufficient unto the day is the evil thereof.'

Many men have rejected those words of Jesus: 'Take no thought for the morrow.' They have rejected those words as a counsel of perfection, as a bit of mysticism. I must take thought for the morrow,' they say. 'I must take out insurance to protect my family. I must lay aside money for my old age. I must plan and prepare to get ahead.'

Right! Of course, you must. The truth is that those words of Jesus, translated over three hundred years ago, don't mean today what they meant during the reign of King James. Three hundred years ago the word, though, frequently meant 'anxiety'. Modern versions of the Bible quote Jesus more accurately as saying: 'Have no anxiety for the tomorrow.'

By all means take thought for the tomorrow, yes, careful thought and planning and preparation. But have no anxiety.

During the Second World War, our military leaders planned for the morrow, but they could not afford to have any anxiety. 'I have supplied the best men with the best equipment we have,' said Admiral Ernest J. King, who directed the United States Navy, 'and have given them what seems to be the wisest mission. That is all I can do.

'If a ship has been sunk,' Admiral King went on, 'I can't bring it up. If it is going to be sunk, I can't stop it. I can use my time much better working on tomorrow's problem than by fretting about yesterday's. Besides, if I let those things get me, I wouldn't last long.'

Whether in war or peace, the chief difference between good thinking and bad thinking is this:

> Good thinking deals with causes and effects and leads to logical, constructive planning; bad thinking frequently leads to tension and nervous breakdowns.

I had the privilege of interviewing Arthur Hays Sulzberger, publisher (1935-1961) of one of the most famous newspapers in the world, the *New York Times*. Mr Sulzberger told me that when the Second World War flamed across Europe, he was so stunned, so worried about the future, that he found it almost impossible to sleep. He would frequently get out of bed in the middle of the night, take some canvas and tubes of paint, look in the mirror, and try to paint a portrait of himself. He didn't know anything about painting, but he painted anyway, to get his mind off his worries. Mr Sulzberger told me that he was never able to banish his worries and find peace until he had adopted as his motto five words from a church hymn: 'One step enough for me.'

Lead, kindly Light...
Keep thou my feet: I do not ask to see
The distant scene; one step enough for me.

At about the same time, a young man in uniform – somewhere in Europe – was learning the same lesson. His name was Ted Bengermino, of Baltimore, Maryland – and he had worried himself into a first-class case of combat fatigue.

'In April, 1945,' wrote Ted Bengermino, 'I had worried until I had developed what doctors call "spasmodic transverse colon" – a condition that produced intense pain. If the war hadn't ended when it did, I am sure I would have had a complete physical breakdown.

'I was utterly exhausted. I was a Graves Registration, non-comissioned officer for the 94th Infantry Division. My work was to help set up and maintain records of all men killed in action, missing in action, and hospitalized. I also had to help disinter the bodies of both Allied and enemy soldiers who had been killed and hastily buried in shallow graves during the pitch of battle. I had to gather up the personal effects of these men and see that they were sent back to parents or closest relatives who would prize these personal effects so much. I was constantly worried for fear we might be making embarrassing and serious mistakes. I was worried about whether or not I would come through all this. I was worried about whether I would live to hold my only child in my arms – a son of sixteen months, whom I had never seen. I was so worried and exhausted that I lost thirty-four pounds. I was so frantic that I was almost out of my mind. I looked at my hands. They were hardly more than skin and bones. I was terrified at the thought of going home a physical wreck. I broke down and sobbed like a child. I was so shaken that tears welled up every time I was alone. There was one period soon after the Battle of the Bulge started that I wept so often that I almost gave up hope of ever being a normal human being again.

'I ended up in an Army dispensary. An Army doctor gave me some advice which has completely changed my life. After giving me a thorough physical examination, he informed me that my troubles were mental. "Ted" he said, "I want you to think of your life as an hourglass. You know there are thousands of grains of sand in the top of the hourglass; and they all pass slowly and evenly through the narrow neck in the middle. Nothing you or I could do would make more than one grain of sand pass through this narrow neck without impairing the hourglass. You and I and everyone else are like this hourglass. When we start in the morning, there are hundreds of tasks which we feel that we must accomplish that day, but if we do not take them one at a time and let them pass through the day slowly and evenly, as do the grains of sand passing through the narrow neck of the hourglass, then we are bound to break our own physical or mental structure."

'I have practised that philosophy ever since that memorable day that an Army doctor gave it to me. "One grain of sand at a time; one task at a time." That advice saved me physically and mentally during the war; and it has also helped me in my present position of public relations and advertising director for the Adcrafters Printing & Offset Co., Inc. I found the same problems arising in business that had arisen during the war: a score of things had to be done at once – and there was little time to do them. We were low in stocks. We had new forms to handle, new stock arrangements, changes of address, opening and closing offices, and so on. Instead of getting taut and nervous, I remembered what the doctor had told me. "One grain of sand at a time. One task at a time." By repeating those words to myself over and over, I accomplished my tasks in a more efficient manner and I did my work without the confused and jumbled feeling that had almost wrecked me on the battlefield.'

One of the most appalling comments on our present way of life is that at one time half of all the beds in our hospitals were reserved for patients with nervous and mental troubles, patients who had collapsed under the crushing burden of accumulated yesterdays and fearful tomorrows. Yet, a vast majority of those people could have avoided those hospitals – could have led happy, useful lives – if they had only heeded the words of Jesus: 'Have no anxiety about the morrow'; or the words of Sir William Osier: 'Live in day-tight compartments.'

You and I are standing this very second at the meeting place of two eternities: the vast past that has endured forever, and the future that is plunging on to the last syllable of recorded time. We can't possibly live in either of those eternities – no, not even for one split second. But, by trying to do so, we can wreck both our bodies and our minds. So let's be content to live the only time we can possibly live: from now until bedtime. 'Anyone can carry his burden, however hard, until nightfall,' wrote Robert Louis Stevenson. 'Anyone can do his work, however hard, for one day. Anyone can live sweetly, patiently, lovingly, purely, till the sun goes down. And this is all that life really means.'

Yes, that is all that life requires of us; but Mrs E.K. Shields, of Saginaw, Michigan, was driven to despair – even to the brink of suicide – before she learned to live just till bedtime. 'In 1937, I lost my husband,' Mrs Shields said as she told me her story. 'I was very depressed – and almost penniless. I wrote my former employer, Mr Leon Roach, of the Roach-Fowler Company of Kansas City, and got my old job back. I had formerly made my living selling World Books to rural and town school boards. I had sold my car two years previously when my husband became ill; but I managed to scrape together enough money to put a down payment on a used car and started out to sell books again.

'I had thought that getting back on the road would help relieve my depression; but driving alone and eating alone was almost more than I could take. Some of the territory was not very productive, and I found it hard to make those car payments, small as they were.

'In the spring of 1938, I was working out of Versailles, Missouri. The schools were poor, the roads bad; I was so lonely and discouraged that at one time I even considered suicide. It seemed that success was impossible. I had nothing to live for. I dreaded getting up each morning and facing life. I was afraid of everything: afraid I could not meet the car payments; afraid I could not pay my room rent; afraid I would not have enough to eat. I was afraid my health was failing and I had no money for a doctor. All that kept me from suicide were the thoughts that my sister would be deeply grieved, and that I did not have enough money to pay my funeral expenses.

'Then one day I read an article that lifted me out of my despondence and gave me the courage to go on living. I shall never cease to be grateful for one inspiring sentence in that article. It said: "Every day is a new life to a wise man." I typed that sentence out and pasted it on the windshield of my car, where I saw it every minute I was driving. I found it wasn't so hard to live only one day at a time. I learned to forget the yesterdays and to not think of the tomorrows. Each morning I said to myself, "Today is a new life."

'I have succeeded in overcoming my fear of loneliness, my fear of want. I am happy and fairly successful now and have a lot of enthusiasm and love for life. I know now that I shall never again be afraid, regardless of what life hands me. I know now that I don't have to fear the future. I know now that I can live one day at a time – and that "Every day is a new life to a wise man."'

Who do you suppose wrote this verse:

Happy the man, and happy he alone,
He, who can call to-day his own:
He who, secure within, can say:
'To-morrow, do thy worst, for I have liv'd to-day.'

Those words sound modern, don't they? Yet, they were written thirty years before Christ was born, by the Roman poet Horace.

One of the most tragic things I know about human nature is that all of us tend to put off living. We are all dreaming of some magical rose garden over the horizon – instead of enjoying the roses that are blooming outside our windows today.

Why are we such fools – such tragic fools?

'How strange it is, our little procession of life!' wrote Stephen Leacock. 'The child says, "When I am a big boy." But what is that? The big boy says, "When I grow up." And then, grown up, he says,

"When I get married." But to be married, what is that after all? The thought changes to, "When I'm able to retire." And then, when retirement comes, he looks back over the landscape traversed; a cold wind seems to sweep over it; somehow he has missed it all, and it is gone. Life, we learn too late, is in the living, in the tissue of every day and hour.'

The late Edward S. Evans of Detroit almost killed himself with worry before he learned that life 'is in the living, in the tissue of every day and hour'. Brought up in poverty, Edward Evans made his first money by selling newspapers, then worked as a grocer's clerk. Later, with seven people dependent upon him for bread and butter, he got a job as an assistant librarian. Small as the pay was, he was afraid to quit. Eight years passed before he could summon up the courage to start out on his own. But once he started, he built up an original investment of fifty-five borrowed dollars into a business of his own that made him $20,000 a year. Then came a frost, a killing frost. He endorsed a big note for a friend – and the friend went bankrupt. Quickly on top of that disaster came another: the bank in which he had all his money collapsed. He not only lost every cent he had, but was plunged into debt for $16,000. His nerves couldn't take it.

'I couldn't sleep or eat,' he told me. 'I became strangely ill. Worry and nothing but worry,' he said, 'brought on this illness. One day as I was walking down the street, I fainted and fell on the sidewalk. I was no longer able to walk. I was put to bed and my body broke out in boils. These boils turned inward until just lying in bed was agony. I grew weaker every day. Finally my doctor told me that I had only two more weeks to live. I was shocked. I drew up my will, and then lay back in bed to await my end. No use now to struggle or worry. I gave up, relaxed, and went to sleep. I hadn't slept two hours in succession for weeks; but now with my earthly problems drawing to an end, I slept like a baby. My exhausting weariness began to disappear. My appetite returned. I gained weight.

'A few weeks later, I was able to walk with crutches. Six weeks later, I was able to go back to work. I had been making $20,000 a year; but I was glad to get a job for $30 a week. I got a job selling blocks to put behind the wheels of automobiles when they are shipped by freight. I had learned my lesson now. No more worry for me – no more regret about what had happened in the past – no more dread of the future. I concentrated all my time, energy, and enthusiasm into selling those blocks.'

Edward S. Evans shot up fast now. In a few years, he was president of the company – the Evans Products Company. It has been listed on the New York Stock Exchange for years. If you ever fly over Greenland you may land on Evans Field – a flying field named in his honour. Yet, Edward S. Evans never would have achieved these victories if he hadn't learned to live in day-tight compartments.

You will recall that the White Queen said: 'The rule is jam tomorrow and jam yesterday but never jam today.' Most of us are like that – stewing about yesterday's jam and worrying about tomorrow's jam – instead of spreading today's jam thick on our bread right now.

Even the great French philosopher, Montaigne, made that mistake. 'My life,' he said, 'has been full of terrible misfortunes most of which never happened.' So has mine – so has yours.

'Think,' said Dante, 'that this day will never dawn again.' Life is slipping away with incredible speed. We are racing through space at the rate of nineteen miles every second. Today is our most precious possession. It is our only sure possession.

That is the philosophy of Lowell Thomas. I recently spent a weekend at his farm; and I noticed that he had these words from 'Psalm cxviii' framed and hanging on the walls of his broadcasting studio where he would see them often:

This is the day which the Lord hath made;
we will rejoice and be glad in it.

The writer John Ruskin had on his desk a simple piece of stone on which was carved one word: TODAY. And while I haven't a piece of stone on my desk, I do have a poem pasted on my mirror where I can see it when I shave every morning – a poem that Sir William Osier always kept on his desk – a poem written by the famous Indian dramatist, Kalidasa:

SALUTATION TO THE DAWN
Look to this day!
For it is life, the very life of life.
In its brief course
Lie all the verities and realities of your existence:
The bliss of growth
The glory of action
The splendour of beauty,
For yesterday is but a dream
And tomorrow is only a vision,
But today well lived makes every yesterday a dream of happiness
And every tomorrow a vision of hope.
Look well, therefore, to this day!
Such is the salutation to the dawn.

So, the first thing you should know about worry is this: if you want to keep it out of your life, do what Sir William Osier did:

'Shut the iron doors on the past and the future. Live in day-tight compartments.'

ASK YOURSELF

Why not ask yourself these questions, and write down the answers?

- Do I tend to put off living in the present in order to worry about the future, or to yearn for some 'magical rose garden over the horizon'?
- Do I sometimes embitter the present by regretting things that happened in the past – that are over and done with?
- Do I get up in the morning determined to 'seize the day' – to get the utmost out of these twenty-four hours?
- Can I get more out of life by 'living in day-tight compartments'?
- When shall I start to do this? Next week? Tomorrow? Today?

2

A Magic Formula for Solving Worry Situations

Would you like a quick, sure-fire recipe for handling worry situations – a technique you can start using right away, before you go any further in reading this book?

Then let me tell you about the method worked out by Willis H. Carrier, the brilliant engineer who launched the air-conditioning industry, and who headed the world-famous Carrier Corporation, in Syracuse, New York. It is one of the best techniques I ever heard of for solving worry problems, and I got it from Mr Carrier personally when we were having lunch together one day at the Engineers' Club in New York.

'When I was a young man,' Mr Carrier said, 'I worked for the Buffalo Forge Company in Buffalo, New York. I was handed the assignment of installing a gas-cleaning device in a plant of the Pittsburgh Plate Glass Company at Crystal City, Missouri – a plant costing millions of dollars. The purpose of this installation was to remove the impurities from the gas so it could be burned without injuring the engines. This method of cleaning gas was new. It had been tried only once before – and under different conditions. In my work at Crystal City, Missouri, unforeseen difficulties arose. It worked after a fashion – but not well enough to meet the guarantee we had made.

'I was stunned by my failure. It was almost as if someone had struck me a blow on the head. My stomach, my insides, began to twist and turn. For a while I was so worried I couldn't sleep.

'Finally, common sense reminded me that worry wasn't getting me anywhere; so I figured out a way to handle my problem without worrying. It worked superbly. I have been using this same anti-worry technique for more than thirty years. It is simple. Anyone can use it. It consists of three steps:

Step I: Figure out the worst that could possibly happen.

'I analysed the situation fearlessly and honestly, and figured out what was the worst that could possibly happen as a result of this failure. No one was going to jail me or shoot me. That was certain. True, there was also a chance that I would lose my position; and there was also a chance that my employers would have to remove the machinery and lose the $20,000 we had invested.

Step II: Reconcile yourself to the worst.

'After figuring out what was the worst that could possibly happen, I reconciled myself to accepting it, if necessary. I said to myself: "This failure will be a blow to my record, and it might possibly mean the loss of my job; but if it does, I can always get another position. Conditions could be much worse; and as far as my employers are concerned – well, they realize that we are experimenting with a new method of cleaning gas, and if this experience costs them $20,000, they can stand it. They can charge it up to research, for it is an experiment."

'After discovering the worst that could possibly happen and reconciling myself to accepting it, if necessary, an extremely important thing happened: I immediately relaxed and felt a sense of peace that I hadn't experienced in days.

Step III: Improve upon the worst.

'From that time on, I calmly devoted my time and energy to trying to improve upon the worst which I had already accepted mentally.

'I now tried to figure out ways and means by which I might reduce the loss of $20,000 that we faced. I made several tests and finally figured out that if we spent another $5,000 for additional equipment, our problem would be solved. We did this, and instead of the firm losing $20,000, we made $15,000.

'I probably would never have been able to do this if I had kept on worrying, because one of the worst features about worrying is that it destroys our ability to concentrate. When we worry, our minds jump here and there and everywhere, and we lose all power of decision. However, when we force ourselves to face the worst and accept it mentally, we then eliminate all these vague imaginings and put ourselves in a position in which we are able to concentrate on our problem.

'This incident that I have related occurred many years ago. It worked so superbly that I have been using it ever since; and, as a result, my life has been almost completely free from worry.'

Now, why is Willis H. Carrier's magic formula so valuable and so practical, psychologically speaking? Because it yanks us down out of the great grey clouds in which we fumble around when we are blinded by worry. It plants our feet good and solid on the earth. We know where we stand. And if we haven't solid ground under us, how in creation can we ever hope to think anything through?

Professor William James, the father of applied psychology, has been dead since 1910. But if he were alive today, and could hear this formula for facing the worst, he would heartily approve it. How do I know that? Because he told his own students: 'Be willing to have it so,' he said, 'because...acceptance of what has happened is the first step in overcoming the consequences of any misfortune.'

The same idea was expressed by Lin Yutang in his widely read book, *The Importance of Living*. 'True peace of mind,' said this Chinese philosopher, 'comes from accepting the worst. Psychologically, I think, it means a release of energy.'

That's it, exactly! Psychologically, it means a new release of energy! When we have accepted the worst, we have nothing more to lose. And that automatically means – we have everything to gain! 'After facing the worst,' Willis H. Carrier reported, 'I immediately relaxed and felt a sense of peace that I hadn't experienced in days. From that time on, I was able to think.'

Makes sense, doesn't it? Yet, millions of people have wrecked their lives in angry turmoil, because they refused to accept the worst; refused to try to improve upon it; refused to salvage what they could from the wreck. Instead of trying to reconstruct their fortunes, they engaged in a bitter and 'violent contest with experience' – and ended up victims of that brooding fixation known as melancholia.

Would you like to see how someone else adopted Willis H. Carrier's magic formula and applied it to his own problem? Well, here is one example, from a New York oil dealer who was a student in my classes.

'I was being blackmailed!' this student began. 'I didn't believe it was possible – I didn't believe it could happen outside of the movies – but I was actually being blackmailed! What happened was this: the oil company of which I was the head had a number of delivery trucks and a number of drivers. At that time, war regulations were strictly in force, and we were rationed on the amount of oil we could deliver to any one of our customers. I didn't know it, but it seems that certain of our drivers had been delivering oil short to our regular customers, and then reselling the surplus to customers of their own.

'The first inkling I had of these illegitimate transactions was when a man who claimed to be a government inspector came to see me one day and demanded hush money. He had got documentary proof of what our drivers had been doing, and he threatened to turn this proof over to the district attorney's office if I didn't cough up.

'I knew, of course, that I had nothing to worry about – personally, at least. But I also knew that the law says a firm is responsible for the actions of its employees. What's more, I knew that if the case came to court, and it was aired in the newspapers, the bad publicity would ruin my business. And I was proud of my business – it had been founded by my father twenty-four years before.

'I was so worried I was sick! I didn't eat or sleep for three days and nights. I kept going around in crazy circles. Should I pay the money – $5,000 – or should I tell this man to go ahead and do his damnedest? Either way I tried to make up my mind, it ended in nightmare.

'Then, on Sunday night, I happened to pick up the booklet on *How to Stop Worrying*, which I had been given in my Carnegie class in public speaking. I started to read it, and came across the story of Willis H. Carrier. "Face the worst," it said. So I asked myself, "What is the worst that can happen if I refuse to pay up, and these blackmailers turn their records over to the district attorney?"

'The answer to that was: "The ruin of my business – that's the worst that can happen. I can't go to jail. All that can happen is that I shall be ruined by the publicity."

'I then said to myself, "All right, the business is ruined. I accept that mentally. What happens next?"

'Well, with my business ruined, I would probably have to look for a job. That wasn't bad. I knew a lot about oil – there were several firms that might be glad to employ me. I began to feel better. The blue funk I had been in for three days and nights began to lift a little. My emotions calmed down. And to my astonishment, I was able to think.

'I was clear-headed enough now to face Step III – improve on the worst. As I thought of solutions, an entirely new angle presented itself to me. If I told my attorney the whole situation, he might find a way out which I hadn't thought of. I know it sounds stupid to say that this hadn't even occurred to me before – but of course I hadn't been thinking, I had only been worrying! I immediately made up my mind that I would see my attorney first thing in the morning – and then I went to bed and slept like a log!

'How did it end? Well, the next morning my lawyer told me to go and see the district attorney and tell him the truth. I did precisely that. When I finished I was astonished to hear the DA say that this blackmail racket had been going on for months and that the man who claimed to be a government agent was a crook wanted by the police. What a relief to hear all this after I had tormented myself for three days and nights wondering whether I should hand over $5,000 to this professional swindler!

'This experience taught me a lasting lesson. Now, whenever I face a pressing problem that threatens to worry me, I give it what I call "the old Willis H. Carrier formula".'

If you think Willis H. Carrier had troubles – listen: you ain't heard nothin' yet. Here is the story of Earl P. Haney, of Winchester, Massachusetts. Here is the story as he told it to me himself on November 17, 1948, in the Hotel Statler in Boston.

'Back in the twenties,' he said, 'I was so worried that ulcers began eating the lining of my stomach. One night, I had a terrible haemorrhage. I was rushed to a hospital connected with the School of Medicine of Northwestern University of Chicago. My weight dropped from 175 pounds to 90 pounds.

'I was so ill I was warned not even to lift my hand. Three doctors, including a celebrated ulcer specialist, said my case was incurable. I lived on alkaline powders and a tablespoonful of half milk and half cream every hour. A nurse put a rubber tube down into my stomach every night and morning and pumped out the contents.

'This went on for months. Finally, I said to myself: "Look here, Earl Haney, if you have nothing to look forward to except a lingering death, you might as well make the most of the little time you have left. You have always wanted to travel around the world before you die; so if you are ever going to do it, you'll have to do it now."

'When I told my physicians I was going to travel around the world and pump out my own stomach twice a day, they were shocked. Impossible! They had never heard of such a thing. They warned me that if I started around the world, I would be buried at sea. "No, I won't," I replied. "I have promised my relatives that I will be buried in the family plot at Broken Bow, Nebraska. So I am going to take my casket with me."

'I arranged for a casket, put it aboard ship, and then made arrangements with the steamship company – in the event of my death – to put my corpse in a freezing compartment and keep it there till the liner returned home. I set out on my trip, imbued with the spirit of old Omar:

Ah, make the most of what we yet may spend,
Before we too into the Dust descend;
Dust into Dust, and under Dust, to lie, Sans Wine,
sans Song, sans Singer, and – sans End!

'The moment I boarded the S.S. President Adams in Los Angeles and headed for the Orient, I felt better. I gradually gave up my alkaline powders and my stomach pump. I was soon eating all kinds of foods – even strange native mixtures and concoctions that were guaranteed to kill me. As the weeks went by, I even smoked long, black cigars and drank highballs. I enjoyed myself more than I had in years! We ran into monsoons and typhoons which should have put me in my casket, if only from fright – but I got an enormous kick out of all this adventure.

'I played games aboard the ship, sang songs, made new friends, stayed up half the night. When we reached China and India, I realized that the business cares that I had faced back home were paradise compared to the poverty and hunger in the Orient. I stopped all my senseless worrying and felt fine. When I got back to

America, I had gained ninety pounds and I had almost forgotten I had ever had a stomach ulcer. I had never felt better in my life. I went back to business and haven't been ill a day since.'

Earl P. Haney told me he realizes now that he was unconsciously using the selfsame principles that Willis H. Carrier used to conquer worry.

'First, I asked myself, "What is the worst that could possibly happen?" The answer was death.

'Second, I prepared myself to accept death. I had to. There was no choice. The doctors said my case was hopeless.

'Third, I tried to improve the situation by getting the utmost enjoyment out of life for the short time I had left. "If," he continued, "if I had gone on worrying after boarding that ship, I have no doubt that I would have made the return voyage inside my coffin. But I relaxed – and I forgot all my troubles. And this calmness of mind gave me a new burst of energy which actually saved my life."'

If you have a worry problem, apply the magic formula of Willis H. Carrier by doing these three things:

- Ask yourself, 'What is the worst that can possibly happen?'
- Prepare to accept it if you have to.
- Then calmly proceed to improve on the worst.

3

How to Analyse and Solve Worry Problems

I keep six honest serving-men
(They taught me all I knew);
Their names are What and Why and When
And How and Where and Who.

– Rudyard Kipling

Will the magic formula of Willis H. Carrier, described earlier solve all worry problems? No, of course not.

Then what is the answer? The answer is that we must equip ourselves to deal with different kinds of worries by learning the three basic steps of problem analysis. The three steps are:

- Get the facts.
- Analyse the facts.
- Arrive at a decision, and then act on that decision.

Obvious stuff? Yes, Aristotle taught it – and used it. And, you and I must use it too if we are going to solve the problems that are harassing us and turning our days and nights into veritable hells.

RULE 1: GET THE FACTS

Why is it so important to get the facts? Because unless we have the facts we can't possibly even attempt to solve our problem intelligently. Without the facts, all we can do is stew around in confusion. My idea? No, that was the idea of the late Herbert E. Hawkes, dean of Columbia College, Columbia University, for twenty-two years. He had helped two hundred thousand students solve their worry problems; and he told me that 'confusion is the chief cause of worry'. He put it this way – he said: 'Half the worry in the world is caused by people trying to make decisions before they have sufficient knowledge on which to base a decision. For example, if I have a problem which has to be faced at 3 o'clock next Tuesday, I refuse to even try to make a decision about it until next Tuesday arrives. In the meantime, I concentrate on getting all the facts that bear on the problem. I don't worry,' he said. 'I don't agonize over my problem. I don't lose any sleep. I simply concentrate on getting the facts. And by the time Tuesday rolls around, if I've got all the facts the problem usually solves itself!'

I asked Dean Hawkes if this meant he had licked worry entirely. 'Yes,' he said. 'I think I can honestly say that my life is now almost totally devoid of worry. I have found,' he went on, 'that if a man will devote his time to securing facts in an impartial, objective way, his worries will usually evaporate in the light of knowledge.'

Let me repeat that:

> If a man will devote his time to securing facts in an impartial, objective way, his worries will usually evaporate in the light of knowledge.

But what do most of us do? If we bother with facts at all – and Thomas Edison said in all seriousness, 'There is no expedient to which a man will not resort to avoid the labour of thinking' – if we bother with facts at all, we hunt like bird dogs after the facts that bolster up what we already think – and ignore all the others! We want only the facts that justify our acts – the facts that fit in conveniently with our wishful thinking and justify our preconceived prejudices!

As Andre Maurois put it: 'Everything that is in agreement with our personal desires seems true. Everything that is not puts us into a rage.'

Is it any wonder, then, that we find it so hard to get at the answers to our problems? Wouldn't we have the same trouble trying to solve a second-grade arithmetic problem, if we went ahead on the assumption that two plus two equals five? Yet, there are a lot of people in this world who make life a hell for themselves and others by insisting that two plus two equals five – or maybe five hundred!

What can we do about it? We have to keep our emotions out of our thinking; and, as Dean Hawkes put it, we must secure the facts in 'an impartial, objective' manner:

That is not an easy task when we are worried. When we are worried, our emotions are riding high. But here are two ideas that I have found helpful when trying to step aside from my problems, in order to see the facts in a clear, objective manner.

- When trying to get the facts, I pretend that I am collecting this information not for myself, but for some other person. This helps me to take a cold, impartial view of the evidence. This helps me eliminate my emotions.
- While trying to collect the facts about the problem that is worrying me, I sometimes pretend that I am a lawyer preparing to argue the other side of the issue. In other words, I try to get all the facts against myself – all the facts that are damaging to my wishes, all the facts I don't like to face.

Then I write down both my side of the case and the other side of the case – and I generally find that the truth lies somewhere in between these two extremities.

Here is the point I am trying to make. Neither you nor I, nor Einstein nor the Supreme Court of the United States is brilliant enough to reach an intelligent decision on any problem without first getting the facts. Thomas Edison knew that. At the time of his death, he had 2,500 notebooks filled with facts about the problems he was facing.

So, Rule 1 for solving our problems is: Get the facts. Let's do what Dean Hawkes did: let's not even attempt to solve our problems without first collecting all the facts in an impartial manner.

However, getting all the facts in the world won't do us any good until we analyse them and interpret them.

RULE 2: ANALYSE THE FACTS

I have found from costly experience that it is much easier to analyse the facts after writing them down. In fact, merely writing the facts on a piece of paper and stating our problem clearly goes a long way toward helping us reach a sensible decision. As Charles Kettering puts it: 'A problem well stated is a problem half solved.'

Let me show you all this as it works out in practice. Since the Chinese say one picture is worth ten thousand words, suppose I show you a picture of how one man put exactly what we are talking about into concrete action.

Let's take the case of Galen Litchfield – a man I have known for several years; one of the most successful American businessmen in the Far East. Mr Litchfield was in China in 1942, when the Japanese invaded Shanghai. And here is his story as he told it to me while a guest in my home:

'Shortly after the Japanese bombed Pearl Harbour,' Galen Litchfield began, 'they came swarming into Shanghai. I was the manager of the Asia Life Insurance Company in Shanghai. They sent us an "army liquidator" – he was really an admiral – and gave me orders to assist this man in liquidating our assets. I didn't have any choice in the matter. I could cooperate – or else… And the "or else" was certain death.

'I went through the motions of doing what I was told, because I had no alternative. But there was one block of securities, worth $750,000, which I left off the list I gave to the admiral. I left that block of securities off the list because they belonged to our Hong Kong organization and had nothing to do with the Shanghai assets. All the same, I feared I might be in hot water if the Japanese found out what I had done. And they soon found out.

'I wasn't in the office when the discovery was made, but my head accountant was there. He told me that the Japanese admiral flew into a rage, and stamped and swore, and called me a thief and a traitor! I had defied the Japanese army! I knew what that meant. I would be thrown into the Bridgehouse!

The Bridgehouse! The torture chamber of the Japanese Gestapo! I had had personal friends who had killed themselves rather than be taken to that prison. I had had other friends who had died in that place after ten days of questioning and torture. Now I was slated for the Bridgehouse myself!

'What did I do? I heard the news on Sunday afternoon. I suppose I should have been terrified. And I would have been terrified if I hadn't had a definite technique for solving my problems. For years, whenever I was worried I had always gone to my typewriter and written down two questions – and the answers to these questions:

- What am I worrying about?
- What can I do about it?

'I used to try to answer those questions without writing them down. But I stopped that years ago. I found that writing down both the questions and the answers clarifies my thinking. So, that Sunday afternoon, I went directly to my room at the Shanghai YMCA, and got out my typewriter. I wrote:

What am I worrying about?

'I am afraid I will be thrown into the Bridgehouse tomorrow morning.

'Then I typed out the second question:

What can I do about it?

'I spent hours thinking out and writing down the four courses of action I could take – and what the probable consequence of each action would be.

- I can try to explain to the Japanese admiral. But he doesn't speak English. If I try to explain to him through an interpreter, I may stir him up again. That might mean death, for he is cruel, would rather dump me in the Bridgehouse than bother talking about it.
- I can try to escape. Impossible. They keep track of me all the time. I have to check in and out of my room at the YMCA. If I try to escape, I'll probably be captured and shot.
- I can stay here in my room and not go near the office again. If I do, the Japanese admiral will be suspicious, will probably send soldiers to get me and throw me into the Bridgehouse without giving me a chance to say a word.
- I can go down to the office as usual on Monday morning. If I do, there is a chance that the Japanese admiral may be so busy that he will not think of what I did. Even if he does think of it, he may have cooled off and may not bother me. If this happens, I am all right. Even if he does bother me, I'll still have a chance to try to explain to him. So, going down to the office as usual on Monday morning, and acting as if nothing had gone wrong, gives me two chances to escape the Bridgehouse.

'As soon as I thought it all out and decided to accept the fourth plan – to go down to the office as usual on Monday morning – I felt immensely relieved.

'When I entered the office the next morning, the Japanese admiral sat there with a cigarette dangling from his mouth. He glared at me as he always did; and said nothing. Six weeks later – thank God – he went back to Tokyo and my worries were ended.

'As I have already said, I probably saved my life by sitting down that Sunday afternoon and writing out all the various steps I could take and then writing down the probable consequence of each step and calmly coming to a decision. If I hadn't done that, I might have floundered and hesitated and done the wrong thing on the spur of the moment. If I hadn't thought out my problem and come to a decision, I would have been frantic with worry all Sunday afternoon. I wouldn't have slept that night. I would have gone down to the office Monday morning with a harassed and worried look; and that alone might have aroused the suspicion of the Japanese admiral and spurred him to act.

'Experience has proved to me, time after time, the enormous value of arriving at a decision. It is the failure to arrive at a fixed purpose, the inability to stop going round and round in maddening circles, that drives men to nervous breakdowns and living hells. I find that 50 per cent of my worries vanish once I arrive at a clear, definite decision; and another 40 per cent usually vanishes once I start to carry out that decision.

'So I banish about 90 per cent of my worries by taking these four steps:

- Writing down precisely what I am worrying about.
- Writing down what I can do about it.
- Deciding what to do.
- Starting immediately to carry out that decision.

RULE 3: ARRIVE AT A DECISION, AND THEN ACT ON THAT DECISION

Galen Litchfield became the Far Eastern Director for Starr, Park and Freeman, Inc., representing large insurance and financial interests. This made him one of the most important American businessmen in Asia; and he confessed to me that he owed a large part of his success to this method of analysing worry and meeting it head-on.

Why is his method so superb? Because it is efficient, concrete, and goes directly to the heart of the problem. On top of all that, it is climaxed by the third and indispensable rule: Do something about it. Unless we carry out our action, all our fact-finding and analysis is whistling upwind – it's a sheer waste of energy.

William James said this: 'When once a decision is reached and execution is the order of the day, dismiss absolutely all responsibility and care about the outcome.' (In this case, William James undoubtedly used the word 'care' as a synonym for 'anxiety.') He meant – once you have made a careful decision based on facts, go into action. Don't stop to reconsider. Don't begin to hesitate, worry and retrace your steps. Don't lose yourself in self-doubting which begets other doubts. Don't keep looking back over your shoulder.

I once asked Waite Phillips, one of Oklahoma's most prominent oil men, how he carried out decisions. He replied: 'I find that to keep thinking about our problems beyond a certain point is bound to create confusion and worry. There comes a time when any more investigation and thinking are harmful. There comes a time when we must decide and act and never look back.'

Why don't you employ Galen Litchfield's technique to one of your worries right now?

(Please pencil the answers to these questions in the space below.)

Question No. 1 – **What am I worrying about?**

Question No. 2 – **What can I do about it?**

Question No. 3 – **Here is what I am going to do about it.**

Question No. 4 – **When am I going to start doing it?**

4

How to Crowd Worry out of Your Mind

I shall never forget one night when Marion J. Douglas was a student in one of my classes. (I have not used his real name. He requested me, for personal reasons, not to reveal his identity.) But here is his real story as he told it to the class. He told us how tragedy had struck at his home, not once, but twice. The first time he had lost his five-year-old daughter, a child he adored. He and his wife thought they couldn't endure that first loss; but, as he said, 'Ten months later God gave us another little girl – and she died in five days.'

This double bereavement was almost too much to bear. 'I couldn't take it,' this father told us. 'I couldn't sleep, I couldn't eat, I couldn't rest or relax. My nerves were utterly shaken and my confidence gone.' At last he went to doctors; one recommended sleeping pills and another recommended a trip. He tried both, but neither remedy helped. He said, 'My body felt as if it were encased in a vise, and the jaws of the vise were being drawn tighter and tighter.' The tension of grief – if you have ever been paralysed by sorrow, you know what he meant.

'But thank God, I had one child left – a four-year-old son.

He gave me the solution to my problem. One afternoon as I sat around feeling sorry for myself, he asked: 'Daddy, will you build a boat for me?' I was in no mood to build a boat; in fact, I was in no mood to do anything. But my son is a persistent little fellow! I had to give in.

'Building that toy boat took about three hours. By the time it was finished, I realized that those three hours spent building that boat were the first hours of mental relaxation and peace that I had had in months!

'That discovery jarred me out of my lethargy and caused me to do a bit of thinking – the first real thinking I had done in months. I realized that it is difficult to worry while you are busy doing something that requires planning and thinking. In my case, building the boat had knocked worry out of the ring. So I resolved to keep busy.

'The following night, I went from room to room in the house, compiling a list of jobs that ought to be done. Scores of items needed to be repaired: bookcases, stair steps, storm windows, window shades, knobs, locks, leaky faucets. Astonishing as it seems, in the course of two weeks I had made a list of 242 items that needed attention.

'During the last two years I have completed most of them. Besides, I have filled my life with stimulating activities. Two nights per week I attend adult-education classes in New York. I have gone in for civic activities in my home town and I am now chairman of the school board. I attend scores of meetings. I help collect money for the Red Cross and other activities. I am so busy now that I have no time for worry.'

No time for worry! That is exactly what Winston Churchill said when he was working eighteen hours a day at the height of the war. When he was asked if he worried about his tremendous responsibilities, he said, 'I'm too busy. I have no time for worry.'

Charles Kettering was in the same fix when he started out to invent a self-starter for automobiles. Mr Kettering was, until his retirement, vice-president of General Motors, in charge of the world-famous General Motors Research Corporation. But in those days, he was so poor that he had to use the hayloft of a barn as a laboratory. To buy groceries, he had to use $1,500 that his wife had made by giving piano lessons; later, had to borrow $500 on his life insurance. I asked his wife if she wasn't worried at a time like that. 'Yes,' she replied, 'I was so worried I couldn't sleep; but Mr Kettering wasn't. He was too absorbed in his work to worry.'

The great scientist, Pasteur, spoke of 'the peace that is found in libraries and laboratories'. Why is peace found there? Because the men in libraries and laboratories are usually too absorbed in their tasks to worry about themselves. Research-men rarely have nervous breakdowns. They haven't time for such luxuries.

Why does such a simple thing as keeping busy help to drive out anxiety? Because of a law – one of the most fundamental laws ever revealed by psychology. And that law is: that it is utterly impossible for any human mind, no matter how brilliant, to think of more than one thing at any given time. You don't quite believe it? Very well, then, let's try an experiment.

Suppose you lean back right now, close your eyes, and try, at the same instant, to think of the Statue of Liberty and of what you plan to do tomorrow morning. (Go ahead, try it.)

You found out, didn't you, that you could focus on either thought in turn, but never on both simultaneously? Well, the same thing is true in the field of emotions. We cannot be pepped up and enthusiastic about doing something exciting and feel dragged down by worry at the very same time. One kind of emotion drives out the other. And it was that simple discovery that enabled Army psychiatrists to perform such miracles during the Second World War.

When men came out of battle so shaken by the experience that they were called 'psychoneurotic,' Army doctors prescribed 'Keep 'em busy' as a cure.

Every waking minute of these nerve-shocked men was filled with activity – usually outdoor activity, such as fishing, hunting, playing ball, golf, taking pictures, making gardens, and dancing. They were given no time for brooding over their terrible experiences.

'Occupational therapy' is the term now used by psychiatry when work is prescribed as though it were a medicine. It is not new. The old Greek physicians were advocating it five hundred years before Christ was born!

The Quakers were using it in Philadelphia in Ben Franklin's time. A man who visited a Quaker sanitarium in 1774 was shocked to see that the patients who were mentally ill were busy spinning flax. He thought these poor unfortunates were being exploited – until the Quakers explained that they found that their patients actually improved when they did a little work. It was soothing to the nerves.

Any psychiatrist will tell you that work – keeping busy – is one of the best anaesthetics ever known for sick nerves. Henry W. Longfellow found that out for himself when he lost his young wife. His wife had been melting some sealing wax at a candle one day, when her clothes caught on fire. Longfellow heard her cries and tried to reach her in time; but she died from the burns. For a while, Longfellow was so tortured by the memory of that dreadful experience that he nearly went insane; but, fortunately for him, his three small children needed his attention. In spite of his own grief, Longfellow undertook to be father and mother to his children. He took them for walks, told them stories, played games with them, and immortalized their companionship in his poem, 'The Children's Hour'. He also translated Dante; and all these duties combined kept him so busy that he forgot himself entirely, and regained his peace of mind. As Tennyson declared when he lost his most intimate friend, Arthur Hallam, 'I must lose myself in action, lest I wither in despair.'

Most of us have little trouble 'losing ourselves in action' while we have our noses to the grindstone and are doing our day's work. But the hours after work – they are the dangerous ones. Just when we're free to enjoy our own leisure, and ought to be happiest – that's when the blue devils of worry attack us. That's when we begin to wonder whether we're getting anywhere in life; whether we're in a rut; whether the boss 'meant anything' by that remark he made today; or whether we're losing our sex appeal.

When we are not busy, our minds tend to become a near-vacuum. Every student of physics knows that 'nature abhors a vacuum'. The nearest thing to a vacuum that you and I will probably ever see is the inside of an incandescent electric-light bulb. Break that bulb – and nature forces air in to fill the theoretically empty space.

Nature also rushes in to fill the vacant mind. With what? Usually with emotions. Why? Because emotions of worry, fear, hate, jealousy, and envy are driven by primeval vigour and the dynamic energy of the jungle. Such emotions are so violent that they tend to drive out of our minds all peaceful, happy thoughts and emotions.

James L. Mursell, professor of education, Teachers College, Columbia, put it very well when he said: 'Worry is most apt to ride you ragged not when you are in action, but when the day's work is done. Your imagination can run riot then and bring up all sorts of ridiculous possibilities and magnify each little blunder. At such a time,' he continued, 'your mind is like a motor operating without its load. It races and threatens to burn out its bearings or even to tear itself to bits. The remedy for worry is to get completely occupied doing something constructive.'

But you don't have to be a college professor to realize this truth and put it into practice. During the Second World War, I met a housewife from Chicago who told me how she discovered for herself that the remedy for worry is to get completely occupied doing something constructive. I met this woman and her husband in the dining car while I was travelling from New York to my farm in Missouri.

This couple told me that their son had joined the armed forces the day after Pearl Harbour. The woman told me that she had almost wrecked her health worrying over that only son. Where was he? Was he safe? Or in action? Would he be wounded? Killed?

When I asked her how she overcame her worry, she replied: 'I got busy.' She told me that at first she had dismissed her maid and tried to keep busy by doing all her housework herself. But that didn't help much. 'The trouble was,' she said, 'that I could do my housework almost mechanically, without using my mind. So I kept on worrying while making the beds and washing the dishes. I realized I needed some new kind of work that would keep me busy both mentally and physically every hour of the day. So I took a job as a saleswoman in a large department store.

'That did it,' she said. 'I immediately found myself in a whirlwind of activity: customers swarming around me, asking for prices, sizes, colours. Never a second to think of anything except my immediate duty; and when night came, I could think of nothing except getting off my aching feet. As soon as I ate dinner, I fell into bed and instantly became unconscious. I had neither the time nor the energy to worry.'

She discovered for herself what John Cowper Powys meant when he said, in *The Art of Forgetting the Unpleasant*: 'A certain comfortable security, a certain profound inner peace, a kind of happy numbness, soothes the nerves of the human animal when absorbed in its allotted task.'

And what a blessing that it is so! Osa Johnson, one of the world's most famous woman explorers, told me how she found release from worry and grief. You may have read the story of her life. It is called *I Married Adventure*. If any woman ever married adventure, she certainly did. Martin Johnson married her when she was sixteen and lifted her feet off the sidewalks of Chanute, Kansas, and set them down on the wild jungle trails of Borneo. For a quarter of a century, this Kansas couple travelled all over the world, making motion pictures of the vanishing wildlife of Asia and Africa. Some years later, they were on a lecture tour, showing their famous films. They took a plane out of Denver, bound for the Coast. The plane plunged into a mountain. Martin Johnson was killed instantly. The doctors said Osa would never leave her bed again. But they didn't know Osa Johnson. Three months later, she was in a wheelchair, lecturing before large audiences. In fact, she addressed over a hundred audiences that season – all from a wheelchair. When I asked her why she did it, she replied: 'I did it so that I would have no time for sorrow and worry.'

Osa Johnson had discovered the same truth that Tennyson had sung about a century earlier: 'I must lose myself in action, lest I wither in despair.'

Admiral Byrd discovered this same truth when he lived all alone for five months in a shack that was literally buried in the great glacial ice cap that covers the South Pole – an ice cap that holds nature's oldest secrets – an icecap covering an unknown continent larger than the United States and Europe combined. Admiral Byrd spent five months there alone. No other living creature of any kind existed within a hundred miles. The cold was so intense that he could hear his breath freeze and crystallize as the wind blew it past his ears. In his book, *Alone*,* Admiral Byrd tells all about those five months he spent in bewildering and soul-shattering darkness. The days were as black as the nights. He had to keep busy to preserve his sanity.

'At night,' he says, 'before blowing out the lantern, I formed the habit of blocking out the morrow's work. It was a case of assigning myself an hour, say, to the Escape Tunnel, half-an-hour to levelling drift, an hour to straightening up the fuel drums, an hour to cutting bookshelves in the walls of the food tunnel, and two hours to renewing a broken bridge in the man-hauling sledge…

'It was wonderful,' he says, 'to be able to dole out time in this way. It brought me an extraordinary sense of command over myself…' And he adds, 'Without that or an equivalent, the days would have been without purpose; and without purpose they would have ended, as such days always end, in disintegration.'

---

*Richard E. Byrd, *Alone* (G.P. Putnam's Sons, 1938).

Note that last again: 'Without purpose, the days would have ended, as such days always end, in disintegration.'*

If you and I are worried, let's remember that we can use good old-fashioned work as a medicine. That was said by no less an authority than the late Dr Richard C. Cabot, formerly professor of clinical medicine at Harvard. In his book, *What Men Live By*, Dr Cabot says, 'As a physician, I have had the happiness of seeing work cure many persons who have suffered from trembling palsy of the soul which results from overmastering doubts, hesitations, vacillation and fear...Courage given us by our work is like the self-reliance which Emerson has made forever glorious.'

If you and I don't keep busy – if we sit around and brood – we will hatch out a whole flock of what Charles Darwin used to call the 'wibber gibbers.' And the 'wibber gibbers' are nothing but old-fashioned gremlins that will run us hollow and destroy our power of action and our power of will.

I knew a businessman in New York who fought the 'wibber gibbers' by getting so busy that he had no time to fret and stew. His name is Tremper Longman. He was a student in one of my classes; and his talk on conquering worry was so interesting, so impressive, that I asked him to have a late supper with me after class; and we sat in a restaurant until long past midnight, discussing his experiences. Here is the story he told me: 'Eighteen years ago, I was so worried I had insomnia. I was tense, irritated, and jittery. I felt I was headed for a nervous breakdown.

'I had reason to be worried. I was treasurer of the Crown Fruit and Extract Company. We had half a million dollars invested in strawberries packed in gallon tins. For twenty years, we had been selling these gallon tins of strawberries to manufacturers of ice cream. Suddenly our sales stopped because the big ice cream makers, such as National Dairy and Borden's, were rapidly increasing their production and were saving money and time by buying strawberries packed in barrels.

'Not only were we left with half-a-million dollars in berries we couldn't sell, but we were also under contract to buy a million dollars more of strawberries in the next twelve months! We had already borrowed $350,000 from the banks. We couldn't possibly pay off or renew these loans. No wonder I was worried!

'I rushed out to Watsonville, California, where our factory was located, and tried to persuade our president that conditions had changed, that we were facing ruin. He refused to believe it. He blamed our New York office for all the trouble – poor salesmanship.

'After days of pleading, I finally persuaded him to stop packing more strawberries and to sell our new supply on the fresh berry market in San Francisco. That almost solved our problems. I should have been able to stop worrying then; but I couldn't. Worry is a habit; and I had that habit.

'When I returned to New York, I began worrying about everything; the cherries we were buying in Italy, the pineapples we were buying in Hawaii, and so on. I was tense, jittery, couldn't sleep; and, as I have already said, I was heading for a nervous breakdown.

'In despair, I adopted a way of life that cured my insomnia and stopped my worries. I got busy. I got so busy with problems demanding all my faculties that I had no time to worry. I had been working seven hours a day. I now began working fifteen and sixteen hours a day. I got down to the office every morning at 8 o'clock and stayed there every night until almost midnight. I took on new duties, new responsibilities. When I got home at midnight, I was so exhausted when I fell in bed that I became unconscious in a few seconds.

'I kept up this programme for about three months. I had broken the habit of worry by that time, so I returned to a normal working day of seven or eight hours. This event occurred eighteen years ago. I have never been troubled with insomnia or worry since then.'

George Bernard Shaw was right. He summed it all up when he said: 'The secret of being miserable is to have the leisure to bother about whether you are happy or not.' So, don't bother to think about it! Spit on your hands and get busy. Your blood will start circulating; your mind will start ticking – and pretty soon this whole positive upsurge of life in your body will drive worry from your mind. Get busy. Keep busy. It's the cheapest kind of medicine there is on this earth – and one of the best.

> Keep busy. The worried person must lose himself in action, lest he wither in despair.

5

A Law That Will Outlaw Many of Your Worries

As a child, I grew up on a Missouri farm; and one day, while helping my mother pit cherries, I began to cry. My mother said, 'Dale, what in the world are you crying about?' I blubbered, 'I'm afraid I am going to be buried alive!'

I was full of worries in those days. When thunderstorms came, I worried for fear I would be killed by lightning. When hard times came, I worried for fear we wouldn't have enough to eat. I worried for fear I would go to hell when I died. I was terrified for fear an older boy, Sam White, would cut off my big ears – as he threatened to do. I worried for fear girls would laugh at me if I tipped my hat to them. I worried for fear no girl would ever be willing to marry me. I worried about what I would say to my wife immediately after we were married. I imagined that we would be married in some country church, and then get in a surrey with a fringe on the top and ride back to the farm...but how would I be able to keep the conversation going on that ride back to the farm? How? How? I pondered over that earth-shaking problem for many an hour as I walked behind the plough.

As the years went by, I gradually discovered that 99 per cent of the things I worried about never happened.

For example, as I have already said, I was once terrified of lightning; but I now know that the chances of my being killed by lightning in any one year are, according to the National Safety Council, only 1 in 350,000.

My fear of being buried alive was even more absurd: I don't imagine that – even back in the days before embalming was the rule – that one person in ten million was buried alive; yet, I once cried for fear of it.

One person out of every eight dies of cancer. If I had wanted something to worry about, I should have worried about cancer – instead of being killed by lightning or being buried alive.

To be sure, I have been talking about the worries of youth and adolescence. But many of our adult worries are almost as absurd. You and I could probably eliminate nine-tenths of our worries right now if we would cease our fretting long enough to discover whether, by the law of averages, there was any real justification for our worries.

The most famous insurance company on earth – Lloyd's of London – has made countless millions of dollars out of the tendency of everybody to worry about things that rarely happen. Lloyd's of London bets people that the disasters they are worrying about will never occur. However, they don't call it betting. They call it insurance. But it is really betting based on the law of averages. This great insurance firm has been going strong for over two hundred years; and unless human nature changes, it will still be going strong fifty centuries from now by insuring shoes and ships and sealing wax against disasters that, by the law of averages, don't happen nearly so often as people imagine.

If we examine the law of averages, we will often be astounded at the facts we uncover. For example, if I knew that during the next five years I would have to fight in a battle as bloody as the Battle of Gettysburg, I would be terrified. I would take out all the life insurance I could get. I would draw up my will and set all my earthly affairs in order. I would say, 'I'll probably never live through that battle, so I had better make the most of the few years I have left.' Yet, the facts are that, according to the law of averages, it is just as dangerous, just as fatal, to try to live from age fifty to age fifty-five in peacetime as it was to fight in the Battle of Gettysburg. What I am trying to say is this: in times of peace, just as many people die per thousand between the ages of fifty and fifty-five as were killed per thousand among the 1,63,000 soldiers who fought at Gettysburg.

I wrote several chapters of this book at James Simpson's Num-Ti-Gah Lodge, on the shore of Bow Lake in the Canadian Rockies. While stopping there one summer, I met Mr and Mrs Herbert H. Salinger, of San Francisco. Mrs Salinger, a poised, serene woman, gave me the impression that she had never worried. One evening in front of the roaring fireplace, I asked her if she had ever been troubled by worry. 'Troubled by it?' she said. 'My life was almost ruined by it. Before I learned to conquer worry, I lived through eleven years of self-made hell. I was irritable and hot-tempered. I lived under terrific tension. I would take the bus every week from my home in San Mateo to shop in San Francisco. But even while shopping, I worried myself into a dither – maybe I had left the electric iron connected on the ironing board; maybe the house had caught fire; maybe the maid had run off and left the children; maybe they had been out on their bicycles and been killed by a car. In the midst of my shopping, I would often worry myself into a cold perspiration and rush out and take the bus home to see if everything was all right. No wonder my first marriage ended in disaster.

'My second husband is a lawyer – a quiet, analytical man who never worries about anything. When I became tense and anxious, he would say to me, "Relax. Let's think this out. What are you really worrying about? Let's examine the law of averages and see whether or not it is likely to happen."

'For example, I remember the time we were driving from Albuquerque, New Mexico, to the Carlsbad Caverns – driving on a dirt road – when we were caught in a terrible rainstorm.

'The car was slithering and sliding. We couldn't control it. I was positive we would slide off into one of the ditches that flanked the road; but my husband kept repeating to me: "I am driving very slowly. Nothing serious is likely to happen. Even if the car does slide into the ditch, by the law of averages, we won't be hurt." His calmness and confidence quietened me.

'One summer we were on a camping trip in the Touquin Valley of the Canadian Rockies. One night, we were camping 7,000 feet above sea level, when a storm threatened to tear our tents to shreds. The tents were tied with guy-ropes to a wooden platform. The outer tent shook and trembled and screamed and shrieked in the wind. I expected every minute to see our tent torn loose and hurled through the sky. I was terrified! But my husband kept saying: "Look, my dear, we are travelling with Brewsters' guides. Brewsters know what they are doing. They have been pitching tents in these mountains for sixty years. This tent has been here for many seasons. It hasn't blown down yet and, by the law of averages, it won't blow away tonight; and even if it does, we can take shelter in another tent. So relax..." I did; and I slept soundly the balance of the night.

'A few years ago an infantile-paralysis epidemic swept over our part of California. In the old days, I would have been hysterical. But my husband persuaded me to act calmly. We took all the precautions we could: we kept our children away from crowds, away from school and the movies. By consulting the Board of Health, we found out that even during the worst infantile-paralysis epidemic that California had ever known up to that time, only 1,835 children had been stricken in the entire state of California. And that the usual number was around two hundred or three hundred. Tragic as those figures are, we nevertheless felt that, according to the law of averages, the chances of any one child being stricken were remote.

'"By the law of averages, it won't happen". That phrase has destroyed 90 per cent of my worries; and it has made the past twenty years of my life beautiful and peaceful beyond my highest expectations.'

> It has been said that nearly all of our worries and unhappiness come from our imagination and not from reality.

As I look back across the decades, I can see that that is where most of my worries came from also. Jim Grant told me that that had been his experience, too. He owned the James A. Grant Distributing Company, of New York City. He ordered from ten to fifteen carloads of Florida oranges and grapefruit at a time. He told me that he used to torture himself with such thoughts as: 'What if there's a train wreck? What if my fruit is strewn all over the countryside? What if a bridge collapses as my cars are going across it?' Of course, the fruit was insured; but he feared that if he didn't deliver his fruit on time, he might risk the loss of his market. He worried so much that he feared he had stomach ulcers and went to a doctor. The doctor told him there was nothing wrong with him except jumpy nerves. 'I saw the light then,' he said, 'and began to ask myself questions. I said to myself: "Look here, Jim Grant, how many fruit cars have you handled over the years?" The answer was: "About 25,000." Then I asked myself: "How many of those cars were ever wrecked?" The answer was: "Oh – maybe five." Then I said to myself: "Only five – out of 25,000? Do you know what that means? A ratio of 5,000 : 1! In other words, by the law of averages, based on experience, the chances are 5,000 to 1 against one of your cars ever being wrecked. So what are you worried about?"

'Then I said to myself: "Well, a bridge may collapse!" Then I asked myself: "How many cars have you actually lost from a bridge collapsing?" The answer was – "None." Then I said to myself: "Aren't you a fool to be worrying yourself into stomach ulcers over a bridge which has never yet collapsed, and over a railroad wreck when the chances are 5,000 to 1 against it!"

'When I looked at it that way,' Jim Grant told me, 'I felt pretty silly. I decided then and there to let the law of averages do the worrying for me – and I have not been troubled with my "stomach ulcer" since!'

When Al Smith was Governor of New York, I heard him answer the attacks of his political enemies by saying over and over: 'Let's examine the record…let's examine the record.' Then he proceeded to give the facts. The next time you and I are worrying about what may happen, let's take a tip from wise old Al Smith – let's examine the record and see what basis there is, if any, for our gnawing anxieties. That is precisely what Frederick J. Mahlstedt did when he feared he was lying in his grave. Here is his story as he told it to one of our classes in New York:

'Early in June, 1944, I was lying in a slit trench near Omaha Beach. I was with the 999th Signal Service Company, and we had just "dug in" in Normandy. As I looked around at that slit trench – just a rectangular hole in the ground – I said to myself, "This looks just like a grave." When I lay down and tried to sleep in it, it felt like a grave. I couldn't help saying to myself, "Maybe this is my grave". When the German bombers began coming over at 11 p.m., and the bombs started falling, I was scared stiff. For the first two or three nights I couldn't sleep at all. By the fourth or fifth night, I was almost a nervous wreck. I knew that if I didn't do something, I would go stark crazy. So I reminded myself that five nights had passed, and I was still alive; and so was every man in our outfit. Only two had even been injured, and they had been hurt, not by German bombs, but by falling flak, from our own anti-aircraft guns. I decided to stop worrying by doing something constructive. So, I built a thick wooden roof over my slit trench, to protect myself from flak. I thought of the vast area over which my unit was spread. I told myself that the only way I could be killed in that deep, narrow slit trench was by a direct hit; and I figured out that the chance of a direct hit on me was not 1 in 10,000. After a couple of nights of looking at it in this way, I calmed down and slept even through the bomb raids!'

The United States Navy used the statistics of the law of averages to buck up the morale of their men. One ex-sailor told me that when he and his shipmates were assigned to high-octane tankers, they were worried stiff. They all believed that if a tanker loaded with high-octane gasoline was hit by a torpedo, it exploded and blew everybody to kingdom come.

But the US Navy knew otherwise; so the Navy issued exact figures, showing that out of 100 tankers hit by torpedoes, 60 stayed afloat; and of the 40 that did sink, only five sank in less than ten minutes. That meant time to get off the ship – it also meant casualties were exceedingly small. Did this help morale? 'This knowledge of the law of averages wiped out my jitters,' said Clyde W. Maas, of St. Paul, Minnesota – the man who told this story. 'The whole crew felt better. We knew we had a chance; and that, by the law of averages, we probably wouldn't be killed.'

> Let's examine the record. Let's ask ourselves: 'What are the chances, according to the law of averages, that this event I am worrying about will ever occur?'

6

Cooperate with the Inevitable

When I was a little boy, I was playing with some of my friends in the attic of an old, abandoned log house in north-west Missouri. As I climbed down out of the attic, I rested my feet on a window sill for a moment – and then jumped. I had a ring on my left forefinger; and as I jumped, the ring caught on a nail head and tore off my finger.

I screamed. I was terrified. I was positive I was going to die. But after the hand healed, I never worried about it for one split second. What would have been the use? I accepted the inevitable.

Now, I often go for a month at a time without even thinking about the fact that I have only three fingers and a thumb on my left hand.

A few years ago, I met a man who was running a freight elevator in one of the downtown office buildings in New York. I noticed that his left hand had been cut off at the wrist. I asked him if the loss of that hand bothered him. He said, 'Oh, no, I hardly ever think about it. I am not married; and the only time I ever think about it is when I try to thread a needle.'

It is astonishing how quickly we can accept almost any situation – if we have to – and adjust ourselves to it and forget about it.

I often think of an inscription on the ruins of a fifteenth-century cathedral in Amsterdam, Holland. This inscription says in Flemish: 'It is so. It cannot be otherwise.'

As you and I march across the decades of time, we are going to meet a lot of unpleasant situations that are so. They cannot be otherwise. We have our choice. We can either accept them as inevitable and adjust ourselves to them, or we can ruin our lives with rebellion and maybe end up with a nervous breakdown.

Here is a bit of sage advice from one of my favourite philosophers, William James: 'Be willing to have it so,' he said. 'Acceptance of what has happened is the first step to overcoming the consequences of any misfortune.'

Elizabeth Connley, of Portland, Oregon, had to find that out the hard way. Here is a letter that she wrote me: 'On the very day that America was celebrating the victory of our armed forces in North Africa,' the letter says, 'I received a telegram from the War Department that my nephew – the person I loved most – was missing in action. A short time later, another telegram arrived saying he was dead.

'I was prostrate with grief. Up to that time, I had felt that life had been very good to me. I had a job I loved. I had helped to raise this nephew. He represented to me all that was fine and good in young manhood. I had felt that all the bread I had cast upon the waters was coming back to me as cake! Then came this telegram. My whole world collapsed. I felt there was nothing left to live for. I neglected my work; neglected my friends. I let everything go. I was bitter and resentful. Why did my loving nephew have to be taken? Why did this good boy – with his life all before him – why did he have to be killed? I couldn't accept it. My grief was so overwhelming that I decided to give up my work, and go away and hide myself in my tears and bitterness.

'I was clearing out my desk, getting ready to quit, when I came across a letter that I had forgotten – a letter from this nephew who had been killed, a letter he had written to me when my mother had died a few years ago. "Of course, we will all miss her," the letter said, "and especially you. But I know you'll carry on. Your own personal philosophy will make you do that. I shall never forget the beautiful truths you taught me. Wherever I am, or how far apart we may be, I shall always remember that you taught me to smile, and to take whatever comes, like a man."

'I read and reread that letter. It seemed as if he were there beside me, speaking to me. He seemed to be saying to me: "Why don't you do what you taught me to do? Carry on, no matter what happens. Hide your private sorrows under a smile and carry on."

'So, I went back to my work. I stopped being bitter and rebellious. I kept saying to myself: "It is done. I can't change it. But I can and will carry on as he wished me to do." I threw all my mind and strength into my work. I wrote letters to soldiers – to other people's boys. I joined an adult-education class at night – seeking out new interests and making new friends. I can hardly believe the change that has come over me. I have ceased mourning over the past that is forever gone. I am living each day now with joy – just as my nephew would have wanted me to do. I have made peace with life. I have accepted my fate. I am now living a fuller and more complete life than I have ever known.'

Elizabeth Connley learned what all of us will have to learn sooner or later:

> Namely, that we must accept and cooperate with the inevitable. 'It is so. It cannot be otherwise.'

That is not an easy lesson to learn. Even kings on their thrones have to keep reminding themselves of it. The late George V had these framed words hanging on the wall of his library in Buckingham Palace: 'Teach me neither to cry for the moon nor over spilt milk.' The same thought is expressed by Schopenhauer in this way: 'A good supply of resignation is of the first importance in providing for the journey of life.'

Obviously, circumstances alone do not make us happy or

unhappy. It is the way we react to circumstances that determines our feelings. Jesus said that the kingdom of heaven is within you. That is where the kingdom of hell is, too.

We can all endure disaster and tragedy and triumph over them – if we have to. We may not think we can, but we have surprisingly strong inner resources that will see us through if we will only make use of them. We are stronger than we think.

The late Booth Tarkington always said: 'I could take anything that life could force upon me except one thing – blindness. I could never endure that.'

Then one day, when he was along in his sixties, Tarkington glanced down at the carpet on the floor. The colours were blurred. He couldn't see the pattern. He went to a specialist. He learned the tragic truth: he was losing his sight. One eye was nearly blind; the other would follow. That which he feared most had come upon him.

And how did Tarkington react to this 'worst of all disasters'? Did he feel, 'This is it! This is the end of my life?' No, to his amazement, he felt quite gay. He even called upon his humour. Floating 'specks' annoyed him; they would swim across his eyes and cut off his vision. Yet, when the largest of these specks would swim across his sight, he would say, 'Hello! There's Grandfather again! Wonder where he's going on this fine morning!'

How could fate ever conquer a spirit like that? The answer is it couldn't. When total darkness closed in, Tarkington said, 'I found I could take the loss of my eyesight, just as a man can take anything else. If I lost all five of my senses, I know I could live on inside my mind. For it is in the mind we see, and in the mind we live, whether we know it or not.'

In the hope of restoring his eyesight, Tarkington had to go through more than twelve operations within one year. With local anaesthetic! Did he rail against this? He knew it had to be done. He knew he couldn't escape it, so the only way to lessen his suffering was to take it with grace. He refused a private room at the hospital and went into a ward, where he could be with other people who had troubles, too. He tried to cheer them up. And when he had to submit to repeated operations – fully conscious of what was being done to his eyes – he tried to remember how fortunate he was. 'How wonderful!' he said. 'How wonderful, that science now has the skill to operate on anything so delicate as the human eye!'

The average man would have been a nervous wreck if he had had to endure more than twelve operations and blindness. Yet, Tarkington said, 'I would not exchange this experience for a happier one.' It taught him acceptance. It taught him that nothing life could bring him was beyond his strength to endure. It taught him, as John Milton discovered, that, 'It is not miserable to be blind, it is only miserable not to be able to endure blindness.'

Margaret Fuller, the famous New England feminist, once offered as her credo: 'I accept the universe!'

When grouchy old Thomas Carlyle heard that in England, he snorted, 'By gad, she'd better!' Yes, and by gad, you and I had better accept the inevitable, too!

If we rail and kick against it and grow bitter, we won't change the inevitable; but we will change ourselves. I know. I have tried it.

I once refused to accept an inevitable situation with which I was confronted. I played the fool and railed against it, and rebelled. I turned my nights into hells of insomnia. I brought upon myself everything I didn't want. Finally, after a year of self-torture, I had to accept what I knew from the outset I couldn't possibly alter.

I should have cried out years ago with old Walt Whitman:

Oh, to confront night, storms, hunger,
Ridicule, accident, rebuffs as the trees and animals do.

I spent twelve years working with cattle; yet I never saw a Jersey cow running a temperature because the pasture was burning up from a lack of rain or because of sleet and cold or because her boyfriend was paying too much attention to another heifer. The animals confront night, storms, and hunger calmly; so they never have nervous breakdowns or stomach ulcers; and they never go insane.

Am I advocating that we simply bow down to all the adversities that come our way? Not by a long shot! That is mere fatalism. As long as there is a chance that we can save a situation, let's fight! But when common sense tells us that we are up against something that is so – and cannot be otherwise – then, in the name of our sanity, let's not 'look before and after and pine for what is not'.

The late Dean Hawkes of Columbia University told me that he had taken a Mother Goose rhyme as one of his mottos:

For every ailment under the sun,
There is a remedy, or there is none;
If there be one, try to find it;
If there be none, never mind it.

While writing this book, I interviewed a number of the leading business executives of America; and I was impressed by the fact that they cooperated with the inevitable and led lives singularly free from worry. If they hadn't done that, they would have cracked under the strain. Here are a few examples of what I mean:

J.C. Penney, founder of the nation-wide chain of Penney stores, said to me: 'I wouldn't worry if I lost every dollar I have because I don't see what is to be gained by worrying. I do the best job I possibly can; and leave the results in the laps of the gods.'

Henry Ford told me much the same thing. 'When I can't handle events,' he said, 'I let them handle themselves.'

When I asked K.T. Keller, then president of the Chrysler Corporation, how he kept from worrying, he replied: 'When I am up against a tough situation, if I can do anything about it, I do it. If I can't, I just forget it. I never worry about the future, because I know no man living can possibly figure out what is going to happen in the future. There are so many forces that will affect that future! Nobody can tell what prompts those forces – or understand them. So why worry about them?' K.T. Keller would be embarrassed if you told him he is a philosopher. He is just a good businessman, yet he has stumbled on the same philosophy that Epictetus taught in Rome nineteen centuries ago. 'There is only one way to happiness,' Epictetus taught the Romans, 'and that is to cease worrying about things which are beyond the power of our will.'

Sarah Bernhardt, the 'divine Sarah', was an illustrious example of a woman who knew how to cooperate with the inevitable. For half a century, she had been the reigning queen of the theatre on four continents – the best-loved actress on earth. Then, when she was seventy-one and broke – she had lost all her money – her physician, Professor Pozzi of Paris, told her he would have to amputate her leg. While crossing the Atlantic, she had fallen on deck during a storm, and injured her leg severely. Phlebitis developed. Her leg shrank. The pain became so intense that the doctor felt her leg had to be amputated. He was almost afraid to tell the stormy, tempestuous 'divine Sarah' what had to be done. He fully expected that the terrible news would set off an explosion of hysteria. But he was wrong. Sarah looked at him a moment, and then said quietly, 'If it has to be, it has to be.' It was fate.

As she was being wheeled away to the operating room her son stood weeping. She waved to him with a gay gesture and said cheerfully: 'Don't go away. I'll be right back.'

On the way to the operating room she recited a scene from one of her plays. Someone asked her if she were doing this to cheer herself up. She said: 'No, to cheer up the doctors and nurses. It will be a strain on them.'

After recovering from the operation, Sarah Bernhardt went on touring the world and enchanting audiences for another seven years.

'When we stop fighting the inevitable,' said Elsie MacCormick in a *Reader's Digest* article, 'we release energy which enables us to create a richer life.'

No one living has enough emotion and vigour to fight the

inevitable and, at the same time, enough left over to create a new life. Choose one or the other.

> You can either bend with the inevitable sleet storms of life – or you can resist them and break!

I saw that happen on a farm I own in Missouri. I planted a score of trees on that farm. At first, they grew with astonishing rapidity. Then a sleetstorm encrusted each twig and branch with a heavy coating of ice. Instead of bowing gracefully to their burden, these trees proudly resisted and broke and split under the load – and had to be destroyed. They hadn't learned the wisdom of the forests of the north. I have travelled hundreds of miles through the evergreen forests of Canada. Yet, I have never seen a spruce or a pine broken by sleet or ice. These evergreen forests know how to bend, how to bow down their branches, how to cooperate with the inevitable.

The masters of ju-jitsu teach their pupils, 'Bend like the willow; don't resist like the oak.'

Why do you think your automobile tyres stand up on the road and take so much punishment? At first, the tyre manufacturers tried to make a tyre that would resist the shocks of the road. It was soon cut to ribbons. Then they made a tyre that would absorb the shocks of the road. That tyre could 'take it'. You and I will last longer, and enjoy smoother riding, if we learn to absorb the shocks and jolts along the rocky road of life.

What will happen to you and me if we resist the shocks of life instead of absorbing them? What will happen if we refuse to bend like the willow and insist on resisting like the oak? The answer is easy. We will set up a series of inner conflicts. We will be worried, tense, strained, and neurotic.

If we go still further and reject the harsh world of reality and retreat into a dream world of our own making, we will then be insane.

During the war, millions of frightened soldiers had either to accept the inevitable or break under the strain. To illustrate, let's take the case of William H. Casselius, of Glendale, New York. Here is a prize-winning talk he gave before one of my classes in New York:

'Shortly after I joined the Coast Guard, I was assigned to one of the hottest spots on this side of the Atlantic. I was made a supervisor of explosives. Imagine it. Me! A cracker salesman becoming a supervisor of explosives! The very thought of finding yourself standing on top of thousands of tonnes of TNT is enough to chill the marrow in a cracker salesman's bones. I was given only two days of instruction; and what I learned filled me with even more terror. I'll never forget my first assignment. On a dark, cold, foggy day, I was given my orders on the open pier of Caven Point, Bayonne, New Jersey.

'I was assigned to Hold No. 5 on my ship. I had to work down in that hold with five longshoremen. They had strong backs, but they knew nothing whatever about explosives. And they were loading blockbusters, each one of which contained a tonne of TNT – enough explosive to blow that old ship to kingdom come. These blockbusters were being lowered by two cable slings. I kept saying to myself: "Suppose one of those cables slipped – or broke! Oh, boy!" Was I scared! I trembled. My mouth was dry. My knees sagged. My heart pounded. But I couldn't run away. That would be desertion. I would be disgraced – my parents would be disgraced – and I might be shot for desertion. I couldn't run. I had to stay. I kept looking at the careless way those longshoremen were handling those blockbusters. The ship might blow up any minute. After an hour or more of this spine-chilling terror, I began to use a little common sense. I gave myself a good talking to. I said, "Look here! So you are blown up. So what! You will never know the difference! It will be an easy way to die. Much better than dying by cancer. Don't be a fool. You can't expect to live forever! You've got to do this job – or be shot. So you might as well like it."

'I talked to myself like that for hours; and I began to feel at ease. Finally, I overcame my worry and fears by forcing myself to accept an inevitable situation.

'I'll never forget that lesson. Every time I am tempted now to worry about something I can't possibly change, I shrug my shoulders and say, "Forget it." I find that it works – even for a cracker salesman.'

Outside of the crucifixion of Jesus, the most famous death scene in all history was the death of Socrates. Ten thousand centuries from now, men will still be reading and cherishing Plato's immortal description of it – one of the most moving and beautiful passages in all literature. Certain men of Athens – jealous and envious of old bare-footed Socrates – trumped up charges against him and had him tried and condemned to death. When the friendly jailer gave Socrates the poison cup to drink, the jailer said: 'Try to bear lightly what needs must be.' Socrates did. He faced death with a calmness and resignation that touched the hem of divinity.

'Try to bear lightly what needs must be.' Those words were spoken 399 years before Christ was born; but this worrying old world needs those words today more than ever before.

I have been reading practically every book and magazine article I could find that dealt even remotely with banishing worry. Would you like to know what is the best single bit of advice about worry that I have ever discovered in all that reading? Well, here it is – summed up in twenty-seven words – words that you and I ought to paste on our bathroom mirrors, so that each time we wash our faces we could also wash away all worry from our minds. This priceless prayer was written by Dr Reinhold Niebuhr:

God grant me the serenity
To accept the things I cannot change,
The courage to change the things I can;
And the wisdom to know the difference.

Cooperate with the inevitable.

HOW TO BREAK THE WORRY HABIT BEFORE IT BREAKS YOU

RULE 1

Crowd worry out of your mind by keeping busy. Plenty of action is one of the best ther¬apies ever devised for curing 'wibber gibbers.'

RULE 2

Don't fuss about trifles. Don't permit little things – the mere termites of life – to ruin your happiness.

RULE 3

Use the law of averages to outlaw your worries. Ask yourself: 'What are the odds against this thing's happening at all?'

RULE 4

Co-operate with the inevitable. If you know a circumstance is beyond your power to change or revise, say to yourself: 'It is so; it cannot be otherwise.'

RULE 5

Put a 'stop-loss' order on your worries. Decide just how much anxiety a thing may be worth – and refuse to give it any more.

RULE 6

Let the past bury its dead. Don't saw sawdust.

7

Eight Words That Can Transform Your Life

A few years ago, I was asked to answer this question on a radio programme: 'What is the biggest lesson you have ever learned?'

That was easy: by far the most vital lesson I have ever learned is the importance of what we think. If I knew what you think, I would know what you are. Our thoughts make us what we are. Our mental attitude is the X-factor that determines our fate. Emerson said: 'A man is what he thinks about all day long.' How could he possibly be anything else?

I now know with a conviction beyond all doubt that the biggest problem you and I have to deal with – in fact, almost the only problem we have to deal with – is choosing the right thoughts. If we can do that, we will be on the highroad to solving all our problems. The great philosopher who ruled the Roman Empire, Marcus Aurelius, summed it up in eight words – eight words that can determine your destiny: 'Our life is what our thoughts make it.'

Yes, if we think happy thoughts, we will be happy. If we think miserable thoughts, we will be miserable. If we think fear thoughts, we will be fearful. If we think sickly thoughts, we will probably be ill. If we think failure, we will certainly fail. If we wallow in self-pity, everyone will want to shun us and avoid us. 'You are not,' said

Norman Vincent Peale, 'you are not what you think you are; but what you think, you are.'

Am I advocating an habitual Pollyanna attitude toward all our problems? No, unfortunately, life isn't so simple as all that. But I am advocating that we assume a positive attitude instead of a negative attitude. In other words, we need to be concerned about our problems, but not worried. What is the difference between concern and worry? Let me illustrate. Every time I cross the traffic-jammed streets of New York, I am concerned about what I am doing – but not worried. Concern means realizing what the problems are and calmly taking steps to meet them. Worrying means going around in maddening, futile circles.

A man can be concerned about his serious problems and still walk with his chin up and a carnation in his buttonhole. I have seen Lowell Thomas do just that. I once had the privilege of being associated with Lowell Thomas in presenting his famous films on the Allenby-Lawrence campaigns in the First World War. He and his assistants had photographed the war on half a dozen fronts; and, best of all, had brought back a pictorial record of T.E. Lawrence and his colourful Arabian army, and a film record of Allenby's conquest of the Holy Land. His illustrated talks entitled, 'With Allenby in Palestine and Lawrence in Arabia' were a sensation in London – and around the world. The London opera season was postponed for six weeks so that he could continue telling his tale of high adventure and showing his pictures at Covent Garden Royal Opera House. After his sensational success in London came a triumphant tour of many countries. Then he spent two years preparing a film record of life in India and Afghanistan. After a lot of incredibly bad luck, the impossible happened: he found himself broke in London. I was with him at the time. I remember we had to eat cheap meals at the Lyons' Corner House restaurants. We couldn't have eaten even there if Mr Thomas had not borrowed money from a Scotsman – James McBey, the renowned artist. Here is the point of the story: even when Lowell

Thomas was facing huge debts and severe disappointments, he was concerned, but not worried. He knew that if he let his reverses get him down, he would be worthless to everyone, including his creditors. So, each morning before he started out, he bought a flower, put it in his buttonhole, and went swinging down Oxford Street with his head high and his step spirited. He thought positive, courageous thoughts and refused to let defeat defeat him. To him, being licked was all a part of the game – the useful training you had to expect if you wanted to get to the top.

Our mental attitude has an almost unbelievable effect even on our physical powers. The famous British psychiatrist, J.A. Hadfield, gives a striking illustration of that fact in his splendid 54-page booklet: *The Psychology of Power*. 'I asked three men,' he writes, 'to submit themselves to test the effect of mental suggestion on their strength, which was measured by gripping a dynamometer.' He told them to grip the dynamometer with all their might. He had them do this under three different sets of conditions.

When he tested them under normal waking conditions, their average grip was 101 pounds.

When he tested them after he had hypnotized them and told them that they were very weak, they could grip only 29 pounds – less than a third of their normal strength. (One of these men was a prize fighter; and when he was told under hypnosis that he was weak, he remarked that his arm felt 'tiny, just like a baby's.')

When Captain Hadfield then tested these men a third time, telling them under hypnosis that they were very strong, they were able to grip an average of 142 pounds. When their minds were filled with positive thoughts of strength, they increased their actual physical powers almost 50 per cent.

Such is the incredible power of our mental attitude.

To illustrate the magic power of thought, let me tell you one of the most astounding stories in the annals of America. I could write a book about it; but let's be brief. On a frosty October night, shortly after the close of the Civil War, a homeless, destitute woman, who was little more than a wanderer on the face of the earth, knocked at the door of 'Mother' Webster, the wife of a retired sea captain, living in Amesbury, Massachusetts.

Opening the door, 'Mother' Webster saw a frail little creature, 'scarcely more than a hundred pounds of frightened skin and bones'. The stranger, a Mrs Glover, explained she was seeking a home where she could think and work out a great problem that absorbed her day and night.

'Why not stay here?' Mrs Webster replied. 'I'm all alone in this big house.'

Mrs Glover might have remained indefinitely with 'Mother' Webster if the latter's son-in-law, Bill Ellis, hadn't come up from New York for a vacation. When he discovered Mrs Glover's presence, he shouted: 'I'll have no vagabonds in this house!' and he shoved this homeless woman out of the door. A driving rain was falling. She stood shivering in the rain for a few minutes, and then started down the road, looking for shelter.

Here is the astonishing part of the story. That 'vagabond' whom Bill Ellis put out of the house was destined to have as much influence on the thinking of the world as any other woman who ever walked this earth. She is now known to millions of devoted followers as Mary Baker Eddy – the founder of Christian Science.

Yet, until this time, she had known little in life except sickness, sorrow, and tragedy. Her first husband had died shortly after their marriage. Her second husband had deserted her and eloped with a married woman. He later died in a poorhouse. She had only one child, a son; and she was forced, because of poverty, illness, and jealousy, to give him up when he was four years old. She lost all track of him and never saw him again for thirty-one years.

Because of her own ill health, Mrs Eddy had been interested for years in what she called 'the science of mind healing'. But the dramatic turning point in her life occurred in Lynn, Massachusetts.

Walking downtown one cold day, she slipped and fell on the icy pavement – and was knocked unconscious. Her spine was so injured that she was convulsed with spasms. Even the doctor expected her to die. If by some miracle she lived, he declared that she would never walk again.

Lying on what was supposed to be her deathbed, Mary Baker Eddy opened her Bible, and was led, she declared, by divine guidance to read these words from Saint Matthew: 'And, behold, they brought to him a man sick of the palsy, lying on a bed: and Jesus…said unto the sick of the palsy; Son, be of good cheer; thy sins be forgiven thee…Arise, take up thy bed, and go unto thine house. And he arose, and departed to his house.'

These words of Jesus, she declared, produced within her such a strength, such a faith, such a surge of healing power, that she 'immediately got out of bed and walked'.

'That experience,' Mrs Eddy declared, 'was the falling apple that led me to the discovery of how to be well myself, and how to make others so. I gained the scientific certainty that all causation was mind, and every effect a mental phenomenon.'

Such was the way in which Mary Baker Eddy became the founder and high priestess of a new religion – Christian Science – the only great religious faith ever established by a woman; a religion that has encircled the globe.

You are probably saying to yourself by now: 'This man Carnegie is proselytizing for Christian Science.' No. You are wrong. I am not a Christian Scientist. But the longer I live, the more deeply I am convinced of the tremendous power of thought. As a result of many years spent in teaching adults, I know men and women can banish worry, fear, and various kinds of illnesses, and can transform their lives by changing their thoughts. I know! I know!! I know!!! I have seen such incredible transformations performed hundreds of times. I have seen them so often that I no longer wonder at them.

For example, one of these incredible transformations which

illustrate the power of thought happened to one of my students. He had a nervous breakdown. What brought it on? Worry. This student told me, 'I worried about everything: I worried because I was too thin; because I thought I was losing my hair; because I feared I would never make enough money to get married; because I felt I would never make a good father; because I feared I was losing the girl I wanted to marry; because I felt I was not living a good life. I worried about the impression I was making on other people. I worried because I thought I had stomach ulcers. I could no longer work; I gave up my job. I built up tension inside me until I was like a boiler without a safety valve. The pressure got so unbearable that something had to give – and it did. If you have ever had a nervous breakdown, pray to God that you never do, for no pain of the body can exceed the excruciating pain of an agonized mind.

'My breakdown was so severe that I couldn't talk even to my own family. I had no control over my thoughts. I was filled with fear. I would jump at the slightest noise. I avoided everybody. I would break out crying for no apparent reason at all.

'Every day was one of agony. I felt that I was deserted by everybody – even God. I was tempted to jump into the river and end it all.

'I decided instead to take a trip to Florida, hoping that a change of scene would help me. As I stepped on the train, my father handed me a letter and told me not to open it until I reached Florida. I landed in Florida during the height of the tourist season. Since I couldn't get in a hotel, I rented a sleeping room in a garage. I tried to get a job on a tramp freighter out of Miami, but had no luck. So, I spent my time at the beach. I was more wretched in Florida than I had been at home; so I opened the envelope to see what my father had written. His note said, "Son, you are 1,500 miles from home, and you don't feel any different, do you? I knew you wouldn't, because you took with you the one thing that is the cause of all your trouble, that is, yourself. There is nothing wrong with either your body or your mind. It is not the situations you have met that have thrown you; it is what you think of these situations. 'As a man thinketh in his heart, so is he.' When you realize that, son, come home, for you will be cured."

'Dad's letter made me angry. I was looking for sympathy, not instruction. I was so mad that I decided then and there that I would never go home. That night as I was walking down one of the side streets of Miami, I came to a church where services were going on. Having no place to go, I drifted in and listened to a sermon on the text: "He who conquers his spirit is mightier than he who taketh a city." Sitting in the sanctity of the house of God and hearing the same thoughts that my Dad had written in his letter – all this swept the accumulated litter out of my brain. I was able to think clearly and sensibly for the first time in my life. I realized what a fool I had been. I was shocked to see myself in my true light: here I was, wanting to change the whole world and everyone in it – when the only thing that needed changing was the focus of the lens of the camera which was my mind.

'The next morning I packed and started home. A week later I was back on the job. Four months later I married the girl I had been afraid of losing. We now have a happy family of five children. God has been good to me both materially and mentally. At the time of the breakdown I was a night foreman of a small department handling eighteen people. I am now superintendent of carton manufacture, in charge of over four hundred and fifty people. Life is much fuller and friendlier. I believe I appreciate the true values of life now. When moments of uneasiness try to creep in (as they will in everyone's life) I tell myself to get that camera back in focus, and everything is okay.

'I can honestly say that I am glad I had the breakdown, because I found out the hard way what power our thoughts can have over our mind and our body. Now I can make my thoughts work for me instead of against me. I can see now that Dad was right when he said it wasn't outward situations that had caused all my suffering, but what I thought of those situations. And as soon as I realized that, I was cured – and stayed cured.' Such was the experience of this student.

I am deeply convinced that our peace of mind and the joy we get out of living depends not on where we are, or what we have, or who we are, but solely upon our mental attitude. Outward conditions have very little to do with it. For example, let's take the case of old John Brown, who was hanged for seizing the United States arsenal at Harpers Ferry and trying to incite the slaves to rebellion. He rode away to the gallows, sitting on his coffin. The jailer who rode beside him was nervous and worried. But old John Brown was calm and cool. Looking up at the Blue Ridge mountains of Virginia, he exclaimed, 'What a beautiful country! I never had an opportunity to really see it before.'

Or take the case of Robert Falcon Scott and his companions – the first Englishmen ever to reach the South Pole. Their return trip was probably the crudest journey ever undertaken by man. Their food was gone – and so was their fuel. They could no longer march because a howling blizzard roared down over the rim of the earth for 11 days and nights – a wind so fierce and sharp that it cut ridges in the polar ice. Scott and his companions knew they were going to die; and they had brought a quantity of opium along for just such an emergency. A big dose of opium, and they could all lie down to pleasant dreams, never to wake again. But they ignored the drug, and died 'singing ringing songs of cheer'. We know they did because of a farewell letter found with their frozen bodies by a searching party, eight months later.

Yes, if we cherish creative thoughts of courage and calmness, we can enjoy the scenery while sitting on our coffin, riding to the gallows; or we can fill our tents with ringing songs of cheer, while starving and freezing to death.

Milton in his blindness discovered that same truth three hundred years ago:

The mind is its own place, and in itself
Can make a heaven of Hell, a hell of Heaven.

Napoleon and Helen Keller are perfect illustrations of Milton's statement: Napoleon had everything men usually crave – glory, power, riches – yet he said at St. Helena, 'I have never known six happy days in my life'; while Helen Keller – blind, deaf, dumb – declared: 'I have found life so beautiful.'

If half a century of living has taught me anything at all, it has taught me that nothing can bring you peace but yourself.

I am merely trying to repeat what Emerson said so well in the closing words of his essay on 'Self-Reliance': 'A political victory, a rise in rents, the recovery of your sick, or the return of your absent friend, or some other quite external event, raises your spirits, and you think good days are preparing for you. Do not believe it. It can never be so. Nothing can bring you peace but yourself.'

Epictetus, the great Stoic philosopher, warned that we ought to be more concerned about removing wrong thoughts from the mind than about removing tumours and abscesses from the body.

Epictetus said that nineteen centuries ago, but modern medicine would back him up. Dr G. Canby Robinson declared that four out of five patients admitted to Johns Hopkins Hospital were suffering from conditions brought on in part by emotional strains and stresses. This was often true even in cases of organic disturbances. 'Eventually,' he declared, 'these trace back to maladjustments to life and its problems.'

Montaigne, the great French philosopher, adopted these seventeen words as the motto of his life: 'A man is not hurt so much by what happens, as by his opinion of what happens.' And our opinion of what happens is entirely up to us.

What do I mean? Have I the colossal effrontery to tell you to your face – when you are mowed down by troubles, and your nerves are sticking out like wires and curling up at the ends – have I the colossal effrontery to tell you that, under those conditions, you can change your mental attitude by an effort of the will? Yes, I mean precisely that! And that is not all. I am going to show you how to do it. It may take a little effort, but the secret is simple.

William James, who has never been topped in his knowledge of practical psychology, once made this observation: 'Action seems to follow feeling, but really, action and feeling go together; and by regulating the action, which is under the more direct control of the will, we can indirectly regulate the feeling, which is not'

In other words, William James tells us that we cannot instantly change our emotions just by 'making up our minds to' – but that we can change our actions. And that when we change our actions, we will automatically change our feelings.

'Thus,' he explains, 'the sovereign voluntary path to cheerfulness, if your cheerfulness be lost, is to sit up cheerfully and to act and speak as if cheerfulness were already there'

Does that simple trick work? Try it yourself. Put a big, broad, honest-to-God smile on your face; throw back your shoulders; take a good, deep breath; and sing a snatch of song. If you can't sing, whistle. If you can't whistle, hum. You will quickly discover what William James was talking about:

> It is physically impossible to remain blue or depressed while you are acting out the symptoms of being radiantly happy!

This is one of the little basic truths of nature that can easily work miracles in all of our lives. I know a woman in California – I won't mention her name – who could wipe out all of her miseries in twenty-four hours if only she knew this secret. She's old, and she's a widow – that's sad, I admit – but does she try to act happy? No; if you ask her how she is feeling, she says, 'Oh, I'm all right.' But the expression on her face and the whine in her voice say, 'Oh, God, if you only knew the troubles I've seen!' She seems to reproach you for being happy in her presence. Hundreds of women are worse off than she is: her husband left her enough insurance to last the rest of her life, and she has married children to give her a home. But I've rarely seen her smile. She complains that all three of her sons-in-law are stingy and selfish – although she is a guest in their homes for months at a time. And she complains that her daughters never give her presents – although she hoards her own money carefully, 'for her old age. She is a blight on herself and her unfortunate family! But does it have to be so? That is the pity of it – she could change herself from a miserable, bitter, and unhappy old woman into an honoured and beloved member of the family – if she wanted to change. And all she would have to do to work this transformation would be to start acting cheerful; start acting as though she had a little love to give away – instead of squandering it all on her own unhappy and embittered self.

H.J. Englert, of Tell City, Indiana, is still alive today because he discovered this secret. Ten years ago Mr Englert had a case of scarlet fever; and when he recovered, he found he had developed nephritis, a kidney disease. He tried all kinds of doctors. 'Even quacks,' he informs me, but nothing could cure him.

Then, a short time ago, he got other complications. His blood pressure soared. He went to a doctor, and was told that his blood pressure was hitting the top at 214. He was told that it was fatal – that the condition was progressive, and he had better put his affairs in order at once.

'I went home,' he says, 'and made sure that my insurance was all paid up, then I apologized to my Maker for all my mistakes, and settled down to gloomy meditations. I made everyone unhappy. My wife and family were miserable, and I was buried deep in depression myself. However, after a week of wallowing in self-pity, I said to myself, "You're acting like a fool! You may not die for a year yet, so why not try to be happy while you're here?"

'I threw back my shoulders, put a smile on my face, and attempted to act as though everything were normal. I admit it was an effort at first – but I forced myself to be pleasant and cheerful; and this not only helped my family, but it also helped me.

'The first thing I knew, I began to feel better – almost as well as I pretended to feel! The improvement went on. And today – months after I was supposed to be in my grave – I am not only happy, well, and alive, but my blood pressure is down! I know one thing for certain: the doctor's prediction would certainly have come true if I had gone on thinking 'dying' thoughts of defeat. But I gave my body a chance to heal itself, by nothing in the world but a change of mental attitude!'

Let me ask you a question: If merely acting cheerful and thinking positive thoughts of health and courage could save this man's life, why should you and I tolerate for one minute more our minor glooms and depressions? Why make ourselves, and everyone around us, unhappy and blue, when it is possible for us to start creating happiness by merely acting cheerful?

Years ago, I read a little book that had a lasting and profound effect on my life. It was called *As a Man Thinketh*, by James Allen, and here's what it said:

'A man will find that as he alters his thoughts toward things and other people, things and other people will alter towards him. Let a man radically alter his thoughts, and he will be astonished at the rapid transformation it will effect in the material conditions of his life. Men do not attract that which they want, but that which they are...The divinity that shapes our ends is in ourselves. It is our very self...All that a man achieves is the direct result of his own thoughts...A man can only rise, conquer and achieve by lifting up his thoughts. He can only remain weak and abject and miserable by refusing to lift up his thoughts.'

According to the book of Genesis, the Creator gave man dominion over the whole wide earth. A mighty big present.

But I am not interested in any such super royal prerogatives. All I desire is dominion over myself – dominion over my thoughts;

dominion over my fears; dominion over my mind and over my spirit. And the wonderful thing is that I know that I can attain this dominion to an astonishing degree, any time I want to, by merely controlling my actions – which in turn control my reactions.

So let us remember these words of William James: 'Much of what we call Evil…can often be converted into a bracing and tonic good by a simple change of the sufferer's inner attitude from one of fear to one of fight.'

Let's fight for our happiness!

Let's fight for our happiness by following a daily programme of cheerful and constructive thinking. Here is such a programme. It is entitled, 'Just for Today.' I found this programme so inspiring that I gave away hundreds of copies. It was written by the late Sibyl R. Partridge. If you and I follow it, we will eliminate most of our worries and increase immeasurably our portion of what the French call *la joie de vivre.*

> If we want to develop a mental attitude that will bring us peace and happiness, think and act cheerfully, and you will feel cheerful.

JUST FOR TODAY

- **Just for today I will be happy.** This assumes that what Abraham Lincoln said is true, that most folks are about as happy as they make up their minds to be. Happiness is from within; it is not a matter of externals.
- **Just for today I will try to adjust myself to what is, and not try to adjust everything to my own desires.** I will take my family, my business, and my luck as they come and fit myself to them.
- **Just for today I will take care of my body.** I will exercise it, care for it, nourish it, not abuse it nor neglect it, so that it will be a perfect machine for my bidding.
- **Just for today I will try to strengthen my mind.** I will learn something useful. I will not be a mental loafer. I will read something that requires effort, thought, and concentration.
- **Just for today I will exercise my soul in three ways;** I will do somebody a good turn and not get found out. I will do at least two things I don't want to do, as William James suggests, just for exercise.
- **Just for today I will be agreeable.** I will look as well as I can, dress as becomingly as possible, talk low, act courteously, be liberal with praise, criticize not at all, nor find fault with anything and not try to regulate nor improve anyone.
- **Just for today I will try to live through this day only, not to tackle my whole life's problems at once.** I can do things for 12 hours that would appal me if I had to keep them up for a lifetime.
- **Just for today I will have a programme.** I will write down what I expect to do every hour. I may not follow it exactly, but I will have it. It will eliminate two pests – hurrying and indecision.
- **Just for today I will have a quiet half-hour all by myself and relax.** In this half-hour, sometimes I will think of God, so as to get a little more perspective into my life.
- **Just for today I will be unafraid;** I will especially not be afraid to be happy, to enjoy what is beautiful, to love, and to believe that those I love, love me.

8

Find Yourself and Be Yourself: Remember There Is No One Else on Earth Like You

I have a letter from Mrs Edith Allred, of Mount Airy, North Carolina: 'As a child, I was extremely sensitive and shy,' she says in her letter. 'I was always overweight and my cheeks made me look even fatter than I was. I had an old-fashioned mother who thought it was foolish to make clothes look pretty. She always said: "Wide will wear while narrow will tear," and she dressed me accordingly. I never went to parties; never had any fun; and when I went to school, I never joined the other children in outside activities, not even athletics. I was morbidly shy. I felt I was "different" from everybody else, and entirely undesirable.

'When I grew up, I married a man who was several years my senior. But I didn't change. My in-laws were a poised and self-confident family. They were everything I should have been but simply was not. I tried my best to be like them, but I couldn't. Every attempt they made to draw me out of myself only drove me further into my shell. I became nervous and irritable. I avoided all friends. I got so bad I even dreaded the sound of the doorbell ringing! I was a failure. I knew it; and I was afraid my husband would find it out. So, whenever we were in public, I tried to be gay, and overacted my part. I knew I overacted; and I would be miserable for days afterwards. At last I became so unhappy that I could see no point in prolonging my existence. I began to think of suicide.'

What happened to change this unhappy woman's life? Just a chance remark!

'A chance remark,' Mrs Allred continued, 'transformed my whole life. My mother-in-law was talking one day of how she brought her children up, and she said, "No matter what happened, I always insisted on their being themselves." That remark – on being themselves – is what did it! In a flash, I realized I had brought all this misery on myself by trying to fit myself into a pattern to which I did not conform.

'I changed overnight! I started being myself. I tried to make a study of my own personality. Tried to find out what I was. I studied my strong points. I learned all I could about colours and styles, and dressed in a way that I felt was becoming to me. I reached out to make friends. I joined an organization – a small one at first – and was petrified with fright when they put me on a programme. But each time I spoke, I gained a little courage. It took a long while – but today I have more happiness than I ever dreamed possible. In rearing my own children, I have always taught them the lesson I had to learn from such bitter experience: No matter what happens, always be yourself!'

This problem of being willing to be yourself is, 'As old as history,' says Dr James Gordon Gilkey, 'and as universal as human life.' This problem of being unwilling to be yourself is the hidden spring behind many neuroses and psychoses and complexes. Angelo Patri has written thirteen books and thousands of syndicated newspaper articles on the subject of child training, and he says: 'Nobody is so miserable as he who longs to be somebody and something other than the person he is in body and mind.'

This craving to be something you are not is especially rampant in Hollywood. Sam Wood, one of Hollywood's best-known directors, said the greatest headache he has with aspiring young actors is exactly this problem: to make them be themselves. They all want to be second-rate Lana Turners or third-rate Clark Gables. 'The public has already had that flavour.' Sam Wood keeps telling them; 'Now it wants something else.'

Before he started directing such pictures as *Goodbye, Mr Chips* and *For Whom the Bell Tolls*, Sam Wood spent years in the real estate business, developing sales personalities. He declares that the same principles apply in the business world as in the world of moving pictures. You won't get anywhere playing the ape. You can't be a parrot. 'Experience has taught me,' says Sam Wood, 'that it is safest to drop, as quickly as possible, people who pretend to be what they aren't.'

I asked Paul Boynton, then employment director for a major oil company, what is the biggest mistake people make in applying for jobs. He ought to know: he has interviewed more than sixty thousand job seekers; and he has written a book entitled, *6 Ways to Get a Job*. He replied: 'The biggest mistake people make in applying for jobs is in not being themselves. Instead of taking their hair down and being completely frank, they often try to give you the answers they think you want.' But it doesn't work, because nobody wants a phony. Nobody ever wants a counterfeit coin.

A certain daughter of a streetcar conductor had to learn that lesson the hard way. She longed to be a singer. But her face was her misfortune. She had a large mouth and protruding buck teeth. When she first sang in public – in a New Jersey night club – she tried to pull down her upper lip to cover her teeth. She tried to act glamorous. The results? She made herself ridiculous. She was headed for failure.

However, there was a man in this night club who heard the girl sing and thought she had talent. 'See here,' he said bluntly, 'I've been watching your performance and I know what it is you're trying to hide. You're ashamed of your teeth!' The girl was embarrassed, but the man continued, 'What of it? Is there any particular crime in having buck teeth? Don't try to hide them! Open your mouth, and the audience will love you when they see you're not ashamed. Besides,' he said shrewdly, 'those teeth you're trying to hide may make your fortune!'

Cass Daley took his advice and forgot about her teeth. From that time on, she thought only about her audience. She opened her mouth wide and sang with such gusto and enjoyment that she became a top star in movies and radio. Other comedians tried to copy her!

The renowned William James was speaking of people who had never found themselves when he declared that the average person develops only 10 per cent of his or her latent mental abilities. 'Compared to what we ought to be,' he wrote, 'we are only half awake. We are making use of only a small part of our physical and mental resources. Stating the thing broadly, human individuals thus live far within their limits. They possess powers of various sorts which they habitually fail to use.'

You and I have such abilities, so let's not waste a second worrying because we are not like other people. You are something new in this world. Never before, since the beginning of time, has there ever been anybody exactly like you; and never again throughout all the ages to come will there ever be anybody exactly like you again. The science of genetics informs us that you are what you are largely as a result of twenty-four chromosomes contributed by your father and twenty-four chromosomes contributed by your mother. These forty-eight chromosomes comprise everything that determines what you inherit. In each chromosome there may be, says Amram Scheinfeld, 'anywhere from scores to hundreds of genes – with a single gene, in some cases, able to change the whole life of an individual.' Truly, we are 'fearfully and wonderfully' made.

Even after your mother and father met and mated, there was only one chance in 300,000 billion that the person who is specifically you would be born! In other words, if you had 300,000 billion brothers and sisters, they might have all been different from you. Is all this guesswork? No. It is a scientific fact. If you would like to read more about it, consult *You and Heredity*, by Amram Scheinfeld.

I can talk with conviction about this subject of being yourself because I feel deeply about it. I know what I am talking about. I know from bitter and costly experience. To illustrate:

When I first came to New York from the cornfields of Missouri, I enrolled in the American Academy of Dramatic Arts. I aspired to be an actor. I had what I thought was a brilliant idea, a shortcut to success, an idea so simple, so fool proof, that I couldn't understand why thousands of ambitious people hadn't already discovered it. It was this: I would study how the famous actors of that day – John Drew, Walter Hampden, and Otis Skinner – got their effects. Then I would imitate the best points of each one of them and make myself into a shining, triumphant combination of all of them. How silly! How absurd! I had to waste years of my life imitating other people before it penetrated through my thick Missouri skull that I had to be myself, and that I couldn't possibly be anyone else.

That distressing experience ought to have taught me a lasting lesson. But it didn't. Not me. I was too dumb. I had to learn it all over again. Several years later, I set out to write what I hoped would be the best book on public speaking for businessmen that had ever been written. I had the same foolish idea about writing this book that I had formerly had about acting: I was going to borrow the ideas of a lot of other writers and put them all in one book – a book that would have everything. So, I got scores of books on public speaking and spent a year incorporating their ideas into my manuscript. But it finally dawned on me once again that I was playing the fool. This hodgepodge of other men's ideas that I had written was so synthetic, so dull, that no businessman would ever plod through it. So I tossed a year's work into the waste basket, and started all over again. This time I said to myself: 'You've got to be Dale Carnegie, with all his faults and limitations. You can't possibly be anybody else.' So, I quit trying to be a combination of other men, and rolled up my sleeves and did what I should have done in the first place: I wrote a textbook on public speaking out of my own experiences, observations, and convictions as a speaker and a teacher of speaking. I learned – for all time, I hope – the lesson that Sir Walter Raleigh learned. (I am not talking about the Sir Walter who threw his coat in the mud for the Queen to step on. I am talking about the Sir Walter Raleigh who was professor of English literature at Oxford, back in 1904.) 'I can't write a book commensurate with Shakespeare,' he said, 'but I can write a book by me.'

Be yourself. Act on the sage advice that Irving Berlin gave the late George Gershwin. When Berlin and Gershwin first met, Berlin was famous but Gershwin was a struggling young composer working for $35 a week in Tin Pan Alley. Berlin, impressed by Gershwin's ability, offered Gershwin a job as his musical secretary at almost three times the salary he was then getting. 'But don't take the job,' Berlin advised. 'If you do, you may develop into a second-rate Berlin. But if you insist on being yourself, someday you'll become a first-rate Gershwin.'

Gershwin heeded that warning and slowly transformed himself into one of the significant American composers of his generation.

Charlie Chaplin, Will Rogers, Mary Margaret McBride, Gene Autry, and millions of others had to learn the lesson I am trying to hammer home in this chapter. They had to learn the hard way – just as I did.

When Charlie Chaplin first started making films, the director of the pictures insisted on Chaplin's imitating a popular German comedian of that day. Charlie Chaplin got nowhere until he acted himself. Bob Hope had a similar experience. He spent years in a singing-and-dancing act – and got nowhere until he began to wisecrack and be himself. Will Rogers twirled a rope in vaudeville for years without saying a word. He got nowhere until he discovered his unique gift for humour and began to talk as he twirled his rope.

When Mary Margaret McBride first went on the air, she tried to be an Irish comedian and failed. When she tried to be just what she was – a plain country girl from Missouri -she became one of the most popular radio stars in New York.

When Gene Autry tried to get rid of his Texas accent and dressed like city boys and claimed he was from New York, people merely laughed behind his back. But when he started twanging his banjo and singing cowboy ballads, Gene Autry started out on a career that made him the world's most popular cowboy both in pictures and on the radio.

> You are something new in this world. Be glad of it. Make the most of what nature gave you.

In the last analysis, all art is autobiographical. You can sing only what you are. You can paint only what you are. You must be what your experiences, your environment, and your heredity have made you. For better or for worse, you must cultivate your own little garden. For better or for worse, you must play your own little instrument in the orchestra of life.

As Emerson said in his essay on 'Self-reliance': 'There is a time in every man's education when he arrives at the conviction that envy is ignorance; that imitation is suicide; that he must take himself for better, for worse, as his portion; that though the wide universe is full of good, no kernel of nourishing corn can come to him but through his toil bestowed on that plot of ground which is given him to till. The power which resides in him is new in nature, and none but he knows what that is which he can do, nor does he know until he has tried.'

That is the way Emerson said it. But here is the way a poet – the late Douglas Malloch – said it:

If you can't be a pine on the top of the hill,
Be a scrub in the valley – but be
The best little scrub by the side of the rill;
Be a bush, if you can't be a tree.

If you can't be a bush, be a bit of the grass,
And some highway happier make;
If you can't be a muskie, then just be a bass –
But the liveliest bass in the lake!

We can't all be captains, we've got to be crew,
There's something for all of us here.
There's big work to do and there's lesser to do
And the task we must do is the near.

If you can't be a highway, then just be a trail,
If you can't be the sun, be a star;
It isn't by size that you win or you fail –
Be the best of whatever you are!

To cultivate a mental attitude that will bring us peace and freedom from worry:

- Let's not imitate others.
- Let's find ourselves and be ourselves.

9

If You Have a Lemon, Make a Lemonade

While writing this book, I dropped in one day at the University of Chicago and asked the chancellor, Robert Maynard Hutchins, how he kept from worrying. He replied, 'I have always tried to follow a bit of advice given to me by the late Julius Rosenwald, president of Sears, Roebuck and Company: 'When you have a lemon, make a lemonade.'

That is what a great educator does. But the fool does the exact opposite. If he finds that life has handed him a lemon, he gives up and says, 'I'm beaten. It is fate. I haven't got a chance.' Then he proceeds to rail against the world and indulge in an orgy of self-pity. But when the wise man is handed a lemon, he says: 'What lesson can I learn from this misfortune? How can I improve my situation? How can I turn this lemon into a lemonade?'

After spending a lifetime studying people and their hidden reserves of power, the great psychologist, Alfred Adler, declared that one of the wonder-filled characteristics of human beings is their power to turn a minus into a plus.

Here is an interesting and stimulating story of a woman I know who did just that. Her name is Thelma Thompson. 'During the war,' she said, as she told me of her experience, 'my husband was stationed at an Army training camp near the Mojave Desert, in California. I went to live there in order to be near him. I hated the place. I loathed it. I had never before been so miserable. My husband was ordered out on manoeuvres in the Mojave Desert, and I was left in a tiny shack alone. Th heat was unbearable – 125 degrees in the shade of a cactus. Not a soul to talk to. The wind blew incessantly, and all the food I ate, and the very air I breathed, were filled with sand, sand, and sand!

'I was so utterly wretched, so sorry for myself, that I wrote to my parents. I told them I was giving up and coming back home. I said I couldn't stand it one minute longer. I would rather be in jail! My father answered my letter with just two lines – two lines that will always sing in my memory – two lines that completely altered my life:

> Two men looked out from prison bars,
> One saw the mud, the other saw the stars.

'I read those two lines over and over. I was ashamed of myself. I made up my mind I would find out what was good in my present situation; I would look for the stars.

'I made friends with the natives, and their reaction amazed me. When I showed interest in their weaving and pottery, they gave me presents of their favourite pieces which they had refused to sell to tourists. I studied the fascinating forms of the cactus and the yuccas and the Joshua trees. I learned about prairie dogs, watched for the desert sunsets, and hunted for seashells that had been left there millions of years ago when the sands of the desert had been an ocean floor.

'What brought about this astonishing change in me? The Mojave Desert hadn't changed. But I had. I had changed my attitude of mind. And by doing so, I transformed a wretched experience into the most exciting adventure of my life. I was stimulated and excited by this new world that I had discovered. I was so excited I wrote a book about it – a novel that was published under the title

Bright Ramparts. I had looked out of my self-created prison and found the stars.'

Thelma Thompson, you discovered an old truth that the Greeks taught five hundred years before Christ was born: 'The best things are the most difficult.'

Harry Emerson Fosdick repeated it again in the Twentieth Century: 'Happiness is not mostly pleasure; it is mostly victory.' Yes, the victory that comes from a sense of achievement, of triumph, of turning our lemons into lemonades.

I once visited a happy farmer down in Florida who turned even a poison lemon into lemonade. When he first got his farm, he was discouraged. The land was so wretched he could neither grow fruit nor raise pigs. Nothing thrived there but scrub oaks and rattlesnakes. Then he got his idea. He would turn his liability into an asset: he would make the most of these rattlesnakes. To everyone's amazement, he started canning rattlesnake meat. When I stopped to visit him a few years ago, I found that tourists were pouring in to see his rattlesnake farm at the rate of twenty thousand a year. His business was thriving. I saw poison from the fangs of his rattlers being shipped to laboratories to make antivenom toxin; I saw rattlesnake skins being sold at fancy prices to make women's shoes and handbags. I saw canned rattlesnake meat being shipped to customers all over the world. I bought a picture postcard of the place and mailed it at the local post office of the village, which had been rechristened 'Rattlesnake, Florida', in honour of a man who had turned a poison lemon into a sweet lemonade.

As I have travelled up and down and back and forth across this nation time after time, it has been my privilege to meet dozens of men and women who have demonstrated their power to turn a minus into a plus.

The late William Bolitho, author of *Twelve Against the Gods*, put it like this: 'The most important thing in life is not to capitalize on your gains. Any fool can do that. The really important thing is to profit from your losses. That requires intelligence; and it makes the difference between a man of sense and a fool.'

Bolitho uttered those words after he had lost a leg in a railway accident. But I know a man who lost both legs and turned his minus into a plus. His name is Ben Fortson. I met him in a hotel elevator in Atlanta, Georgia. As I stepped into the elevator, I noticed this cheerful-looking man, who had both legs missing, sitting in a wheelchair in a corner of the elevator. When the elevator stopped at his floor, he asked me pleasantly if I would step to one corner, so he could manage his chair better. 'So sorry,' he said, 'to inconvenience you,' and a deep, heart-warming smile lighted his face as he said it.

When I left the elevator and went to my room, I could think of nothing but this cheerful cripple. So I hunted him up and asked him to tell me his story.

'It happened in 1929,' he told me with a smile. 'I had gone out to cut a load of hickory poles to stake the beans in my garden. I had loaded the poles on my Ford and started back home. Suddenly one pole slipped under the car and jammed the steering apparatus at the very moment I was making a sharp turn. The car shot over an embankment and hurled me against a tree. My spine was hurt. My legs were paralysed.

'I was twenty-four when that happened, and I have never taken a step since.'

Twenty-four years old, and sentenced to a wheelchair for the rest of his life! I asked him how he managed to take it so courageously, and he said, 'I didn't.' He said he raged and rebelled. He fumed about his fate. But as the years dragged on, he found that his rebellion wasn't getting him anything except bitterness. 'I finally realized,' he said, 'that other people were kind and courteous to me. So the least I could do was to be kind and courteous to them.'

I asked if he still felt, after all these years, that his accident had been a terrible misfortune, and he promptly said, 'No.' He said, 'I'm almost glad now that it happened.' He told me that after he got over the shock and resentment, he began to live in a different world. He began to read and developed a love for good literature. In fourteen years, he said, he had read at least fourteen hundred books; and those books had opened up new horizons for him and made his life richer than he ever thought possible. He began to listen to good music; and he is now thrilled by great symphonies that would have bored him before. But the biggest change was that he had time to think. 'For the first time in my life,' he said, 'I was able to look at the world and get a real sense of values. I began to realize that most of the things I had been striving for before weren't worthwhile at all.'

As a result of his reading, he became interested in politics, studied public questions, made speeches from his wheelchair! He got to know people and people got to know him. And – still in his wheelchair – he got to be secretary of state for the state of Georgia!

While conducting adult-education classes in New York City, I have discovered that one of the major regrets of many adults is that they never went to college. They seem to think that not having a college education is a great handicap. I know that this isn't necessarily true because I have known thousands of successful men who never went beyond high school. So I often tell these students the story of a man I knew who had never finished even grade school. He was brought up in blighting poverty. When his father died, his father's friends had to chip in to pay for the coffin in which he was buried. After his father's death, his mother worked in an umbrella factory ten hours a day and then brought piecework home and worked until eleven o'clock at night.

The boy brought up in these circumstances went in for amateur dramatics put on by a club in his church. He got such a thrill out of acting that he decided to take up public speaking. This led him into politics. By the time he reached thirty, he was elected to the New York State legislature. But he was woefully unprepared for such a responsibility. In fact, he told me that frankly he didn't know what it was all about. He studied the long, complicated bills that he was supposed to vote on – but, as far as he was concerned, those bills might as well have been written in the language of the Choctaw Indians. He was worried and bewildered when he was made a member of the committee on forests before he had ever set foot in a forest. He was worried and bewildered when he was made a member of the State Banking Commission before he had ever had a bank account. He himself told me that he was so discouraged that he would have resigned from the legislature if he hadn't been ashamed to admit defeat to his mother. In despair, he decided to study sixteen hours a day and turn his lemon of ignorance into a lemonade of knowledge. By doing that, he transformed himself from a local politician into a national figure and made himself so outstanding that the *New York Times* called him 'the best-loved citizen of New York'.

I am talking about Al Smith.

Ten years after Al Smith set out on his programme of political self-education, he was the greatest living authority on the government of New York State. He was elected Governor of New York for four terms – at that time a record never attained by any other man. In 1928, he was the Democratic candidate for President. Six great universities – including Columbia and Harvard – conferred honorary degrees upon this man who had never gone beyond grade school.

Al Smith himself told me that none of these things would ever have come to pass if he hadn't worked hard sixteen hours a day to turn his minus into a plus.

Nietzsche's formula for the superior man was 'not only to bear up under necessity but to love it'.

The more I have studied the careers of men of achievement the more deeply I have been convinced that a surprisingly large number of them succeeded because they started out with handicaps that spurred them on to great endeavour and great rewards. As William James said: 'Our very infirmities help us unexpectedly.'

Yes, it is highly probable that Milton wrote better poetry because he was blind and that Beethoven composed better music because he was deaf.

Helen Keller's brilliant career was inspired and made possible because of her blindness and deafness.

If Tchaikovsky had not been frustrated – and driven almost to suicide by his tragic marriage – if his own life had not been pathetic, he probably would never have been able to compose his immortal *Symphonie Pathetique*?

If Dostoevsky and Tolstoy had not led tortured lives, they would probably never have been able to write their immortal novels.

'If I had not been so great an invalid,' wrote the man who changed the scientific concept of life on earth – 'if I had not been so great an invalid, I should not have done so much work as I have accomplished.' That was Charles Darwin's confession that his infirmities had helped him unexpectedly.

The same day that Darwin was born in England, another baby was born in a log cabin in the forests of Kentucky. He, too, was helped by his infirmities. His name was Lincoln – Abraham Lincoln. If he had been reared in an aristocratic family and had had a law degree from Harvard and a happy married life, he would probably never have found in the depths of his heart the haunting words that he immortalized at Gettysburg, nor the sacred poem that he spoke at his second inauguration – the most beautiful and noble phrases ever uttered by a ruler of men: 'With malice toward none; with charity for all...'

Harry Emerson Fosdick says in his book, *The Power to See It Through*, 'There is a Scandinavian saying which some of us might well take as a rallying cry for our lives: "The north wind made the Vikings." Wherever did we get the idea that secure and pleasant living, the absence of difficulty, and the comfort of ease, ever of themselves made people either good or happy? Upon the contrary, people who pity themselves go on pitying themselves even when they are laid softly on a cushion, but always in history character and happiness have come to people in all sorts of circumstances, good, bad, and indifferent, when they shouldered their personal responsibility. So, repeatedly the north wind has made the Vikings.'

Suppose we are so discouraged that we feel there is no hope of our ever being able to turn our lemons into lemonade then here are two reasons why we ought to try, anyway – two reasons why we have everything to gain and nothing to lose.

Reason one: We may succeed.

Reason two: Even if we don't succeed, the mere attempt to turn our minus into a plus will cause us to look forward instead of backward; it will replace negative thoughts with positive thoughts; it will release creative energy and spur us to get so busy that we won't have either the time or the inclination to mourn over what is past and forever gone.

Once when Ole Bull, the world-famous violinist, was giving a concert in Paris, the A string on his violin suddenly snapped. But Ole Bull simply finished the melody on three strings. 'That is life,' says Harry Emerson Fosdick. 'To have your A string snap and finish on three strings.'

That is not only life. It is more than life. It is life triumphant!

If I had the power to do so, I would have these words of William Bolitho carved in eternal bronze and hung in every schoolhouse in the land:

'The most important thing in life is not to capitalize on your gains. Any fool can do that. The really important thing is to profit from your losses. That requires intelligence; and it makes the difference between a man of sense and a fool.'

> When fate hands us a lemon, let's try to make a lemonade.

SEVEN WAYS TO CULTIVATE A MENTAL ATTITUDE THAT WILL BRING YOU PEACE AND HAPPINESS

RULE 1

Let's fill our minds with thoughts of peace, courage, health, and hope, for 'our life is what our thoughts make it.'

RULE 2

Let's never try to get even with our enemies, because if we do we will hurt ourselves far more than we hurt them. Let's do as General Eisenhower does: let's never waste a minute thinking about people we don't like.

RULE 3

A. Instead of worrying about ingratitude, let's expect it. Let's remember that Jesus healed ten lepers in one day – and only one thanked Him. Why should we expect more gratitude than Jesus got?

B. Let's remember that the only way to find happiness is not to expect gratitude – but to give for the joy of giving.

C. Let's remember that gratitude is a 'cultivated' trait; so if we want our children to be grateful, we must train them to be grateful.

RULE 4

Count your blessings – not your troubles!

RULE 5

Let's not imitate others. Let's find ourselves and be ourselves, for 'envy is ignorance' and 'imitation is suicide.'

RULE 6

When fate hands us a lemon, let's try to make a lemonade.

RULE 7

Let's forget our own unhappiness – by trying to create a little happiness for others. 'When you are good to others, you are best to yourself.'

10

How to Keep from Worrying about Criticism

FOOL THINGS I HAVE DONE

I have a folder in my private filing cabinet marked 'FTD' – short for 'Fool Things I Have Done'. I put in that folder written records of the fool things I have been guilty of. I sometimes dictate these memos to my secretary, but sometimes they are so personal, so stupid, that I am ashamed to dictate them, so I write them out in longhand.

I can still recall some of the criticisms of Dale Carnegie that I put in my 'FTD' folders 15 years ago. If I had been utterly honest with myself, I would now have a filing cabinet bursting out at the seams with these 'FTD' memos. I can truthfully repeat what King Saul said thirty centuries ago: 'I have played the fool and have erred exceedingly.'

When I get out my 'FTD' folders and reread the criticisms I have written of myself, they help me deal with the toughest problem I shall ever face: the management of Dale Carnegie.

I used to blame my troubles on other people; but as I have grown older – and wiser, I hope – I have realized that I myself, in the last analysis, am to blame for almost all my misfortunes. Lots of people have discovered that, as they grow older. 'No one but myself,' said

Napoleon at St. Helena, 'can be blamed for my fall. I have been my own greatest enemy – the cause of my own disastrous fate.'

Let me tell you about a man I knew who was an artist when it came to self-appraisal and self-management. His name was H.P. Howell. When the news of his sudden death in the drugstore of the Hotel Ambassador in New York was flashed across the nation on 31 July 1944, Wall Street was shocked, for he was a leader in American finance – chairman of the board of the Commercial National Bank and Trust Company and a director of several large corporations. He grew up with little formal education, started out in life clerking in a country store, and later became credit manager for US Steel – and was on his way to position and power.

'For years I have kept an engagement book showing all the appointments I have during the day,' Mr Howell told me when I asked him to explain the reasons for his success. 'My family never makes any plans for me on Saturday night, for the family knows that I devote a part of each Saturday evening to self-examination and a review and appraisal of my work during the week. After dinner I go off by myself, open my engagement book, and think over all the interviews, discussions, and meetings that have taken place since Monday morning. I ask myself: "What mistakes did I make that time? What did I do that was right – and in what way could I have improved my performance? What lessons can I learn from that experience?" I sometimes find that this weekly review makes me very unhappy. Sometimes I am astonished by my own blunders. Of course, as the years have gone by, these blunders have become less frequent. This system of self-analysis, continued year after year, has done more for me than any other thing I have ever attempted.'

Maybe H.P. Howell borrowed his idea from Ben Franklin. Only Franklin didn't wait until Saturday night. He gave himself a severe going-over every night. He discovered that he had 13 serious faults. Here are three of them: wasting time, stewing around over trifles, arguing and contradicting people. Wise old Ben Franklin realized that, unless he eliminated these handicaps, he wasn't going to get very far. So he battled with one of his shortcomings every day for a week, and kept a record of who had won each day's slugging match. The next week, he would pick out another bad habit, put on the gloves, and when the bell rang he would come out of his corner fighting. Franklin kept up this battle with his faults every week for more than two years.

No wonder he became one of the best-loved and most influential men this nation ever produced!

Elbert Hubbard said: 'Every man is a damn fool for at least five minutes every day. Wisdom consists in not exceeding that limit.'

The small man flies into a rage over the slightest criticism, but the wise man is eager to learn from those who have censured him, reproved him, and disputed the passage with him. Walt Whitman put it this way: 'Have you learned lessons only of those who admired you, and were tender with you, and stood aside for you? Have you not learned great lessons from those who rejected you, and braced themselves against you, or disputed the passage with you?'

Instead of waiting for our enemies to criticize us or our work, let's beat them to it. Let's be our own most severe critic. Let's find and remedy all our weaknesses before our enemies get a chance to say a word. That is what Charles Darwin did. In fact, he spent fifteen years criticizing – well, the story goes like this:

When Darwin completed the manuscript of his immortal book, *The Origin of Species*, he realized that the publication of his revolutionary concept of creation would rock the intellectual and religious worlds. So, he became his own critic and spent another fifteen years, checking his data, challenging his reasoning, criticizing his conclusions.

Suppose someone denounced you as 'a damn fool' – what would you do? Get angry? Indignant? Here is what Lincoln did: Edward

M. Stanton, Lincoln's secretary of war, once called Lincoln a damn fool. Stanton was indignant because Lincoln had been meddling in Stanton's affairs. In order to please a selfish politician, Lincoln had signed an order transferring certain regiments. Stanton not only refused to carry out Lincoln's orders, but swore that Lincoln was a damn fool for ever signing such orders. What happened? When Lincoln was told what Stanton had said, Lincoln calmly replied: 'If Stanton said I am a damned fool, then I must be, for he is nearly always right. I'll just step over and see for myself.'

Lincoln did go to see Stanton. Stanton convinced him that the order was wrong, and Lincoln withdrew it. Lincoln welcomed criticism when he knew it was sincere, founded on knowledge, and given in a spirit of helpfulness.

You and I ought to welcome that kind of criticism, too, for we can't even hope to be right more than three times out of four. At least, that was all Theodore Roosevelt said he could hope for, when he was in the White House. Einstein, the most profound thinker of our day, confessed that his conclusions were wrong 99 per cent of the time!

'The opinions of our enemies,' said La Rochefoucauld, 'come nearer to the truth about us than do our own opinions.'

I know that statement may be true many times; yet when anyone starts to criticize me, if I do not watch myself, I instantly and automatically leap to the defensive – even before I have the slightest idea what my critic is going to say. I am disgusted with myself every time I do it. We all tend to resent criticism and lap up praise, regardless of whether either the criticism or the praise is justified. We are not creatures of logic. We are creatures of emotions. Our logic is like a birch-bark canoe, tossed about on a deep, dark, stormy sea of emotion.

If we hear that someone has spoken ill of us, let's not try to defend ourselves. Every fool does that. Let's be original – and humble – and brilliant! Let's confound our critic and win applause for ourselves by saying: 'If my critic had known about all my other faults, he would have criticized me much more severely than he did.'

In previous chapters, I have talked about what to do when you are unjustly criticized. But here is another idea: when your anger is rising because you feel you have been unjustly condemned, why not stop and say: 'Just a minute...I am far from perfect. If Einstein admits he is wrong 99 per cent of the time, maybe I am wrong at least 80 per cent of the time. Maybe I deserve this criticism. If I do, I ought to be thankful for it, and try to profit by it.'

Charles Luckman, a former president of the Pepsodent Company, spent a million dollars a year putting Bob Hope on the air. He didn't look at the letters praising the programme, but he insisted on seeing the critical letters. He knew he might learn something from them.

The Ford Company was so eager to find out what was wrong with its management and operations that it polled the employees and invited them to criticize the company.

I know a former soap salesman who used even to ask for criticism. When he first started out selling soap for Colgate, orders came slowly. He worried about losing his job. Since he knew there was nothing wrong with the soap or the price, he figured that the trouble must be himself. When he failed to make a sale, he would often walk around the block trying to figure out what was wrong. Had he been too vague? Did he lack enthusiasm? Sometimes he would go back to the merchant and say: 'I haven't come back here to try to sell you any soap. I have come back to get your advice and your criticism. Won't you please tell me what I did that was wrong when I tried to sell you soap a few minutes ago? You are far more experienced and successful than I am. Please give me your criticism. Be frank. Don't pull your punches.'

This attitude won him a lot of friends and priceless advice.

What do you suppose ever happened to him? He rose to be

president of the Colgate-Palmolive-Peet Soap Company – one of the world's largest makers of soap. His name is E.H. Little.

It takes a big man to do what H.P. Howell, Ben Franklin, and E.H. Little did. And now, while nobody is looking, why not peep into the mirror and ask yourself whether you belong in that kind of company!

> Let's keep a record of the fool things we have done and criticize ourselves. Since we can't hope to be perfect, let's do what E.H. Little did: let's ask for unbiased, helpful, constructive criticism.

11

Four Good Working Habits That Will Help Prevent Fatigue and Worry

Good Working Habit No. 1:

Clear your desk of all papers except those relating to the immediate problem at hand.

Roland L. Williams, president of Chicago and Northwestern Railway, once said, 'A person with his desk piled high with papers on various matters will find his work much easier and more accurate if he clears that desk of all but the immediate problem on hand. I call this good housekeeping, and it is the number-one step toward efficiency.'

If you visit the Library of Congress in Washington, DC, you will find five words painted on the ceiling – five words written by the poet Pope:

'Order is Heaven's first law.'

Order ought to be the first law of business, too. But is it? No, the average desk is cluttered up with papers that haven't been looked at for weeks. In fact, the publisher of a New Orleans newspaper once told me that his secretary cleared up one of his desks and found a typewriter that had been missing for two years!

The mere sight of a desk littered with unanswered mail and

reports and memos is enough to breed confusion, tension, and worries. It is much worse than that. The constant reminder of a million things to do and no time to do them, can worry you not only into tension and fatigue, but it can also worry you into high blood pressure, heart trouble, and stomach ulcers.

Dr John H. Stokes, professor, Graduate School of Medicine, University of Pennsylvania, read a paper before the National Convention of the American Medical Association – a paper entitled, 'Functional Neuroses as Complications of Organic Disease.' In that paper, Dr Stokes listed 11 conditions under the title: 'What to Look for in the Patient's State of Mind'. Here is the first item on that list:

The sense of must or obligation; the unending stretch of things ahead that simply have to be done.

But how can such an elementary procedure as clearing your desk and making decisions help you avoid this high pressure, this sense of must, this sense of an 'unending stretch of things ahead that simply have to be done'? Dr William L. Sadler, the famous psychiatrist, told of a patient who, by using this simple device, avoided a nervous breakdown. The man was an executive in a big Chicago firm. When he came to Dr Sadler's office, he was tense, nervous, worried. He knew he was heading for a tailspin, but he couldn't quit work. He had to have help.

'While this man was telling me his story,' Dr Sadler says, 'my telephone rang. It was the hospital calling; and, instead of deferring the matter, I took time right then to come to a decision. I always settle questions, if possible, right on the spot. I had no sooner hung up than the phone rang again. Again an urgent matter, which I took time to discuss. The third interruption came when a colleague of mine came to my office for advice on a patient who was critically ill. When I had finished with him, I turned to my caller and began to apologize for keeping him waiting. But he had brightened up. He had a completely different look on his face.'

'Don't apologize, doctor!' this man said to Sadler. 'In the last 10 minutes, I think I've got a hunch as to what is wrong with me. I'm going back to my office and revise my working habits. But before I go, do you mind if I take a look in your desk?'

Dr Sadler opened up the drawers of his desk. All empty – except for supplies. 'Tell me,' said the patient. 'Where do you keep your unfinished business?'

'Finished!' said Sadler.

'And where do you keep your unanswered mail?'

'Answered!' Sadler told him. 'My rule is never to lay down a letter until I have answered it. I dictate the reply to my secretary at once.'

Six weeks later, this same executive invited Dr Sadler to come to his office. He was changed – and so was his desk. He opened the desk drawers to show there was no unfinished business inside of the desk. 'Six weeks ago,' this executive said, 'I had three different desks in two different offices – and was snowed under by my work. I was never finished. After talking to you, I came back here and cleared out a wagonload of reports and old papers. Now I work at one desk, settle things as they come up, and don't have a mountain of unfinished business nagging at me and making me tense and worried. But the most astonishing thing is I've recovered completely. There is nothing wrong any more with my health!'

Charles Evans Hughes, former chief justice of the United States Supreme Court, said: 'Men do not die from overwork. They die from dissipation and worry.' Yes, from dissipation of their energies – and worry – because they never seem to get their work done.

Good Working Habit No. 2:

Do things in the order of their importance.

Henry L. Doherty, founder of the nation-wide Cities Service Company, said that regardless of how much salary he paid, there were two abilities he found it almost impossible to find:

- The ability to think.
- The ability to do things in the order of their importance.

Charles Luckman, the lad who started from scratch and climbed in 12 years to president of the Pepsodent Company, got a salary of a $1,00,000 a year, and made a million dollars besides – that lad declared that he owed much of his success to developing the two abilities that Henry L. Doherty said he found almost impossible to find. Charles Luckman said: 'As far back as I can remember, I have got up at 5 o'clock in the morning because I can think better then than any other time – I can think better then and plan my day, plan to do things in the order of their importance.'

Frank Bettger, one of America's most successful insurance salesmen, didn't wait until 5 o'clock in the morning to plan his day. He planned it the night before – set a goal for himself – a goal to sell a certain amount of insurance that day. If he failed, that amount was added to the next day – and so on.

I know from long experience that one is not always able to do things in the order of their importance, but I also know that some kind of plan to do first things first is infinitely better than extemporizing as you go along.

If George Bernard Shaw had not made it a rigid rule to do first things first, he would probably have failed as a writer and might have remained a bank cashier all his life. His plan called for writing five pages each day. That plan inspired him to go right on writing five pages a day for nine heart-breaking years, even though he made a total of only $30 in those nine years – about a penny a day. Even Robinson Crusoe wrote out a schedule of what he would do each hour of the day.

Good Working Habit No. 3:

When you face a problem, solve it then and there if you have the facts necessary to make a decision. Don't keep putting off decisions.

One of my former students, the late H.P. Howell, told me that when he was a member of the board of directors of US Steel, the meetings of the board were often long-drawn-out affairs – many problems were discussed, few decisions were made. The result: each member of the board had to carry home bundles of reports to study.

Finally, Mr Howell persuaded the board of directors to take up one problem at a time and come to a decision. No procrastination – no putting off. The decision might be to ask for additional facts; it might be to do something or do nothing. But a decision was reached on each problem before passing on to the next. Mr Howell told me that the results were striking and salutary – the docket was cleared. The calendar was clean. No longer was it necessary for each member to carry home a bundle of reports. No longer was there a worried sense of unresolved problems.

A good rule, not only for the board of directors of US Steel, but for you and me.

Good Working Habit No. 4:

Learn to organize, deputize, and supervise.

Many business persons are driving themselves to premature graves because they have never learned to delegate responsibility to others, insisting on doing everything themselves. As a result, details and confusion overwhelm them. They are driven by a sense of hurry, worry, anxiety, and tension. It is hard to learn to delegate responsibilities. I know. It was hard for me – awfully hard. I also know from experience the disasters that can be caused by delegating authority to the wrong people. But difficult as it is to delegate authority, executives must do it if they are to avoid worry, tension, and fatigue.

Executives who build up big businesses and don't learn to

organize, deputize, and supervise, usually pop off with heart trouble in their fifties or early sixties – heart trouble caused by tension and worries. Want a specific instance? Look at the death notices in your local paper.

12

How to Banish the Boredom That Produces Fatigue, Worry, and Resentment

One of the chief causes of fatigue is boredom. To illustrate, let's take the case of Alice, an executive who lives on your street. Alice came home one night, utterly exhausted. She acted fatigued. She was fatigued. She had a headache. She had a backache. She was so exhausted she wanted to go to bed without waiting for dinner: Her mother pleaded. She sat down at the table. The telephone rang. The boyfriend! An invitation to a dance! Her eyes sparkled. Her spirits soared. She rushed upstairs, put on her Alice-blue gown, and danced until 3 o'clock in the morning; and when she finally did get home, she was not the slightest bit exhausted. She was, in fact, so exhilarated she couldn't fall asleep.

Was Alice really and honestly tired eight hours earlier, when she looked and acted exhausted? Sure she was. She was exhausted because she was bored with her work, perhaps bored with life. There are millions of Alices. You may be one of them.

* * *

It is a well-known fact that your emotional attitude usually has far more to do with producing fatigue than has physical exertion. A few years ago, Joseph E. Barmack, Ph.D, published in the 'Archives of Psychology' a report of some of his experiments showing how boredom produces fatigue. Dr Barmack put a group of students through a series of tests in which, he knew, they could have little interest. The result? The students felt tired and sleepy, complained of headaches and eye strain, felt irritable. In some cases, even their stomachs were upset. Was it all imagination? No. Metabolism tests were taken of these students. These tests showed that the blood pressure of the body and the consumption of oxygen actually decrease when a person is bored, and that the whole metabolism picks up immediately as soon as he begins to feel interest and pleasure in his work!

We rarely get tired when we are doing something interesting and exciting. For example, I recently took a vacation in the Canadian Rockies up around Lake Louise. I spent several days trout fishing along Corral Creek, fighting my way through brush higher than my head, stumbling over logs, struggling through fallen timber – yet after eight hours of this, I was not exhausted. Why? Because I was excited, exhilarated. I had a sense of high achievement: six cutthroat trout. But suppose I had been bored by fishing, then how do you think I would have felt? I would have been worn out by such strenuous work at an altitude of 7,000 feet.

Even in such exhausting activities as mountain climbing, boredom may tire you far more than the strenuous work involved. For example, Mr S.H. Kingman, president of the Farmers and Mechanics Savings Bank of Minneapolis, told me of an incident that is a perfect illustration of that statement. In July, 1953, the Canadian government asked the Canadian Alpine Club to furnish guides to train the members of the Prince of Wales Rangers in mountain climbing. Mr Kingman was one of the guides chosen to train these soldiers. He told me how he and the other guides – men ranging from forty-two to fifty-nine years of age – took these young army men on long hikes across glaciers and snow fields and up a sheer cliff of 40 feet, where they had to climb with ropes and tiny footholds and precarious handholds. They climbed Michael's Peak, the Vice-President Peak, and other unnamed peaks in the Little Yoho Valley in the Canadian Rockies. After fifteen hours of mountain climbing, these young men, who were in the pink of condition (they had just finished a six-week course in tough commando training), were utterly exhausted.

Was their fatigue caused by using muscles that had not been hardened by commando training? Any man who had ever been through commando training would hoot at such a ridiculous question! No, they were utterly exhausted because they were bored by mountain climbing. They were so tired that many of them fell asleep without waiting to eat. But the guides – men who were two and three times as old as the soldiers – were they tired? Yes, but not exhausted. The guides ate dinner and stayed up for hours, talking about the day's experiences. They were not exhausted because they were interested.

When Dr Edward Thorndike of Columbia was conducting experiments in fatigue, he kept young men awake for almost a week by keeping them constantly interested. After much investigation, Dr Thorndike is reported to have said: 'Boredom is the only real cause of diminution of work.'

If you are a mental worker, it is seldom the amount of work you do that makes you tired. You may be tired by the amount of work you do not do. For example, remember the day last week when you were constantly interrupted. No letters answered. Appointments broken. Trouble here and there. Everything went wrong that day. You accomplished nothing whatever, yet you went home exhausted – and with a splitting head.

The next day everything clicked at the office. You accomplished forty times more than you did the previous day. Yet, you went home fresh as a snowy-white gardenia. You have had that experience. So have I.

The lesson to be learned? Just that: Our fatigue is often caused not by work, but by worry, frustration, and resentment.

While writing this chapter, I went to see a revival of Jerome Kern's delightful musical comedy, *Show Boat*. Captain Andy, captain of the Cotton Blossom, says in one of his philosophical interludes: 'The lucky folks are the ones that get to do things they enjoy doing.' Such folk are lucky because they have more energy, more happiness, less worry, and less fatigue. Where your interests are, there is your energy also. Walking ten blocks with a nagging wife or husband can be more fatiguing than walking ten miles with an adoring sweetheart.

And so what? What can you do about it? Well, here is what one stenographer did about it – a stenographer working for an oil company in Tulsa, Oklahoma. For several days each month, she had one of the dullest jobs imaginable: filling out printed forms for oil leases, inserting figures and statistics. This task was so boring that she resolved, in self-defence, to make it interesting. How? She had a daily contest with herself. She counted the number of forms she filled out each morning, and then tried to excel that record in the afternoon. She counted each day's total and tried to better it the next day. Result? She was soon able to fill out more of these dull printed forms than any other stenographer in her division. And what did all this get her? Praise? No. Thanks? No. Promotion? No. Increased pay? No...But it did help to prevent the fatigue that is spawned by boredom. It did give her a mental stimulant. Because she had done her best to make a dull job interesting, she had more energy, more zest, and got far more happiness out of her leisure hours.

I happen to know this story is true, because I married that girl.

Here is the story of another stenographer who found it paid to act as if her work were interesting. She used to fight her work. But no more. She is Miss Vallie G. Golden, of Elmhurst, Illinois. Here is her story, as she wrote it to me:

'There are four stenographers in my office and each of us is assigned to take letters from several men. Once in a while we get jammed up in these assignments. One day, when an assistant department head insisted that I do a long letter over, I started to rebel. I tried to point out to him that the letter could be corrected without being retyped – and he retorted that if I didn't do it over, he would find someone else who would! I was absolutely fuming! But as I started to retype this letter, it suddenly occurred to me that there were a lot of other people who would jump at the chance to do the work I was doing. Also, that I was being paid a salary to do just that work. I began to feel better. I suddenly made up my mind to do my work as if I actually enjoyed it – even though I despised it. Then I made this important discovery: if I do my work as if I really enjoy it, then I do enjoy it to some extent. I also found I can work faster when I enjoy my work over time. So there is seldom any need for me to work overtime. This new attitude of mine gained me the reputation of being a good worker. And when one of the department superintendents needed a private secretary, he asked for me for the job – because, he said, I was willing to do extra work without being sulky! This matter of the power of a changed mental attitude,' wrote Miss Golden, 'has been a tremendously important discovery to me. It has worked wonders!'

Miss Golden used the wonder-working 'as if' philosophy of Professor Hans Vaihinger. He taught us to act 'as if we were happy – and so on.

If you act as if you are interested in your job, that bit of acting will tend to make your interest real. It will also tend to decrease your fatigue, your tensions, and your worries.

A few years ago, Harlan A. Howard made a decision that completely altered his life. He resolved to make a dull job interesting – and he certainly had a dull one: washing plates, scrubbing counters, and dishing out ice cream in the high school lunchroom while the other boys were playing ball or kidding the girls. Harlan Howard despised his job – but since he had to stick to it, he resolved to study ice cream – how it was made, what ingredients were used, why some ice creams were better than others. He studied the chemistry of ice cream, and became a whiz in the high school chemistry course. He was so interested now in food chemistry that he entered the Massachusetts State College and majored in the field of food technology. When the New York Cocoa Exchange offered a hundred-dollar prize for the best paper on uses of cocoa and chocolate – a prize open to all college students – who do you suppose won it? That's right. Harlan Howard.

When he found it difficult to get a job, he opened a private laboratory in the basement of his home in Amherst, Massachusetts. Shortly after that, a new law was passed. The bacteria in milk had to be counted. Harlan A. Howard was soon counting bacteria for the fourteen milk companies in Amherst – and he had to hire two assistants.

Where will he be twenty-five years from now? Well, the men who are now running the business of food chemistry will be retired then, or dead; and their places will be taken by young lads who are now radiating initiative and enthusiasm. Twenty-five years from now, Harlan A. Howard will probably be one of the leaders in his profession, while some of his classmates to whom he used to sell ice cream over the counter will be sour, unemployed, cussing the government, and complaining that they never had a chance. Harlan A. Howard might never have had a chance, either, if he hadn't resolved to make a dull job interesting.

Years ago, there was another young man who was bored with his dull job of standing at a lathe, turning out bolts in a factory. His first name was Sam. Sam wanted to quit, but he was afraid he couldn't find another job. Since he had to do this dull work, Sam decided he would make it interesting. So he ran a race with the mechanic operating a machine beside him. One of them was to trim off the rough surfaces on his machine, and the other was to trim the bolts down to the proper diameter. They would switch machines occasionally and see who could turn out the most bolts. The foreman, impressed with Sam's speed and accuracy, soon gave him a better job. That was the start of a whole series of promotions. Thirty years later, Sam – Samuel Vauclain – was president of the Baldwin Locomotive Works. But he might have remained a mechanic all his life if he had not resolved to make a dull job interesting.

H.V. Kaltenborn – the famous radio news analyst – once told me how he made a dull job interesting. When he was twenty-two years old, he worked his way across the Atlantic on a cattle boat, feeding and watering the steers. After making a bicycle tour of England, he arrived in Paris, hungry and broke. Pawning his camera for $5, he put an ad in the Paris edition of the *New York Herald* and got a job selling stereopticon machines. I can remember those old-fashioned stereoscopes that we used to hold up before our eyes to look at two pictures exactly alike. As we looked, a miracle happened. The two lenses in the stereoscope transformed the two pictures into a single scene with the effect of a third dimension. We saw distance. We got an astounding sense of perspective.

Well, as I was saying, Kaltenborn started out selling these machines from door to door in Paris – and he couldn't speak French. But he earned $5,000 in commissions the first year, and made himself one of the highest-paid salesmen in France that year. H. V. Kaltenborn told me that this experience did as much to develop within him the qualities that make for success as did any single year of study at Harvard. Confidence? He told me himself that after that experience, he felt he could have sold the *Congressional Record* to French housewives.

That experience gave him an intimate understanding of French life that later proved invaluable in interpreting, on the radio, European events.

How did he manage to become an expert salesman when he couldn't speak French? Well, he had his employer write out his sales talk in perfect French, and he memorized it. He would ring a doorbell, a housewife would answer, and Kaltenborn would begin repeating his memorized sales talk with an accent so terrible it was funny. He would show the housewife his pictures, and when she asked a question, he would shrug his shoulders and say, 'An American...an American.' He would then take off his hat and point to a copy of the sales talk in perfect French that he had pasted in the top of his hat. The housewife would laugh, he would laugh – and show her more pictures. When H.V. Kaltenborn told me about this, he confessed that the job had been far from easy. He told me that there was only one quality that pulled him through: his determination to make the job interesting. Every morning before he started out, he looked into the mirror and gave himself a pep talk: 'Kaltenborn, you have to do this if you want to eat. Since you have to do it – why not have a good time doing it? Why not imagine every time you ring a doorbell that you are an actor before the footlights and that there's an audience out there looking at you? After all, what you are doing is just as funny as something on the stage. So, why not put a lot of zest and enthusiasm into it?'

Mr Kaltenborn told me that these daily pep talks helped him transform a task that he had once hated and dreaded into an adventure that he liked and made highly profitable.

When I asked Mr Kaltenborn if he had any advice to give to the young men of America who are eager to succeed, he said: 'Yes, go to bat with yourself every morning. We talk a lot about the importance of physical exercise to wake us up out of the half-sleep in which so many of us walk around. But we need, even more, some spiritual and mental exercises every morning to stir us into action. Give yourself a pep talk every day.'

Is giving yourself a pep talk every day silly, superficial, childish? No, on the contrary, it is the very essence of sound psychology. 'Our life is what our thoughts make it.' These words are just as true today as they were eighteen centuries ago when Marcus Aurelius first wrote them in his book on Meditations: 'Our life is what our thoughts make it.'

By talking to yourself every hour of the day, you can direct yourself to think thoughts of courage and happiness, thoughts of power and peace. By talking to yourself about the things you have to be grateful for, you can fill your mind with thoughts that soar and sing.

> By thinking the right thoughts, you can make any job less distasteful.

Your boss wants you to be interested in your job so that he will make more money. But let's forget about what the boss wants. Think only of what getting interested in your job will do for you. Remind yourself that it may double the amount of happiness you get out of life, for you spend about one half of your waking hours at your work, and if you don't find happiness in your work, you may never find it anywhere.

Keep reminding yourself that getting interested in your job will take your mind off your worries, and, in the long run, will probably bring promotion and increased pay. Even if it doesn't do that, it will reduce fatigue to a minimum and help you enjoy your hours of leisure.

SIX WAYS TO PREVENT FATIGUE AND WORRY AND KEEP YOUR ENERGY AND SPIRITS HIGH

RULE 1

Rest before you get tired.

RULE 2

Learn to relax at your work.

RULE 3

Learn to relax at home.

RULE 4

Apply these four good working habits:

a. Clear your desk of all papers except those relating to the immediate problem at hand.
b. Do things in the order of their importance.
c. When you face a problem, solve it then and there if you have the facts necessary to make a decision.
d. Learn to organize, deputize, and supervise. To prevent worry and fatigue, put enthusiasm into your work.

RULE 5

Remember, no one was ever killed by lack of sleep. It is worrying about insomnia that does the damage – not the insomnia.

